English/CSCT

# Table of Contents

Ondaatje, M.

<u>The Cinnamon Peeler: Selected Poems</u>, Ondaatje, M.

© 1994 McClelland & Stewart Ltd.

Ondaatje, M.

<u>The Cinnamon Peeler: Selected Poems</u>, Ondaatje, M.

© 1994 McClelland & Stewart Ltd.

Ondaatje, M.

<u>The Cinnamon Peeler: Selected Poems</u>, Ondaatje, M.

© 1994 McClelland & Stewart Ltd.

Ondaatje, M.

<u>The Cinnamon Peeler: Selected Poems</u>, Ondaatje, M.

© 1994 McClelland & Stewart Ltd.

Ondaatje, M.

<u>The Cinnamon Peeler: Selected Poems</u>, Ondaatje, M.

© 1994 McClelland & Stewart Ltd.

Ondaatje, M.

# THE COLLECTED WORKS OF BILLY THE KID

## Scripting the Docudrama

*Manina Jones*

7. FABLE, EDMUND, JR. *The True Life of Billy the Kid.* Denver: Denver Publishing Co.

This title was recorded with the Copyright Office of the Library of Congress on September 7, 1881, but there is no record that the copyright deposit copies were received by the Library. Was this item ever printed? If so, is there a copy extant?  (13)

> — from J. C. Dykes, *Billy the Kid:*
> *The Bibliography of a Legend*

IN HER 1969 ARTICLE, "The Documentary Poem: A Canadian Genre," Dorothy Livesay announced the existence of a class of Canadian poetry she called, alluding to a tradition of Canadian non-fiction film and radio, the "documentary." This genre, Livesay argued, uses particularized historical and geographical data, is based on research, focuses on a theme or precept and a representative protagonist rather than an individualized hero, and is marked by dramatic and didactic presentation (280). "What interests me in these developments," Livesay wrote, "is the evidence they present of a conscious attempt to create a dialectic between the objective facts and the subjective feelings of the poet" (267). A factual, historical situation, in other words, gives rise to the poet's fictional, creative musings.

Fifteen years after the publication of Livesay's article, Stephen Scobie's survey of numerous examples of recent writing in the genre, "Amelia, or: Who Do You Think You Are? Documentary and Identity in Canadian Literature," demonstrated the prophetic nature of Livesay's observations.[1] Scobie extends Livesay's discussion, and modifies it in light of developments in contemporary literary theory and Canadian writing. While he agrees with Livesay that "The documentary poem appeals to the authoritativeness of fact" ("Amelia," 270), he notes that the very idea of "objective fact" or "historical reality" that provides the basis for Livesay's subjective-objective distinction is now being rethought:

26

The whole notion of 'fact' may itself be no more than a fiction, a linguistic construct — and thus subject, like all linguistic constructs, to the deconstructive play of Derridean 'différance'. . . . So, while the attraction of the documentary may begin with an appeal to the authoritativeness of fact, consideration of the difficulties involved in ever satisfactorily *writing* fact leads quickly to that borderblur area between fact and fiction, in which the categories collapse into each other. ("Amelia," 272)

It is significant to this discussion that both Scobie and Livesay comment on the importance of the document, not just as a source for, but as an active component of the documentary. In the first paragraph of Livesay's essay she observes that "Today we find, linked with the use of documentary material as the basis for poetry, the employment of *the actual data itself*, rearranged for the eye and ear" (267; emphasis added). Her first — and, it might be argued, prototypical — examples of documentary poetry are John Robert Colombo's *The Mackenzie Poems* and F. R. Scott's *Trouvailles*, both instances of "found poetry," a genre whose central gesture is the (re)presentation of non-fiction documents in poetic form. Scobie notes that under his definition, "The idea of the 'document' remains within the poems, as a source of historical fact, as an element of intertextuality" ("Amelia," 269). The documentary poem, then, literally takes written "evidence" of the historical situation into (its) account.

I would argue for a class of documentary writing that takes this principle literally, not simply by sustaining the *idea* of the document, but by self-consciously transcribing "outside" non-fiction documents into a poetic context. This version of the documentary — we might provisionally call it the "documentary-collage" — would include such works as Lionel Kearns's *Convergences*, Robert Kroetsch's *The Ledger* and *Seed Catalogue*, Don Gutteridge's *A True History of Lambton County*, Birk Sproxton's *Headframe*, Don McKay's *Lependu*, Fred Wah's *Pictograms from the Interior of B.C.* and Michael Ondaatje's *The Collected Works of Billy the Kid*, all of which quote historical records of one sort or another.

In these works, Livesay's "dialectic between the objective facts and the subjective feelings of the poet" is recast as a dialectic between the status of the document as an authoritative univocal "representative" of some "outside" reality, and its status as text, which *constructs* a dialogic historical reality subject to interpretive instabilities and contradictions. This dialectic corresponds to Dominick LaCapra's distinction between the uncritically "documentary model" of history in which "the basis of research is 'hard' fact derived from the critical sifting of sources" and which "is limited to plausibly filling gaps in the record" (18), and the "rhetorical model," which emphasizes "the way 'documents' are themselves texts that 'process' or rework 'reality' and require a critical reading" (19-20). Linda Hutcheon corroborates LaCapra's historical argument in her consideration of the "head-on" meeting in contemporary Canadian fiction of "the documentary impulse of realism" and

27

"the problematizing of reference begun by self-reflexive modernism" (24). She writes that

> If we only have access to the past today through its traces — documents, the testimony of witnesses, and other archival materials — then in a way we only have other representations of the past from which to construct our own narrative representations or explanations. Postmodernism nevertheless tries to understand present culture as the product of previous codings and representations. (23)

The documentary-collage enacts exactly the process Hutcheon describes. Rather than ignoring the textual nature of unquestioned "sources" as do LaCapra's "documentary history" and Hutcheon's "documentary realism," the documentary-collage requires that we engage in a self-conscious re-reading of the documents of the past in a present context. Both (realistically or representationally) documentary and (self-reflexively) document-ary, it participates in the process by which, as Hutcheon puts it, "The representation of history becomes the history of representation too" (23).

MICHAEL ONDAATJE'S LONG POEM *The Collected Works of Billy the Kid*, published in 1970, is a work of documentary-collage. It is a "collected works," an assembled group of writings linked to the historical-legendary figure of Billy the Kid. Rather than functioning simply as "documentary evidence" of objective, verifiable events, these writings themselves compose a series of self-consciously textual events. *The Collected Works of Billy the Kid* is, therefore, a kind of "docudrama," a drama of documents, a play of texts that perversely fulfils Livesay's requirement that the documentary poem be dramatic. The work's central figure — or, perhaps more appropriately, *de*-centred figure — Billy the Kid, is, as Livesay also requires, a "representative hero." He is a hero of representation, for these documents are his "collected works" not because he composed them, but because he is composed *of* them. The signifier "Billy the Kid" becomes the shifting locus of their intersection, the place where problems of documentation become unavoidable.

Ondaatje, of course, has the advantage of working with a figure of legend, one which is obviously already filtered through layers of story and whose "true character" is therefore problematic. The poem reveals, however, that history too is "legendary," always already subject to such filterings. The root of the word legend, *legenda*, means "what is to be read"; Billy the Kid is a legendary figure in the rhetorical sense, constructed in readings and in writings. Because of the multiple, unstable and potentially contradictory nature of readings and writings (and readings *as* writings), however, Billy the Kid is subject to a kind of *de*-constructive

28

3

drama that the text also enacts: he is both encoded by it and refuses to stick to the script.

While LaCapra's totalizing "documentary history" is engaged in "plausibly filling gaps in the record," then, Ondaatje's poem asks its readers to seek them out. It approaches the problem of beginnings, for example, by addressing the reader directly: "Find the beginning, the slight silver key to unlock it, to dig it out. Here then is a maze to begin, be in" (20). Finding a beginning involves the reader in examining her own orientation in relation to the text, in finding a place for herself. This discursive positioning may be seen in grammatical terms. In the passage quoted above, for example, "here" is a spatial deictic, and "then" is a temporal deictic, as well as a conjunction. Both are examples of what Émile Benveniste calls "pronomial" forms that "do not refer to 'reality' or to 'objective' positions in space or time," but rather to a "reality of discourse" established by the "utterances that contain them" (218-19). "Billy the Kid" is, I would argue, the poem's central "pronomial" form, since his character is not a simple fixed entity that exists independently of its representations, but is, rather, continually placed and displaced by the reading of "his" collected works. In the invitation "Here then is a place to begin . . . ," the shifting relationship between the reader's proximate position "here" and a temporally distant "then" becomes a function of the poem's present reading, which gives past writings a "new beginning" in our "finding" of them as "a maze to begin, be in."

"Be in" is "begin" with a gap, a letter left out. As readers we are looking less for keys than keyholes, entrance not into a teleological structure that terminates in a single exit, but through and into uncertainties. We might recall in this regard the poem's description of the entrance to the Boot Hill cemetery, literally a place one might enter to visit those who have passed/past away:

> . . . There is an elaborate gate
> but the path keeps to no main route for it tangles
> like branches of a tree among the gravestones. (9)

The tangled path, which might be associated with "a maze to begin" leads, not directly to the dead themselves, but "among the gravestones," *signs* of the dead, markers of their absence, memorials to them. Later, the poem uses the path metaphor again, this time to mock the kind of literalist biographical "graverobbing" that would attempt to resurrect its subject, but in fact issues in a kind of dead end:

> Imagine if you dug him up and brought him out. You'd see very little. There'd be the buck teeth. Perhaps Garret's bullet no longer in thick wet flesh would roll in the skull like a marble. From the head there'd be a *trail* of vertebrae like a row of pearl buttons. . . . (97; emphasis added)

Ondaatje's introduction to *The Long Poem Anthology* quotes a comment on documentary cinema by film-maker Jean-Luc Godard that sends us again to the figure

29

of the "tangled path." Typical of Godard, the quotation reverses conventional wisdom on documentary film, but in a way which is quite appropriate to Ondaatje's re-versing of prosaic documentary material and methods. Godard notes that the documentary is "a road leading to fiction, but it's still not a road, it's bushes and trees" (cited in "What is in the Pot," 16).

Photographic and cinematic patterns in *The Collected Works* have been thoroughly and usefully traced by other critics.[2] The poem's near obsession with poetic images of photographic images suggests the layering of documentary evidence, as well as a concern with writing as a problematic method of documenting Billy's career, of showing it by telling it. Godard's comment on documentary cinema implicates fiction in the process of investigation and interpretation involved in "scripting" the documentary. In this light, we might consider *The Collected Works* as a kind of documentary "screen-play." It begins, after all, with an empty frame, a blank screen (5), and ends with a list of "CREDITS" which identify the poem's documentary sources (110). The quotation that appears below the open frame is taken from one such source, the credits tell us, L. A. Huffman's book *Huffman, Frontier Photographer*:

> I send you a picture of Billy made with the Perry shutter as quick as it can be worked — Pyro and soda developer. I am making daily experiments now and find I am able to take passing horses at a lively trot square across the line of fire. . . . I will send you proofs sometime. I shall show you what can be done from the saddle without ground glass or tripod — please notice when you get the specimens that they were made with the lense wide open and many of the best exposed when my horse was in motion.   (5)

The very act of quotation, notes Victor Li, "disperses meaning, first, by transgressing the protective limits of the 'univocal' or 'autonomous' text," and then, by citing it in a different context, destroying its apparent univocality, "multiplying and scattering its single voice" (297). This is exactly the case for the Huffman quotation. Its ostensibly simple, referentially documentary quality is first and most clearly ruptured by the absence of the photograph in question, signalled by an open frame. As the title of Judith Owens's paper on the poem, " 'I Send You a Picture': Ondaatje's Portrait of Billy the Kid," implies, the document's "new" context shifts it from the apparently historical and factual reference of the photograph to an obviously fictional, poetic referent (the poem as a whole), a shift which also changes the pronominal reference of "I" to Ondaatje's as the text's "compiler" or "editor," if not, strictly speaking, its author. The quotation's reference is further multiplied if we decide *not* to treat the poem as a whole, but as a collection of documents — themselves neither "univocal" nor "autonomous" — successively "projected" like the frames of a film, onto the blank space from which Billy as photograph and referent is absent.

The diction of the passage "speaks to" several other contexts relevant to our

30

consideration of the poem. Its language is not just that of photography, for example, but of photography as scientific experimentation: "I am making daily *experiments* . . . I will send you *proofs* sometime . . . when you get the *specimens*" (5; emphasis added). Frank Davey writes that "much of the impulse in the twentieth-century documentary long poem begins . . . in the modernist envy of the scientist's access to self evident testimony and precise measurement" (34). It is no coincidence that a lexicon similar to Huffman's (and Davey's) relates to two other related "truth-seeking" activities: the detective's investigation of a crime, and the process of legally trying a criminal, where, as E. L. Doctorow puts it, "society arranges with all its investigative apparatus to apprehend factual reality" (227). The aim of such a process, after all, is to reach a *verdict*, both a conclusive finding and, literally, a "true saying."

I T IS PRECISELY THESE THREE AREAS — scientific experimentation, criminal investigation and legal trial — that Parker Tyler brings together in his discussion of documentary film. He, for example, calls the detective story "a method paralleling the experimental method of science itself; a tentative, and not always successful search for the relevant, conclusive facts" (261). He later notes that in the detective story,

> if the crimes treated are, literally or symbolically, already on the books, the verisimilitude tends to compass the fiction itself. For this simple reason: the murderer as individual is technically a fiction until legally convicted; even a suspect . . . is a legal-fiction criminal only, as anxious as a certain group is to consider him a real one. This theoretically imbeds fiction in the chosen theme of fact. Crime detection is therefore allied to the method of scientific knowledge already mentioned as a category of documentary. The whole process of apprehension and trial is an experiment conducted to make a present hypothesis secure in a past fact by connecting, beyond any reasonable doubt, the doer with the deed.   (263-64)

The realist documentary must present the evidence necessary to prove its case, to demonstrate that it is the one true story — history. Success, to continue the legal trope, is based on the strength of its conviction. Ondaatje, however, objects to what he calls the "CBC kind of documentary" because in it the element of fiction or uncertainty is not sustained, or indeed was never entertained in the first place. According to Ondaatje, this is the kind of documentary that "knows what it is going to say before the actual filming begins" (Solecki interview, 15). The "documentary method" of *The Collected Works*, on the other hand, ensures that Billy the Kid remains a "legal-fiction criminal only" by, in effect, trying the evidence without settling on a verdict. Like the documentary described by Godard, textual evidence becomes a kind of road to fiction; the document, like the found poem, is a "finding," but not a conclusive finding.

31

Billy the Kid's crimes are, quite literally, on the books, as the bibliographical credits and J. C. Dykes's *Bibliography of a Legend* indicate: they are part of the historical record. They are also *in* the book *The Collected Works of Billy the Kid*: it contains an itemized list of "the killed / (by me)" (6). When, in that book, we return to the *scenes* of the crimes, then, we should not be surprised to find that they are also scenes of writing. For example, a passage midway through the poem asks about "A motive? some reasoning we can give to explain all this violence. Was there a source for all this? yup—" (54). Stephen Scobie suggests that "simplistic psychological 'explanations' of the source of Billy's violence" are being mocked here ("Two Authors," 194). It should be added that the above-quoted passage is followed by an italicized account describing the savage murder of Tunstall. The documentary "source" of all *this* violence is Walter Noble Burns's book *The Saga of Billy the Kid* which the passage quotes verbatim (see Burns, 48). We are turned away, then, from psychologically rooted clues that require a present psyche to interpret, to intertextual ones, which send us "elsewhere." Jean Weisgarber points out of quotation in general that it both invokes questions of significance and sends us "elsewhere" to investigate them: "It is rather like a question mark, a marginal note, a signpost directing us to some unexplored ground and arousing our curiosity" (143). The question posed by *The Collected Works* is not, therefore, What made Billy the Kid so mean? but rather, What makes him *mean*? That is, How does his figure acquire significance?

Paulita Maxwell's testimony allots her the role of "character" witness in the fictional trial. She explains the absence of another photograph in judicial terms: "I never liked the picture. I don't think it does Billy justice" (19). Her account describes the way the excluded photograph "constructs" Billy: "The picture *makes him* rough and uncouth" (19; emphasis added). Her own version of Billy is quite different, and, as an "eyewitness account," seems at first to supersede the photograph: "his face *was really* boyish and pleasant" (19; emphasis added). That testimony is itself, however, equivocal, subject to its own interpretive agenda. The phrasing of the complete quotation draws attention to the fact that it is not the objective, unmediated expression *on* Billy's face that was boyish and pleasant, but "The expression *of* his face," Paulita's expression of it in her own description (19; emphasis added). In fact, Ondaatje's use of the quotation (taken from Burns, 194-95) stresses that this is not really even "Paulita's" testimony, since it is appropriated first by Burns and then re-cited by *The Collected Works*, which rends it into lines and renders it "poetic." As Victor Li comments, "Quotation makes intertextuality visible" (297). The quotation's meaning is not simply transplanted from one citation to another, but is determined by successive contextualizations.

Another of the alternative stories *The Collected Works* presents is the comic book tale "Billy the Kid and the Princess." In the comic book story the Princess (a "real princess" — a real comic book princess) tells Billy, "I must not go

32

on being formal with you" (102). In a sense she states Ondaatje's mandate, too: he must avoid the marks of formal closure that denote the completion of story. The comic book tale, for example, while it is formally set off by a page border (page 20, we might note, tells us how Billy and Charlie Bowdre "criss-cross" borders), defies that frame by ending with an ellipsis and a conjunction: "Before Billy the Kid can defend himself, La Princesa Marguerita has taken him in her arms and. . . ." (102). In a film, of course, the two would fade off into the sunset, indicating that the story continues beyond the confines of its present telling.

In a related passage — and relationships among stories are another way of violating closure — Paulita Maxwell sets out to put an end to the proliferating stories about her relationship with Billy, stories which she, ironically, perpetuates by *relating* them, laying the groundwork for the comic book legend, not to mention Burns's and Ondaatje's tellings:

> An old story that identifies me as Billy the Kid's sweetheart has been going the rounds for many years. . . . But I was not Billy the Kid's sweetheart. . . . There was a story that Billy and I had laid our plans to elope to old Mexico. . . . There was another tale that we proposed to elope riding double on one horse. Neither story was true. . . . (96)

One place that promises to give us a first-hand, and therefore genuinely *true*, story is the "Exclusive Interview" with *The Texas Star* in which, we are told in a bold headline, "THE KID TELLS ALL" (81). The interview, however (invented by Ondaatje), is more a justification of the failure of the experimental/legal trial than a verdict in itself. When the interviewer asks Billy "Did you have any reason for going on living, or were you just experimenting?" Billy replies that "in the end that is all that's important — that you keep testing yourself, as you say — experimenting on how good you are, and you can't do that when you want to lose" (83). The experiment, in other words, is not directed toward completion, but is an ongoing activity in which Billy the Kid's character is only ever offered on a "trial" basis.

The Kid explains that "I could only be arrested if they had proof, definite proof, not just stories" (81). The Huffman quote that "opens" the volume tells us "I will send you [photographic] proofs sometime" (5). The arrival of conclusive "proofs," however, is infinitely deferred by the poem since, as Billy says in the interview, "there is no legal proof to all this later stuff. The evidence used was unconstitutional" (83). That is, it fails to constitute him conclusively. When Judge Houston offers Billy amnesty, he refuses: "All Houston was offering me was protection from the law, and at that time the law had no quarrels with me, so it seemed rather silly" (81). The judge proposes to give Billy the Kid what he already has; Houston offers him *parole*. In French, of course, *parole* means "word," or, more particularly as defined by structuralist linguistics, it means *individual* utterances as opposed to *langue*, the language system as a whole (Culler, 8). As we have seen,

33

it is in the contentious, provisional utterances or "works" on/of Billy the Kid that he is both described and de-scripted.

These works do violence to the principle of identity that is central to the project of "connecting the doer with the deed." When a description in the poem is given from two perspectives, both apparently Billy's, Dennis Cooley asks "how can Billy know what he doesn't know, be privileged with two visions?" (225). One answer is that Billy is not "at one with himself"; his eye-witness/I-witness account is dubious indeed, and the lyric I itself comes under suspicion. In order to avoid the law, Billy says, "All I had to do was ride off in the opposite direction" (81). And that is exactly what "he" (the pronoun itself clearly becomes equivocal) does, since the documents in *The Collected Works* both conflict with each other and gesture outward to other intertextual "sources." Françoise Gaillard comments that opposed to the logic of identity is a "logic of juxtaposition," which fosters conflicting meanings:

> Here there is no 'right place' of meaning, simply an infinite number of positions no sooner occupied than abandoned. Every act of judgement takes on a shifting, fluctuating, unstable form. This general indecision entails the destruction of the monadic subject. (145)

Patrick Garrett, we might note in this regard, tells us that Billy "could never remain in one position more than five minutes" (44). In film, if all the images projected on the screen are identical, the effect is stasis, a "freeze frame." The differential, juxtapositional logic of *The Collected Works* ensures that such recuperation to stasis or "arrested" movement is not possible.

Indeed, in several places "I," the pronoun that would at least theoretically identify Billy as a self-conscious, self-present speaker, is, like the photographs, omitted altogether, as if in recognition that "he" escapes the integration it seems to signify. The "pronomial form," literally flickers between presence and absence. One instance of this "disappearing I" occurs after an introduction that draws attention to Billy as a character on the move whose "performance" in reading is likely to be self-revealing — but self-revealing less in a confessional sense than in the sense that it causes his *audience* to "expose" themselves in their roles as producers rather than passive consumers of Billy's character and story:

> Up with the curtain
> down with your pants
> William Bonney
> is going to dance.  (63)

Billy's address to the audience significantly "avoids the subject": "Hlo folks — 'd liketa sing my song about the lady Miss A D . . ." (64). Further, when Billy's lover Angie attempts an unusual sexual position at the Chisum home, this "indecisive" dialogue occurs: "Come on Angie I'm drunk 'm not a trapeze artist. Yes you are.

34

No" (68). As the exchange implies, Billy's identity swings between contradictions; it violates identity itself. Finally, the absent pronoun is equated with a dartboard, literally a field of play which once again invokes audience/participants: "Am the dartboard / for your midnight blood" (85). In the same poem an attempted representation elliptically disintegrates before our eyes: "a pencil, harnessing my face / goes stumbling into dots" (85).

Billy describes himself as "locked inside my sensitive skin," but even that boundary breaks down. Just as Billy cannot be located linguistically as a unified entity, and is formally disintegrated through the fragmentation of his collected works, so he is physically "opened up." Even the human frame does not contain him. Pat Garrett's bullet enters Billy in a poem:

> leaving skin in a puff
> behind and the slow
> as if fire pours out
> red grey brain the hair slow
> startled by it all pour    (73)

The effect of such a brutal violation is not what one might think. The game is not up: this is not the end either of Billy the Kid or *The Collected Works of Billy the Kid*. When Billy is asked what happens after you die he replies, "I guess they'll just put you in a box and you will stay there forever" (83). If that guess is right, a coffin becomes the ultimate frame-up, the final case against him, but *The Collected Works* is resistant to such simplistic conclusions. To quote Robert Kroetsch, it "resists endings, violently" (57).

IT IS NO WONDER THEN, in light of all this inconclusive evidence, that deputy John W. Poe has last-minute doubts about the man Garrett shot. *The Collected Works* quotes his version of an exchange that takes place after the shooting: "'It was the Kid who came in there on to me,' Garrett told Poe, 'and I think I got him.' 'Pat,' replied Poe, 'I believe you have killed the wrong man'" (103). *The Collected Works of Billy the Kid* depends on the apprehended Billy *always* being the "wrong man." In T. D. McLulich's article, "Ondaatje's Mechanical Boy: Portrait of the Artist as Photographer," he states that "Billy is simply *there*, his existence a fact to be neutrally recorded by the author" (116). The opposite case might also be maintained: that Billy is *never* simply *there*, that his recording in both past and present documents is never neutral, based as it is on both acknowledged and unacknowledged pre-texts.

Terry Gilliam's recent "science-fiction" film *Brazil* provides a suggestive analogy for the docudramatic process of *The Collected Works*. The film's hero, Buttle, is a renegade heating engineer who subverts the department system by "freelancing."

35

In one of *Brazil*'s closing sequences, Buttle finally escapes the government representatives who pursue him. As he walks calmly down a city street, the wind stirs stray pieces of paper around his feet. Gradually, as the number of papers increases, the wind picks up and blows them against his body. He can't remove them. As more and more papers stick he is completely covered; he becomes a paper mummy. Finally, Buttle falls struggling to the ground. A friend rushes to help him, but as he begins to pull the papers off he discovers only more papers. Nothing lies beneath them. The papers disperse. There is, one might say, no Buttle, only re-Buttle. Like Buttle, Billy the Kid is seen as a body of texts; he becomes documentary material. Ondaatje's "documentary history," to its credit, leaves something to be desired: Billy the Kid remains . . . WANTED.

## NOTES

[1] In a recent issue of *Event*, Susan Glickman objects to the fact that "there has been so much blather about the use of documentary sources in Canadian poetry as something new and in some way especially 'Canadian'. . . . What I am dubious about is the claim that this tradition is in any significant way *new*" (107). Glickman's latter point, if taken to its logical end, is certainly a valid one. Indeed, Susan Rudy Dorscht observes of Eli Mandel's "The Long Poem: Journal and Origin" that the poem/essay demonstrates "that there are no poems that are not documentary: that the poems that we write are constructed out of what Livesay called the 'actual data itself.'" What distinguishes much of contemporary documentary poetry, and particularly the documentary-collage, is its self-conscious violation of the inside-text/outside-text distinction and its interrogation of those texts that "prescribe" it.

[2] Perry Nodelman and T. D. MacLulich, for example, both see the volume as a kind of photograph album which assembles a series of still images (Nodelman, 68; MacLulich, 108), and the latter reads it as "a warning against the dehumanizing consequences of photographic voyeurism" (109). Lorraine York similarly sees the image of the photo as a metaphor both for Billy's destructive attempt to control and fix his own world, and for Ondaatje's attempt to fix Billy's character (104, 106), while Dennis Cooley conducts an engaging analysis of the contrast between still photography and cinematic reference in the poem as representative of controlled modern and archaic postmodern perspectives, respectively. Stephen Tatum, finally, sees a parallel between the poem's "violent manipulations of time and ideas" and rapid editing techniques in cinema and television, commenting that this style "usefully parallel[s] the violence in the outlaw's life (and death)" (152).

## WORKS CITED

Benveniste, Émile. "The Nature of Pronouns," *Problems in General Linguistics*, trans. Mary Elizabeth Meek (Coral Gables, Fla.: Univ. of Miami Press, 1971), 219-22.

Burns, Walter Noble. *The Saga of Billy the Kid* (Garden City, N.Y.: Doubleday, Page, 1926).

Cooley, Dennis. "'I am here on the edge': Modern Hero/Postmodern Poetics in *The Collected Works of Billy the Kid*," in *Spider Blues: Essays on Michael Ondaatje*, ed. Sam Solecki (Montreal: Véhicule, 1985), 211-39.

Culler, Jonathan. *Structuralist Poetics: Structuralism, Linguistics and the Study of Literature* (London: Routledge, 1975).

36

Davey, Frank. "Countertextuality in the Long Poem," *Open Letter* 6th series, nos. 2-3 (Summer-Fall 1985), 33-44.

Doctorow, E. L. "False Documents," *American Review* 26 (November 1977), 215-32.

Dorscht, Susan Rudy. "A Way of Writing I(t) Again: The Concept of Agency in Eli Mandel's 'The Long Poem: Journal and Origin.'" Paper delivered at "The Politics of Art: Eli Mandel's Poetry and Criticism," a conference held jointly by Wilfrid Laurier University and the University of Guelph, October 20-21, 1988.

Dykes, J. C. *Billy the Kid: The Bibliography of a Legend* (Albuquerque: Univ. of New Mexico Press, 1951).

Gaillard, Françoise. "An Unspeakable (Hi)story," *Yale French Studies* 59 (1980), 137-54.

Glickman, Susan. "The Ring and the Book: Fact and Fiction in Canadian Poetry," *Event* 17.3 (Fall 1988), 105-09.

Hutcheon, Linda. "The Politics of Representation in Canadian Art and Literature," *Robarts Centre Working Papers* (North York: York University, 1988).

Kroetsch, Robert. "The Exploding Porcupine: Violence of Form in English-Canadian Fiction," *Open Letter* 5th series, no. 4 (1983), 57-64.

LaCapra, Dominick. *History & Criticism* (Ithaca and London: Cornell Univ. Press, 1985).

Li, Victor. "The Rhetoric of Presence: Reading Pound's *Cantos* I to III," *English Studies in Canada* 14.3 (September 1988), 296-309.

Livesay, Dorothy. "The Documentary Poem: A Canadian Genre," in *Contexts of Canadian Criticism*, ed. Eli Mandel (Chicago and London: Univ. of Chicago Press, 1971), 267-81.

MacLulich, T. D. "Ondaatje's Mechanical Boy: Portrait of the Artist as Photographer," *Mosaic* 14.2 (1981), 107-19.

Nodleman, Perry M. "The Collected Photographs of Billy the Kid," *Canadian Literature* 87 (Winter 1980), 68-79.

Ondaatje, Michael. *The Collected Works of Billy the Kid* (Toronto: Anansi, 1970).

————. "What is in the Pot." Introduction to *The Long Poem Anthology*, ed. Michael Ondaatje (Toronto: Coach House, 1979), 11-18.

Owens, Judith. "'I Send You a Picture': Ondaatje's Portrait of Billy the Kid," *Studies in Canadian Literature* 8.1 (1983), 117-39.

Scobie, Stephen. "Amelia, or: Who Do You Think You Are? Documentary and Identity in Canadian Literature," *Canadian Literature* 100 (Spring 1984), 264-85.

————. "Two Authors in Search of a Character: bpNichol and Michael Ondaatje," in *Spider Blues: Essays on Michael Ondaatje*, ed. Sam Solecki (Montreal: Véhicule, 1985), 185-210.

Solecki, Sam. "An Interview with Michael Ondaatje," in *Spider Blues: Essays on Michael Ondaatje*, ed. Sam Solecki (Montreal: Véhicule, 1985), 13-27.

Tatum, Stephen. *Inventing Billy the Kid: Visions of the Outlaw in America, 1881-1981* (Albuquerque: Univ. of New Mexico Press, 1982).

Tyler, Parker. "Documentary Technique in Film Fiction," in *The Documentary Tradition: From Nanook to Woodstock*, ed. Lewis Jacobs (New York: Hopkinson and Blake, 1974), 251-66.

37

Weisgerber, Jean. "The Use of Quotations in Recent Literature," *Comparative Literature* 22 (1970), 30-45.

York, Lorraine M. "'Making and Destroying': The Photographic Image in Michael Ondaatje's Works," in her *"The Other Side of Dailiness": Photography in the Works of Alice Munro, Timothy Findley, Michael Ondaatje, and Margaret Laurence* (Downsview, Ont.: ECW, 1988), 93-120.

*

*The author wishes to acknowledge the assistance of the Social Sciences and Humanities Research Council during the preparation of this paper.*

# GLOSSOLALIA

*Anne M. Kelly*

### I

Tongue: blunt-tipped,
slippery organ
of muscle and tastebuds;
homo sapiens use it
for declarations
of lingual sounds — in English,
the 'l' of love, or the 't'
of hate.

It is often kept hidden
behind a row of teeth.

### II

In most supermarkets, you can buy a tongue.

Look for a nice fresh one.
If it is discoloured
or bruised, the animal
to whom it belonged
may have been butchered
incorrectly.

Do not listen to old wives' tales.
You need not cover your ears
when you cook a tongue. The tongue
cannot say anything;

38

# DECONSTRUCTING THE "DESERT OF FACTS": DETECTION AND ANTIDETECTION IN *COMING THROUGH SLAUGHTER*

NANCY E. BJERRING
*Fanshawe College*

Michael Ondaatje's *Coming Through Slaughter* is one of many postmodern texts that parody the world-view and narrative devices of the detective story. In an early and important article entitled "The Detective and the Boundary: Some Notes on the Postmodern Literary Imagination," William V. Spanos offers a convincing explanation for the appeal of the detective story genre for contemporary writers. Deriving much of his argument from Sartre and other existentialist theorists, he hypothesizes that postmodern writers subvert the "post-Renaissance humanistic structure of consciousness" (170) in order to contest the authority of prescriptive systems of validation, whether they be religious, aesthetic, or scientific. The scientific world-view comes in for particular scrutiny, since popularized versions of the values of science, such as the centrality of objectivity, rational analysis, inductive reasoning, and so on, inform virtually all classical detective stories. In contrast, Spanos argues,

the postmodern literary imagination at large insists on the *mystery* — the ominous and threatening uncanniness that resists naming — and that the paradigmatic literary archetype it has discovered is the ant┄ctive story (and its antipsychoanalytical analogue), the formal purpo┄ hich is to evoke the impulse to "detect" and/or to psychoanalyze ┄er to violently frustrate it by refusing to solve the crime (or find th┄ause of the neurosis). (171)

In addition, Spanos points out, postmodernism also rejects "the rigidly causal plot of the well-made work of the humanistic tradition" (171) in order to deny the reader the comfort of "the eternal simultaneity of essential art" (177) or the "iconic poetic of transcendence" (181). Postmoderns, therefore, refuse to substitute what might be called the truth-claims of art for the truth-claims of science.

Linda Hutcheon also acknowledges the importance to postmodern fiction of the structures of the detective story. Her *Narcissistic Narrative: The Metafictional Paradox* identifies this form as one of the "paradigms" of self-reflexive metafiction, since postmodern texts often employ, for the purposes explanation and verification is human reason, and the method of explanation is the exercise of inductive reasoning (ratiocination after Edgar Allan Poe, or the application of "little grey cells," after Hercule Poirot); 4. the detective is uniquely rational, and he or she possesses an extraordinarily powerful ability to assess and evaluate evidence, as well as an almost poetic ability to introject the criminal mind so as to deduce how it has functioned during the criminal act, while yet rejecting criminality itself; 5. the ordinary run of human events is disrupted by a crime, usually involving an unnatural death or disappearance; 6. a whole community of individuals is implicated in the crime (that is, there are numerous suspects); 7. the detective separates this community into the many innocent and the one guilty; and 8. the community is restored to order and calm after the identification, punishment, and purgation of the criminal.[2] These archetypes may be classified as those that provide the primarily ideological foundations, themselves clearly derived from the scientific world-view (1, 2, 3), and those that provide the narrative structures (4, characterization, and 5–8, plot). The "workability" of the appropriated scientific paradigms is reinforced by the care that writers like Sayers took to ensure that their complicated plots were subject to the rational decoding of the readers themselves, as well as that of the fictional detective. The ideological and narrative assumptions of this worldview were taken as givens, without needing to be overtly established in each text.

As I have argued, the postmodern world-view, as represented in literary texts as well as in texts from many other fields, such as psychoanalysis, literary criticism, philosophy, historiography, and so on, rejects the notion that any intellectual system can securely establish any truth, or, rather, that any human construct or epistemological system can exhaust the richness of an experience or event. As Linda Hutcheon argues in her recent book *A Poetics of Postmodernism: History, Theory, Fiction*:

> The local, the limited, the temporary, the provisional are what define postmodern "truth" . . . . The point is not exactly that the world is meaningless . . . . but that any meaning that exists is of our own creation. (43)

Although Hutcheon does not address scientific discourse as such, the same postmodern strictures may be applied to it as to any discursive system. As Christopher Norris puts it in *Deconstruction: Theory and Practice*:

> 'Science', in Derrida's usage, is a discourse linked to the repressive ideology of reason, which in turn (as Nietzsche argued) took rise from the Greek equation between truth and logic. What is in question, for Nietzsche and Derrida, is not some 'alternative' logic of figurative language but an open plurality of discourse where all such priorities dissolve into the disconcerting 'free play' of signs. (59)

---

of parody, the sort of decoding intelligence detective fiction always employs, which weighs evidence in order to "discover meaning, 'unravel plots'" (32). The parody emerges when the postmodern antidetective, emulating the classical detective in his or her analyses of causes and crimes, typically encounters frustration, self-delusion, and self-reproach, but ends up proliferating rather than conquering such confusion. Whereas the classical detective "solves" the mysteries of being, the postmodern antidetective bogs down, even wallows in the mystery.

On the other hand, classical detective fiction itself frequently includes an analysis of the processes and pitfalls involved in the elucidation of some truth about a crime and its perpetrator. Many detective stories contain a running commentary on the action, usually provided by the extremely self-conscious detective him/herself — the poet/detective Dalgliesh, for example, in the series of novels by P.D. James. A device that is even more relevant as an illustration of Hutcheon's thesis about *narcissistic* narratives is the self-reflexive commentary provided by a fictional *author* of detective stories who is also a character in the detective novel — Harriet Vane, for instance, in the Peter Wimsey novels of Dorothy L. Sayers. A character such as Harriet provides an apt model for emulation by the puzzled writer-sleuths or antidetectives in texts such as *Pale Fire, Les faux monnayeurs,* and *Coming Through Slaughter.* In *Gaudy Night,* for example, Harriet considers the possibility of recharacterizing her fictional hero, Wilfrid, but fears that if she gives him "violent and lifelike feelings, he'll throw the whole book out of balance" (291). Harriet is, of course, coming to grips with the same narrative problem as is her creator, whose own essay, also entitled "Gaudy Night," examines Sayers's qualms about humanizing *her* fictional hero, Lord Peter.[1] Typically, the postmodern narrator-sleuth of *Coming Through Slaughter* conflates his fictional, biographical, and autobiographical impulses, including with his creation and recreation of Bolden, the protagonist, his own accompanying, somewhat paranoid self-identification:

> . . . When he went mad he was the same age as I am now.
> The photograph moves and becomes a mirror. When I read he stood in front of mirrors and attacked himself, there was the shock of memory. For I had done that. Stood, and with a razor-blade cut into cheeks and forehead, shaved hair. Defiling people we did not wish to be. (133)

Narrative devices and characters already formulated in classical detective fiction, then, provide ready examples for postmodern extrapolation and parody.

The major tenets of the world-view of the classical detective story may be briefly summarized as follows: 1. all events, whether physical, chemical, psychological, or social, can ultimately be explained; 2. the explanations can be verified; that is, their truth can be established; 3. the source of such

15

In a summary statement destined to be beloved by postmodern critics, Stephen Hawking says in his recent *A Brief History of Time* that current scientific theorists have "redefined the task of science to be the discovery of laws that will enable us to predict events up to the limits set by the uncertainty principle" (173), which principle, he points out, "signaled an end to . . . a model of the universe that would be completely deterministic: one certainly cannot predict future events exactly if one cannot even measure the present state of the universe precisely" (55).

Postmodernism, then, calls into question the likelihood of authoritatively interpreting anything, let alone human existence, through any one discursive mode. No wonder parody, as Hutcheon defines it — "repetition with critical distance that allows ironic signalling of difference at the very heart of similarity" (*Poetics* 26) — has been embraced by postmodern discourse. Parody both mimics and criticizes that which it parodies, countering any truth claims that the conventions themselves may be implicitly asserting.

Postmodern parodies of the detective story genre subvert the generic form in two crucial respects: they call into question the capacity of human reason and its traditional methods to explain and verify the events of experience, both past and present; and they continually remind the reader of the inevitable failure of fictional discourse either definitively to record experience itself or to propose convincing solutions, rational or otherwise, to what Spanos calls the "'mystery,' the 'crime' of contingent existence" (167). The questioning of reason undertaken by these texts establishes their opposition to the scientific world-view, and their subversive parodies of the transcendent claims of art deny an alternative epistemology based on the humanistic over-valorization of the work of art.

*Coming Through Slaughter*, by providing us with two sleuths, the police detective Webb and the antidetective narrator of the text, confronts precisely these two recurrent issues. Both characters are in search of a missing person, Buddy Bolden, jazz musician. In the fictional policeman Webb, we find the conventional detective: linear, certain, inevitably rational; he assembles the facts of the case in order to get his man and return him to Storyville where he "belongs." In the quasi-fictional antidetective-narrator, we have a postmodern deconstructionist, simultaneous, tentative, inevitably personal; he inspects and invents the data in order to "re-story" rather than "restore" his long-dead protagonist. His search impels him to re-story Storyville as well (for the narrator of a fictional text that deals with historical people and events, the real name of this New Orleans red-light district is ominously perfect), and at the same time to ponder what it means for Buddy and perhaps any artist to "belong" anywhere.

Like any conventional detective, Webb relies upon a practical application of the inductive methods of the scientific world-view. When Buddy

goes missing, Webb successfully marshals all his evidence-gathering skills to retrieve him. Yet *Coming Through Slaughter* deliberately plays with this convention in order to demonstrate the kind of "truth" that Webb obtains through this methodology, and its failure to achieve Webb's goal, which apparently is to bring Buddy back to Storyville as husband, father, and well-known artist who mirrors his community's "truths." Of course, Webb finds Buddy and returns him to his family and career, yet his success edges Buddy toward another chosen and ultimately permanent disappearance into silence. It is worth emphasizing here that, given the parameters within which Webb is operating, he *is* successful: Buddy is found. But Webb has not foreseen that perhaps Buddy cannot return and be "re-storied." And even Webb can not bring Buddy back after he retires into final silence in the State Hospital.

Parodies of scientific sleuthing abound in the text — Webb's very name reminds us that all he wants is "the facts, ma'am, just the facts."[3] His hobby of collecting magnets surely parodies the hobby of the classical detective, who grows orchids, collects incunabula, or knits.[4] Closer to science, however, is Webb's use of his magnets to "explain the precision of the forces in the air" (35); he keeps a giant magnet that sets the others twisting and twitching while Buddy applauds. Clearly we are being invited to draw a parallel between this gravitational performance of metal and air and Buddy's musical manipulation of the same forces. For Buddy, who "was obsessed with the magic of air, . . . could see the air, could tell where it was freshest in a room by the colour" (14), air is not merely the arena of gravitationally warring forces, but a medium to remake into music. When Buddy pushes and pulls air through the metal surfaces of his cornet in order to generate sound, he, not gravity, is the animating force. Yet Webb's magnet, which causes other magnets to "twitch and thrust up and swivel" (35), suggests a parody of Buddy's music, which compels human beings to do the same thing.

Perhaps the more telling parody of Webb's empirically biassed worldview emerges in his hilarious explanation of the death and disappearance of Nora's mother. Using an example from real life, albeit with a certain prescience — the accidental death of Isadora Duncan, strangled in 1927 when her scarf caught in the wheel of a Bugatti — in conjunction with clues about the possessions of the deceased — her pet snake — Webb concocts an inductively valid yet wildly improbable hypothesis about her death: the snake accidentally strangles Mrs. Bass, but lives to slither away. Webb observes to Buddy: "No trace of a weapon. If the snake was human it wouldn't get much more than manslaughter . . . Sometimes Bolden I think I am a genius" (28; ellipsis in original). Ever the man who needs a solution to explain appearances, Webb closes the case.

The narrator, however, is also prepared to appropriate the methods of the scientific world-view. For example, the text presents us with three sonographs as an alternative frontispiece. Appended is a standard scientific explanation:

> The top left sonograph shows a "squawk." Squawks are common emotional expressions that have many frequencies or pitches, which are vocalized simultaneously. Note that the top right sonograph is a whistle. Note that the number of frequencies is small and this gives a "pure" sound — not a squawk. Whistles are like personal signatures for dolphins and identify each dolphin as well as its location. The middle sonograph shows a dolphin making two kinds of signals simultaneously. The vertical stripes are echolocation clicks (sharp, multi-frequency sounds) and the dark, mountain-like humps are the signature whistles. No one knows how a dolphin makes both whistles and echolocation clicks simultaneously. (6)

At the beginning of the book, the reader has no idea what this theory has to do with Bolden and his world. Later on in the text, when we juxtapose this description with other opinions about Bolden's music, such as Dude Botley's reference to "hymns and blues cooked up together" (81), we might compare these squawks, whistles, and the simultaneous emission of the two to Buddy's ability to express the common experiences of Storyville, his own personal story, and a simultaneous "meta-version" of both, the generation of which remains a mystery to both science and history. The narrator thereby claims Buddy as a fellow postmodern. Challenging the traditional stance that the function of art is to synthesize, to transcend experience by formalizing it into an ordered structure, Buddy exercises the postmodernist's knack of decentring conventional formal structures, denying his listeners the comfort of synthesis and order. The narrator proposes that Buddy's music is synchronic rather than diachronic, provisional rather than final, performance rather than product. The fundamental difference between Webb's and the narrator's use of the methods of science is that Webb is convinced of the truth-value and the "workability" of his case-closing rational explanations; the narrator, by using the language of science as a metaphor for Buddy's postmodernism, is merely co-opting another discursive technique to be assembled and evaluated with all the rest.

There is, however, a sinister side to Webb's sleuthing. Even before Buddy disappears from Storyville, Webb has been analyzing him, accounting for Buddy's success as a musician:

> A month after Bolden had moved Webb went to the city and, unseen, tracked Buddy for several days. Till the Saturday when he watched his nervous friend walk jauntily out of the crowd into the path of a parade and begin to play. So hard and beautifully that Webb didn't even have to wait for the reactions of the people, he simply turned and walked till

he no longer heard the music or the roar he imagined crowding round to suck that joy. Its power. (36)

Interestingly, Webb seems immune to the power of Buddy's music; in this passage, Webb sees Buddy emerging from the crowd itself as an artist who can mirror the people back to themselves, so to speak. For Webb, Buddy is the sort of artist who offers the listener a suspiciously traditional solution to the "crime of contingent existence"; quite simply, for Webb the solution is provided by the entertainment value of art — Buddy's music offers diversion from a murder, perhaps, or an amusing revision of the "stories found in the barber shop" (43). The narrator, on the other hand, sees Buddy the proto-postmodern, an experimenter with the avant-garde gestures of decentring, deconstruction, and disorder. Although Buddy's performances do not engage Webb, his disappearance does; obviously upset by the random irrationality of the act, he immediately starts to look for Buddy, hoping "to stumble on the clues that were left by Bolden's disappearance" (22). He interviews Nora and Crawley, Cornish and Bellocq, collecting a photograph from the latter so that he might have an empirically verifiable "copy" of Buddy to hand round like a wanted poster.

The narrator, on the other hand, although he renounces the possibility of ever establishing the "true story" of Buddy's disappearance, temporary silence, reappearance, and ultimate silence, ransacks archives to assemble documents and transcripts of eyewitness accounts, visits the "scene of the crime," even takes photographs of the landscape. He "re-stories" the characters (both fictional and historical), the institutions, and the gestures. He mingles history with fiction and document with narrative, yet offers no authoritative synthesis of them. He even practices deconstructive criticism himself, offering analyses of both Buddy's music and Bellocq's photographs.

In trying to "find" Buddy, after all, the narrator is at a certain disadvantage: the "real" Buddy is dead. He left no personal evidence of his music — he refused to make any recordings of his jazz. The evidence that the narrator must sift through is inevitably second-hand, fragmentary, inaccurate, subjective, or absent. Buddy's newspaper, The Cricket, which chronicles its "sub-history" of Storyville with "stray facts, manic theories, and well-told lies" (24), serves as a metaphor for the narrator's search.

Like the classical detective, Webb achieves the identification with the "criminal" that marks the great fictional sleuths, from Auguste Dupin through Holmes and Wimsey to Marple and Dalgliesh. Webb, too, is able to introject the criminal mind while yet rejecting the criminal act:

> Webb circled, trying to understand not where Buddy was but wha⁴ he was doing, quite capable of finding him but taking his time, taking almost two years, entering the character of Bolden through every voice he spoke to. (63)

Webb collects the evidence and pursues his leads until he finds Buddy, and then he manoeuvres him to return to New Orleans. In Buddy's words, Webb "could reach me this far away, could tilt me upside down till he was directing me like wayward traffic back home. . . . He came here and placed my past and future on this table like a road" (86). Temporarily, Buddy seems prepared to accept Webb's simple, one-way solution. The narrator, too, attempts to introject:

> Why did my senses stop at you? There was the sentence, 'Buddy Bolden who became a legend when he went berserk in a parade . . .' What was there in that, before I knew your nation your colour your age, that made me push my arm forward and spill it through the front of your mirror and clutch myself? Did not want to pose in your accent but think in your brain and body, and you like a weatherbird arcing round in the middle of your life to exact opposites and burning your brains out . . . . (134; first ellipsis in original)

This slightly paranoid self-identification with the missing person is a post-modern gesture in itself, reminiscent again of such texts as *The Crying of Lot 49* or *Pale Fire*. Art-making itself may turn out to be the crime for which Buddy is punished by the official diagnosis of madness.

Yet Buddy is neither a typical criminal, nor the victim of a criminal act. As Webb discovers, he has not been abducted or hypnotized into committing unwanted crimes; his disappearance was chosen. And although he has disrupted his family life and career by leaving Storyville, this disruption is probably not the worst of crimes. Eventually we wonder why it is so important to Webb to find Buddy and take him back to Storyville. Why, for that matter, does Buddy, apparently in love with Robin Brewitt, agree to return with Webb? Webb may need Buddy the artist, but it would appear that Buddy also needs Webb the lawman.

In the last half of the text, after Webb has retrieved Buddy, most of Buddy's soliloquies are directed to Webb or to the part of himself that is Webb-like. Although Buddy has allowed himself to be relocated, he is uncertain why he has done so. He muses:

> Our friendship had nothing accidental did it. Even at the start you set out to breed me into something better. Which you did. You removed my immaturity at just the right time and saved me a lot of energy and I sped away happy and alone in a new town away from you, and now you produce a leash, curl the leather round and round your fist, and walk straight into me. And you pull me home. . . . All the time I hate what I am doing and want the other. . . . All you've done is cut me in half, pointing me here. Where I don't want these answers. (89)

Buddy acknowledges here that by returning to Storyville he has perhaps succumbed to entrapment. What Webb has tempted him with (and what he has loved — and been infuriated by — in Nora as well) is the affirmation of certainties, of simple actions and simple solutions, of probabilities and patterns, those "sure lanes of the probable" (15–16), which simultaneously attract and repel him. In short, he finds the relatively simple world-view of the classical detective story enticing, but he intuitively knows that its assumptions help him neither to make his music nor to live his life. Buddy discloses this approach-avoidance attitude most clearly in the thoughts he addresses to Webb about another man's music:

> John Robichaux! Playing his waltzes. And I hate to admit it but I enjoyed listening to the clear forms. Every note part of the large curve, so carefully patterned that for the first time I appreciated the possibilities of a mind moving ahead of the instruments in time and waiting with pleasure for them to catch up. I had never been aware of that mechanistic pleasure, that trust.
>
> Did you ever meet Robichaux? I never did. I loathed everything he stood for. He dominated his audiences. He put his emotions into patterns which a listening crowd had to follow. . . . When I played parades we would be going down Canal Street and at each intersection people would hear just the fragment I happened to be playing. . . . I wanted them to be able to come in where they pleased and leave when they pleased and somehow hear the germs of the start and all the possible endings at whatever point in the music that I had reached *then*. (93–94)

Eventually Buddy muses that "in terror we lean in the direction that is most unlike us" (96), and it would seem that when Buddy is lured back to his familiar life in Storyville, he rejects its appealing entrapment by renouncing it all in one grand gesture — music, family, social role: certainty in any of its guises.

When he goes to Shell Beach, Buddy sets aside his art, and, moreover, denies its access to anything final, finished, and absolute. When he chooses the Brewitts, he characterizes them as "The silent ones. Post music. After ambition" (39). He claims that he must rediscover "that fear of certainties [he] had when [he] first began to play" (86), proposing that in adapting to such certainties as ambition and fame, he is offering his audiences merely his "own recycled air" (86).[5] In this renunciation of the truth-claims of his music, Buddy allies himself with Bellocq, who, according to Buddy,

> was offering me black empty spaces. . . .
>
> Whatever I say about him you will interpret as the working of an enemy and what I loved Webb were the possibilities in his silence. . . . He tempted me out of the world of audiences where I had tried to catch everything thrown at me. He offered mole comfort, mole deceit. (91)

To Buddy, Bellocq is someone who can get beyond the established norms and boundaries of everyday life in order to expose life at the margins, to his shirt his java jacket and driven itself onto the wall" (151). With this last grim symbol of entrapment, the narrator depicts Webb pinned to the wall, contained by yet another certain structure. Perhaps seeing in Buddy's behaviour a garbled parody of those "sure lanes of the probable" (15–16), Webb is sickened by his own complicity in Buddy's fate.

The narrator has provided us with a contrasting image in his description of the (fictional) suicide of Bellocq. Vomiting smoke, Bellocq dives against the structure of flames that he has created:

He has expected the wall to be there and his body has prepared itself and his mind has prepared itself so his shape is constricted against an imaginary force looking as if he has come up against an invisible structure in the air.
Then he falls, dissolving out of his pose. Everything has gone wrong.
The wall is not there to catch or hide him. Nothing is there to clasp him into a certainty. (67)

Each character is true to his world-view at the last — Bellocq surrendering to nothingness, and Webb constrained by structure.

The narrator's motives for rediscovering Buddy are not so simple. Certainly he wishes to claim Buddy and Bellocq as avatars of postmodernism, misunderstood in an earlier, inimical age. But the narrator also claims that Buddy's mind was "on the pinnacle of something" (133) when it collapsed; while hardly a resonant claim regarding the truth-value of the work of art, even that indeterminate "something" implies that Buddy's music has reached some sort of apogee after which only silence is possible. Buddy's moments of total identification with the dancer bring him to the condition of silence in the midst of sound, privacy in the public eye:

Then silent. For something's fallen in my body and I can't hear the music as I play it. The notes more often now. She hitting each note with her body before it is even out so I know what I do through her. . . . this is what I wanted, always, loss of privacy in the playing, leaving the stage, the rectangle of band on the street, this hearer who can throw me in the direction and the speed she wishes like an angry shadow. (130)

Is the narrator implying that Buddy has actually achieved access to some transcendent truth, thereby undermining both Buddy's and his own postmodern denials of final solutions? Susan Sontag, in her essay "The Aesthetics of Silence," proposes that

the highest good for the artist is to reach the point where those goals of excellence become insignificant to him, emotionally and ethically, and he is more satisfied by being silent than by finding a voice in art. . . . Silence is the artist's ultimate other-worldly gesture: by silence he frees

reveal in his photographs simultaneously the text and the sub-text beneath it, or the anti-text that abuts it.[6] For the narrator, Bellocq is a fellow deconstructionist; for Webb and Cornish and Nora, Bellocq has modelled the ruin that Buddy mimics.

Strictly speaking, there are two mysteries to be solved in Coming Through Slaughter: the first is the disappearance of Buddy, which is solved by Webb. The second is the establishment of an actual criminal act — has Buddy committed some crime for which he must be punished? Can his art-making be established as innocent or criminal? Buddy has apparently left Storyville to escape those tempting certainties of family, fame, and adulation. Trained by Bellocq to love "the possibilities in his silence" (91), Buddy drops into his "post music" phase at the Brewitts. To Webb, this retreat from fame and responsibility is irrational, "landscape suicide" (22). By bringing Buddy back, Webb may be unconsciously seeking the archetypal scapegoat of the classical detective tale. Many of these tales present a reconstruction of the crime by the detective himself, since the reassembling of all the suspects and the recreation of all the circumstances of the crime invariably invokes the self-incrimination of the perpetrator. For Webb, once Buddy is found and put back into the community, either his nature will prove to be innocent — that is, he will regain centre stage, where his music will be a conduit of the "truth" about human nature — or his innate criminality, his postmodern denial of the truth-value of art, will manifest itself. Webb, of course, has misconceived the role that the musician ought to play in this community; he fails to realize that Buddy will not offer the eternal verities stereotypically demanded of the artist. Buddy has moved on past the edge, like a "naïve explorer looking for footholds" (64), and in trying to restore Buddy to the centre after he has "decentred" himself, Webb is seriously implicated in Buddy's collapse. Although bursting a blood vessel in the throat is neither an illegal nor an insane act, Buddy is carted off like a criminal and madman, first to the House of Detention and later to the East Louisiana State Hospital. Apparently self-incriminated, the artist reserves the right to remain silent.

In an attempt to expose Webb's world-view, the narrator offers a coda to Webb's "solution" to the mystery of Buddy. In 1924 Webb returns yet again to the scene of the crime, and inadvertently learns a new piece of information about Buddy. In conversation with Bella Cornish, Webb learns that Buddy has not died in the hospital as Nora has told him, but lives on, vacantly, touching things like "the taps on the bath, the door frame, benches, things like that" (150). Webb, horrified and sickened, "arched away his body stiff and hard trying to break through the wall every nerve on the outside . . ." (150). After Webb has rushed off to vomit, Bella sees "the damp mark on her right where his sweat had in those few minutes gone through his skin himself from servile bondage to the world, which appears as patron, client, consumer, antagonist, arbiter, and distorter of his work. (6)

Sontag goes on to suggest that the artist who yearns after the condition of silence is in some way superior to those who continue to chatter and ask the questions to which the silent artist knows there are no satisfying answers; that is, although Sontag does not use the terminology, it may be the ultimate postmodern gesture to renounce all subsequent gestures. Buddy apparently goes into training for this silence at the Brewitts's (although he still compulsively practises *Cakewalking Babies* on Robin's back [59]), then perfects it in the State Hospital, retiring into some Zen-like state of mystic otherness. A less comforting hypothesis is that Buddy blows his mind "by playing too hard and too often drunk too wild too crazy" (134), in some personally devastating postmodern attempt to renounce once and for all both the demands of fame and the artist's access to truths of any sort, and hence winds up a certified lunatic in the East Louisiana State Hospital.

Toward the end of the text, Willy Cornish is quoted as asking, "He had all that talent and wisdom.... What good is all that if we can't learn or know?" (145), repeating the inevitable humanist query, "But what can we learn from the tragedy of Buddy?" Allowing himself the last word in the text (although not the final words in the book), the narrator announces that "There are no prizes" (156). The antidetective does not solve the mystery, and indeed cannot solve the mystery, because no one solution will suffice. As Stefano Tani says in *The Doomed Detective*:

> To choose not to choose [not to solve the mystery] is the widest choice the anti-detective can make, because to let the mystery exist does not restrict his freedom to a single choice and, at the same time, potentially implies all solutions without choosing any. The anti-detective arrives reluctantly at this non-solution, however, forced to it by the proliferation of meanings (clues) in the events he goes through. . . . (46–47)

If the on-the-spot sleuth cannot restore Buddy safely to Storyville, the postmodern sleuth, cautious and sympathetic though he is, must renounce the definitive "re-storying" of his protagonist as well. As "M.O." reminds us in a last narrative joke, like his fictional narrator, he is ultimately polishing another document "to suit the truth of fiction" (last page, unpaginated).

NOTES

1 In the essay "Gaudy Night," reprinted in Haycraft, Sayers remarks:

> If the story was to go on, Peter had got to become a complete human being, with a past and a future, with a consistent family and social history, with a complicated psychology and even the rudiments of a religious outlook. And all

this would have to be squared somehow or other with such random attributes as I had bestowed upon him over a series of years in accordance with the requirements of various detective plots. (211)

2 For good general discussions of the archetypes of detective fiction, see, among others, Cawelti and Tani. Such collections of critical essays as Haycraft and Landrum et al. also provide background on classical detective fiction and its variants.

3 The observation that Webb's name may be borrowed from *Dragnet*, in which Sgt. Joe Friday was played by Jack Webb, is also made by Maxwell (111).

4 The hobbies of Nero Wolfe, Lord Peter Wimsey, and Miss Marple respectively.

5 The major episode preceding Buddy's departure from Storyville is his violent encounter with Pickett. This assault may be interpreted as being all about "certainties" — Pickett's beauty, for example, and his determined conservation of that beauty, destroyed by Buddy's murderous attack, and, most devastating of all, the certainty of Nora, undermined by her possible affair with Pickett. As the narrator puts it,

> IF Nora had been with Pickett. Had really been with Pickett as he said. Had jumped off Bolden's cock and sat down half an hour later on Tom Pickett's mouth on Canal Street. Then the certainties he loathed and needed were liquid at the root.... Pickett earlier so confident he knew her thoroughly, her bones, god he knew even the number of bones she had in her body. (78)

If Buddy is "almost completely governed by fears of certainty" (15), his violent lashing out against all containing structures (windows, glass, mirrors, skin, even the metal walls of his cornet) can be seen as attempts to destroy certain structures, assumptions and acts.

6 Ondaatje acknowledges his debt to *Storyville Portraits*, a collection of Bellocq's photographs edited by John Szarkowski, on the second last page of the text, as "an inspiration of mood and character. Private and fictional magnets drew him and Bolden together." This collection of Bellocq's photographs of the Storyville whores is extremely interesting. The prints have all been developed recently, since no contemporary versions developed by Bellocq have been found. The photographs often include elements of background "normally" cropped out of portraits, such as laundry hanging in a back alley behind an obvious, studio-style paper backdrop, in front of which the female subject of the portrait sits. As the editor of *Storyville Portraits* makes clear in the introduction, no one has any idea whether or not Bellocq intended to leave in such "extraneous" (we would now say "postmodern") features.

WORKS CITED

Cawelti, John G. *Adventure, Mystery, and Romance: Formula Stories as Art and Popular Culture*. Chicago: U of Chicago P, 1976.
Hawking, Stephen. *A Brief History of Time*. New York: Bantam, 1988.
Haycraft, Howard, ed. *The Art of the Mystery: A Collection of Critical Essays*. New York: Biblo, 1976.
Hutcheon, Linda. *A Poetics of Postmodernism: History, Theory, Fiction*. New York: Routledge, 1988.
———. *Narcissistic Narrative: The Metafictional Paradox*. Waterloo, Ont.: Wilfrid Laurier UP, 1980.

Landrum, Larry N. et al, eds. *Dimensions of Detective Fiction*. N.p.: Popular, 1976.

Maxwell, Barry. "Surrealistic Aspects of Michael Ondaatje's *Coming Through Slaughter*." *Mosaic* 18.3 (1985): 101–14.

Norris, Christopher. *Deconstruction: Theory and Practice*. London: Methuen, 1982.

Ondaatje, Michael. *Coming Through Slaughter*. Toronto: Anansi, 1976.

Sayers, Dorothy L. *Gaudy Night*. London: New English Library, 1978.

———. "Gaudy Night." *The Art of the Mystery: A Collection of Critical Essays*. Ed. Howard Haycraft. New York: Biblo, 1976. 208–21.

Sontag, Susan. "The Aesthetics of Silence." *Styles of Radical Will*. New York: Farrar, 1969. 3–34.

Spanos, William V. "The Detective and the Boundary: Some Notes on the Postmodern Literary Imagination." *Casebook on Existentialism 2*. Ed. William V. Spanos. New York: Harper, 1976. 163–89.

Szarkowski, John, ed. *Storyville Portraits: Photographs from the New Orleans Red-Light District, Circa 1912*. New York: The Museum of Modern Art, 1970.

Tani, Stefano. *The Doomed Detective: The Contribution of the Detective Novel to Postmodern American and Italian Fiction*. Carbondale: U of Southern Illinois P, 1984.

# Introduction

## 'the slight silver key'

Only his writing was calm. His writing which had in more ways than one saved his life.

Woody Allen, *Deconstructing Harry*

Teacher: Last question – even simpler. 'Where is the father?'

François Truffaut, *The 400 Blows*

According to the proverb, each book has its history. This one began or, perhaps more accurately, took on momentum because of what might be called two non-events: the relative lack of attention to poetry in the special Ondaatje issue of *Essays on Canadian Writing* (Summer 1994) and, four years later, the relative silence in 1998 in Canada and abroad surrounding the publication of *Handwriting*, to my mind one of the decade's most original books of English poetry. Given the warm critical reception of the early poetry and the international success of *The English Patient* as novel and film, I find it difficult to explain this neglect. Though on my bad days I tend to agree with Randall Jarrell that modern society isn't aware of its poets, I'm still surprised when a significant body of work by a writer of Ondaatje's stature and reputation – the two aren't synonymous – is ignored even by academic critics, the linebackers of poetry's crumbling last line of defence. Part of the problem, of course, is that poetry is more difficult than fiction to treat ideologically, to reduce to the expectations and demands of the critically fashionable identity politics or one of the currently dominant critical 'isms.' It can't be turned as easily as fiction into a discourse that 'proves' some point of gender, class, politics, or social critique. In a word, poetry is more resistant to contemporary critical theory, unless it follows Kenneth Burke in its orientation, than prose. It also requires what Frank Kermode calls 'close literary criticism, nose to the text,'[1] an attitude that smacks of the old New Criticism and is therefore almost automatically suspect. Despite this situation, I still expected that at least readers with an interest in postmodernism or post-colonialism would be as attentive to Handwriting as to The English Patient and Anil's Ghost – and they haven't been. Feminist-oriented critics such as Lorraine York and Christian Bök, who have written about the poetry, have done little beyond stating the obvious about the presence of violent males, passive, uncreative, or commodified females, a male gaze, and traditional gender assumptions. York even seems to suggest that feminists have avoided Ondaatje's work because of the phalanx of intimidating male critics – myself included – standing guard over it.[2] Though both York and Bök are occasionally perceptive, one senses that for the most part the literary texts are primarily occasions for the scoring of points, with the author's total going up or down depending on his perceived attitude to women. In Paul de Man's words, the focus is on 'the external politics of literature,' to the detriment of attention to the text itself.[3] These aren't so much misreadings as swerves away from reading towards a preconceived thematization.

This situation has provoked me to take another look at a body of work that I have admired for nearly four decades and to write a book in which I make as strong a critical case as I can for Ondaatje's poetry. I shall simultaneously provide what Billy the Kid called 'the slight silver key' to Ondaatje's central concerns; examine the relationship between the life and the poetry; offer a chronological overview of his body of poetic work; comment on influence, development, and continuity; and give close readings of those poems that seem to require them. Though the focus will be on the poems, I will refer throughout to The Collected Works of Billy the Kid, Coming through Slaughter, Running in the Family, In the Skin of a Lion, The English Patient, and Anil's Ghost, as well as Ondaatje's critical writing, whenever they help to illuminate the reading of a poem or whenever I can use them to show continuity and development. Implicit throughout will also be a continuing act of self-criticism as I revisit some of my own early work on Ondaatje.

Some readers may wonder why I have organized Ragas of Longing around individual chapters devoted to the volumes of poetry. I was originally tempted to structure the book, like The Last Canadian Poet: An Essay on Al Purdy, on the basis of central topics or topoi, but I decided

to turn to this format because Ondaatje organizes his collections very carefully and they repay readings that respect them as wholes and see the poems and volumes as related one to another. I think that George Elliott Clarke overstates the point, but he's on the right scent when he comments, 'Ondaatje's works are so alike that each is best read as an adjunct of the others. They form a canon: they must be read in the light and the shadow of each other before their individual illuminations or obscurities can be seen.'[4] I would qualify this perspective slightly by seeing Ondaatje's personal 'canon' as an evolving one in which each book of poems builds on its predecessor while simultaneously preparing the ground for the following, often quite different, volume. Signature words, images, motifs, and topoi recur from book to book, often linking scenes that echo across decades. I agree with Ondaatje's comment that each new book has 'a new vocabulary, a new set of clothes,'[5] but I would add that it also uses much of the old lexis and wardrobe. As a result, his career as a poet has what might be called a deep narrative and a certain narrative trajectory that is best studied, because most obvious, when the books are read in chronological order.

Such an approach also helps to foreground the evolution of Ondaatje's treatment of himself and what one might call his family romance. The presence of the life in the work will be one of the threads holding the book together. Needless to say, poets write about their lives in a variety of ways, with Anne Sexton and Robert Lowell at one end of the autobiographical spectrum and Wallace Stevens and Zbigniew Herbert at the other. The former are confessional; the latter deal obliquely and impersonally with urgent personal needs. As Stevens put it, 'The subjects of one's poems are the symbols of one's self or of one's selves.'[6] In other words, if a poet like Lowell tries to say it all in as unmediated a fashion as possible, a poet like Stevens deals with his life obliquely and symbolically. As I will argue, Ondaatje uses both approaches. In Secular Love the style creates the impression of an unmediated narrative; elsewhere the life is less an explicit presence or reference than an intimated autobiographical pressure behind image and scene. The 'plot' of the narrative in Handwriting – whose first word, implicit in my main title – taken from Handwriting – whose first word, 'ragas,' points to a song of exile and whose closing phrase, 'of longing,' intimates the desire to return. Some readers may wonder why I have ignored The Collected Works of Billy the Kid, which is strongly, if indirectly, marked by Ondaatje's life. For two reasons: first, I don't think of the book as 'poetry' despite the presence in it of a handful of lyrics I admire; and, second, it has drawn a substantial body of perceptive critical commentary, beginning with Stephen Scobie's 'Two Authors in Search of a Character: bp Nichol and Michael Ondaatje.' By contrast, the 'real' poems became critical orphans after *In the Skin of a Lion* (1987), when Ondaatje achieved international popularity.[7]

My own view, and it will be elaborated in this study, is that Ondaatje has produced a substantial body of verse with an original style and a profound vision, as well as a handful of contemporary classics; among these are 'King Kong meets Wallace Stevens,' 'Light,' 'Burning Hills,' '"The gate in his head,"' 'White Dwarfs,' 'Light,' 'Moon Lines, after Jiménez,' 'The Cinnamon Peeler,' 'Rock Bottom,' 'To a Sad Daughter,' 'The Story,' 'Last Ink,' and 'Letters & Other Worlds' (I agree with Stephen Scobie's comment that the last is among 'the greatest of Ondaatje's poems.')[8] From his early poems to his latest, readers would not mistake his voice – cool, laconic, controlled, wryly humorous, and inflected by striking metaphors – for that of another poet. The adjustments in that voice from poem to poem and over time are co-extensive with 'the structural and symbolic aesthetic strategies to which [he] has been driven in copping' with what Helen Vendler has called 'some personal *donnée* which the poet could not avoid treating.'[9] Czeslaw Milosz's suggestion 'It is possible that there is no other memory than the memory of wounds' may be an exaggeration, but in Ondaatje's case it hits close to the mark; 'wounds,' after all, is one of his signature images, and readers as different as Susan Glickman, Ed Jewinski, and Lorraine York have suggested the presence of a primal wound in the poems' figure in the carpet.[10] His vision of human life is post-Christian, postmodern, and fundamentally tragic – 'There are no prizes' (*CTS*, 156). Reading him, I'm reminded of Bertrand Russell's comment about Joseph Conrad's world view: 'I felt, though I do not know whether he would have accepted such an image, that he thought of civilized and morally tolerable human life as a dangerous walk on a thin crust of barely cooled lava which at any moment might break and let the unwary sink into fiery depths.'[11] It is worth recalling that Conrad, another fatherless exile writing in a foreign language, is referred to in *Rat Jelly*, *Running in the Family*, and *In the Skin of a Lion*. Order in Ondaatje's poems, as in Conrad's novels, is often tenuous and temporary, menaced by violence or chaos.

Something of this sense of threat is apparent in one of the finer lyrics in *The Collected Works of Billy the Kid*:

I have seen pictures of great stars,
drawings which show them straining to the centre
that would explode their white
if temperature and the speed they moved at
shifted one degree.

Or in the East have seen
the dark grey yards where trains are fitted
and the clean speed of machines
that make machines, their
red golden pouring which when cooled
mists out to rust or grey.

The beautiful machines pivoting on themselves
sealing and fusing to others
and men throwing levers like coins at them.
And there is there the same stress as with stars,
the one altered move that will make them maniac.     (41)

Because Billy, the machines, and the stars are on some deep level synonymous, the poem suggests that an explosion threatens the self, the world, and the universe. All are fundamentally unstable. Ondaatje's is a tragic world in which errors ('the one altered move') are both inevitable – life is like *that* – and irremediable because they can never be corrected, except in a way that is paradoxically negligible and vital, in the work of art. His theory of art is predicated on a causal relationship between suffering and creativity; several of his most powerful poems are elegies; and the survivors in his novels resemble minor characters in Shakespearean tragedies in looking back over their shoulders at corpses and what Edgar (a 'character' in *Running in the Family*) calls 'The weight of this sad time' (*King Lear* V. iii. 324). The more fatalistic aspect of his vision can be heard in the epigraph, from Christopher Dewdney, to 'Pure Memory / Chris Dewdney': 'Listen, it was so savage and brutal and powerful that even though it happened out of the blue I knew there was nothing arbitrary about it' (*TTK*, 100).

In this context, it seems particularly fitting that when asked to contribute a poem and a commentary to the *Globe and Mail's* 'How Poems Work' column, Ondaatje chose Elizabeth Bishop's hard-edged villanelle 'One Art.'[12]

The art of losing isn't hard to master;
So many things seem filled with the intent
To be lost that their loss is no disaster.

Lose something every day. Accept the fluster
Of lost door keys, the hour badly spent.
The art of losing isn't hard to master.

Then practice losing farther, losing faster:
Places, and names, and where it was you meant
To travel. None of these will bring disaster.

I lost my mother's watch. And look! My last, or
Next-to-last, of three loved houses went.
The art of losing isn't hard to master.

I lost two cities, lovely ones. And, vaster,
Some realms I owned, two rivers, a continent.
I miss them, but it wasn't a disaster.

— Even losing you (the joking voice, a gesture
I love) I shan't have lied. It's evident
The art of losing's not too hard to master
Though it may look like (Write it!) like disaster.

The last sentence of Ondaatje's brief commentary could also serve as an epigraph to his body of work: 'And in the end we are left with this precise wonder, not a word wasted or misused, that has pretty well said everything, quickly, casually, in that cautious self-protective voice that in the end blurts out the great hurt of everything.' It seems appropriate that his selected poems begin and end with elegies. Reading the villanelle in the context of Ondaatje's poems, I can't help thinking that had he written it, the clause 'Then practice losing farther' might be read homophonically as suggesting 'Then practice losing father.' Bishop's great loss, like Louis MacNeice's, was her mother; hence the poignant pun on 'mother's watch.'

'The great hurt of everything' is also at the heart of Ondaatje's vision, though we can often narrow it down to the essential underlying *donnée*, which is the breakup of his parents' marriage, their divorce, and his subsequent childhood exile from Ceylon in 1954, an exile that

also included a permanent separation from his father, Philip Mervyn Ondaatje. The writer suggests as much in 1993 in the following uncharacteristically self-revealing, though ultimately ambiguous, comment to Eleanor Wachtel about the moves from Ceylon to England and from England to Canada: 'They were all traumatic moves for me, but I don't think I showed it very much. They were traumatic in retrospect. They weren't *bad* traumatic; it was suddenly, "Okay, now you've got to grow up, now you've got to wear long trousers and a tie." It was a physical change more than a mental one.'[13] This observation isn't entirely convincing. I have the impression that Ondaatje realized at the end of the second sentence that he was showing more of his hand than he wanted to and decided to pull back. He did so, however, with an oxymoronic phrase that doesn't quite make sense since there is no such thing as a *good* trauma, just as there is no good wound. To take two examples, 'Letters & Other Worlds,' the elegy for his father, and *Running in the Family* contradict the suggestion that the trauma was more physical than psychological or emotional. The childhood exile from family, father, culture, and island isn't the only subject he has dealt with in his poetry and fiction, but it recurs often enough in a variety of forms to constitute a significant, perhaps dominant structure of feeling and figure in the carpet. It is not a coincidence that he is formally most experimental and imaginatively most daring when responding to the pressure of unresolved personal issues.

I would argue that the absence of the father is an absent presence somewhere behind the missing parental figures in *The Collected Works of Billy the Kid*, *Coming through Slaughter*, *In the Skin of a Lion*, *The English Patient*, and *Anil's Ghost*. In *Running in the Family* the son returns to Sri Lanka primarily to assemble all the available rumours, gossip, memories, and facts about the dead father. He's also the shadow behind the alcoholic Pat Garrett (*The Collected Works of Billy the Kid*), Dashiell Hammett ('White Dwarfs'), and Buddy Bolden (*Coming through Slaughter*). W.M. Verhoeven makes roughly the same point but without mentioning the father: 'Again and again persons (or their identities) get lost in Ondaatje's stories – lost in legend, lost in the bush, lost in the past, lost in history, lost in memory, lost in myth – and in each case people go after them in order to recover them, to remember them, or to recreate them.'[14] T.S. Eliot, discussing some recurrent imagery in Seneca and Chapman, makes the following comment that illuminates this aspect of Ondaatje's work: 'I suggest that what gives [this imagery] such intensity as it has in each case is its saturation ... with feelings too obscure for the authors even to know quite what they were.[15] I'm not suggesting, however, that Ondaatje isn't aware of what he is doing, though in poetry there is often an element of the poet knowing more than he thinks he knows. Stevens captures something of this: 'While there is nothing automatic about the poem, nevertheless it has an automatic aspect in the sense that it is what I wanted it to be without knowing before it was written what I wanted it to be, even though I knew before it was written what I wanted to do.[16] I'm more interested here in the possibility of an emotional or psychological economy in which certain emotions or memories are so strong and important that they saturate or overdetermine aspects of a poem. Eliot, of course, is also probably right in seeing that some feelings may result in recurrent images and scenes of remarkable compression and complexity whose full implications the author doesn't understand. These feelings or memories may also be sufficiently important to the writer to require more than one work for their expression. As George Whalley suggests, the poet's 'transmutation' of his feelings to the words and images with which they have associated in his memory and imagination 'is probably never complete; there is always an untranslatable residue. This no doubt explains how poems and even novels tend to be written in families, as a series of approximations to a recurrent complex of feeling.'[17]

It's worth adding that, while this 'complex of feeling' may have its source in the writer's life, it often finds expression in poems that do not seem to refer to the life at all. An extreme case is 'The Waste Land,' which Eliot described to Elizabeth Bishop as less a 'criticism of the contemporary world' than 'a piece of rhythmical grumbling' and which John Berryman guessed in 1948 would eventually 'prove to be personal' and 'also appear then more terrible and more pitiful even than it does now.'[18]

In Ondaatje's body of work, the father is also a metaphor for a lost place and culture. As several readers have suggested, this magical tropical world, completely different from the England and Canada to which he emigrated in 1954 and 1962 respectively, appears in Ondaatje's early work in a variety of displaced forms and images. The early interest in the work of Henri Rousseau, 'le Douanier,' for instance, becomes more nuanced if we think of it in relation to Sri Lanka, as perhaps does the interest in exile, isolation, and Australia in the man with seven toes (1969). A similar case can be made for Ondaatje's excited reading of One Hundred Years of Solitude in his article 'García Márquez and the Bus to Aracataca,' where Macondo recalls Ceylon

and the wayward Buendias seem distant cousins to the manic Ondaatjes and Gratiaens of the two major elegies ('Letters & Other Worlds' and 'Light') and Running in the Family. As I shall argue in my discussion of Ondaatje's first book, The Dainty Monsters, his work in the 1960s regularly shows the poet swerving away from a direct confrontation with disturbing aspects of his past by finding oblique or symbolic ways of treating them. It's as if he knows that he's not emotionally ready to name the Ceylon of his youth and Philip Mervyn Ondaatje, or perhaps hasn't mastered 'the structural and symbolic strategies' that would allow him to deal with this troubling and, for the moment, intractable material. Yet in a brief prose commentary on 'Peter,' he makes the following revealing comment:

My only emotion about my own work is curiosity. I see my poems as I would a home-movie. I am still conscious of all the bits and pieces / relatives and friends that were just to the left of the camera and that never got into the picture.

I can't remember what was off-screen when writing 'Peter'; the poem grew by itself and went its own way. It probably contains my most interesting hang-ups and I still remain curious about it. I do remember that my appendix burst a few days after I finished the poem.[19]

The imagery in the first paragraph is revealing: a poem is like 'a home-movie,' and even when it isn't about 'relatives and friends,' they constitute both a frame for it and a felt absent presence. The comment about 'Peter' is equally interesting since it suggests a relationship between 'my most interesting hang-ups' and the mythic story of a feral child who becomes an artist and a killer. A handful of sentences written in 1970 may not be much to go on, but they do suggest that other poems of the first decade also might have an autobiographical subtext. It is worth noting, in contrast, that in Leonard Cohen, written at the same time, Ondaatje is reluctant to relate Cohen's work to his life, and he comments that 'nothing is more irritating than to have your work translated by your life' (3). It will be another three years, in 1973 in the dedication to Rat Jelly and in 'Letters & Other Worlds,' before the past will be explicitly acknowledged in the names of his parents.

Inseparable from this issue is the problem of how to write about himself. With the exception of a handful of casual domestic poems, Ondaatje's early work is notable for the absence of poems of intimacy or self-revelation. In an era dominated by confessional poetry – Lowell's

*Life Studies* appeared in 1959, Plath's *Ariel* in 1965 – Ondaatje's poems of the sixties and early seventies, even when they have a first-person speaker, are rarely genuinely subjective or revealing of his personal life; even when subjective, they are almost never intimate, and the 'I' is almost a third-person pronoun. Not coincidentally, his creative energies in this period find full expression primarily in the increasingly experimental mental sequences 'Peter' (1967), *the man with seven toes* (1969), and *The Collected Works of Billy the Kid* (1970), where one senses that the characters are authorial masks. Most readers will recall Billy's teasing suggestion that we 'Find the beginning, the slight silver key to unlock it, to dig it out. Here then is a maze to begin, be in' (20). There seem to me to be two possibilities here. Either Billy is having some postmodern fun with us since he knows that his reality – in this book and in legend – is nothing but an endless verbal and representational maze and therefore without a key. Or Ondaatje is offering this possibility as a feint, distracting us from the significance of the book's final image, a photograph of Michael the Kid dressed as a cowboy in Ceylon circa 1950. Though the photograph appears at the end, a case can be made that we should also imagine it on the opening blank page, where a photograph of Billy is described but not reproduced. However we respond to this final image, my impression is that we can't avoid seeing that it has autobiographical implications for the text. It may not help us to read the sequence autobiographically, but doing so reminds us implicitly of the presence of the subjective concerns that have found indirect dramatic and symbolic expression in the story of a fatherless outlaw whose 'collected works,' like those of Peter and Philip Michael Ondaatje, are expressions of violence and tenderness. After 'Letters & Other Worlds' it will be difficult not to read Pat Garrett, Billy's alcoholic stepfather, as an early avatar of Ondaatje's father as well as of the father as artist. It's worth noting that Billy's parents are never mentioned and that Buddy Bolden is almost autochthonous, though his mother is referred to.

I also want to suggest that we need to read one other of Ondaatje's early works in the light of his life, the master's thesis he wrote on the young Scots poet and critic Edwin Muir in the mid-sixties at Queen's University.[20] It is the most important of Ondaatje's four works of criticism, the others being the monograph on Cohen, an essay on Howard O'Hagan, and 'What is in the Pot,' his introduction to *The Long Poem Anthology.* I need to discuss the thesis and to quote from it at some length because it is not widely known. Today this early work reads very much like Ondaatje's argument with an alter ego, an older writer aspects of

whose life and writing found echoes in himself. Muir's vision of life as chaotic, meaningless, and marked by violence and suffering anticipates Ondaatje's. And Muir's melancholy and remorseful voice must have appealed to him, not least because his Scots accent, like Ondaatje's, marked him as an outsider in English poetry. Ondaatje's comments on Muir's writing are still valid enough to constitute a useful guide to the Scots poet's neglected books. But to anyone familiar with Ondaatje's writing, the commentary also reads like a palimpsest on his own developing central concerns and obsessions and as an early guide to his evolving poetics. My hunch is that Ondaatje wasn't so much learning from or in any substantive way being influenced by Muir as he was finding confirmation for some of his own inclinations and developing thoughts about life and writing. Reading Muir, he indirectly discovered himself, both what he had lived through as a man and what he might become as a writer. His quotations from Muir's work are almost uncanny in anticipating some of his own later writing.

Similarly, some of his comments on the Scots poet's work are equally applicable to his own: 'With each poem, he approaches Ithaca along a new road and discovers a new wound' (103). On the connection between Muir's life and poetry: 'The mental and physical destruction of his family in Glasgow was so grotesque that Muir was unable to write of it in his poetry' (12). In the following description of Wyre, the island home of Muir's childhood, I find it difficult not to sense the presence of Ceylon and Ondaatje's family behind the primary Scots references. 'Wyre was important for Muir's myth-making because it was an island where "there was no distinction between the ordinary and the fabulous." Muir could blend myths with everyday events and turn characters like "Sutherland" into heroes ... Wyre was therefore a landscape very close to the fabulous – when seen with the innocent eyes of a child, and his childhood made the rest of Muir's life seem bathetic' (5).[21] Substitute one or two nouns and a name, and this passage might be a description of the Ceylon of *Running in the Family* which the young Ondaatje was compelled to leave. In other words, for Muir, as for Ondaatje, the personal story or myth includes an idyllic and for the most part innocent childhood on an island, followed by a fall into modern British society. Muir's lines 'My childhood all a myth / Enacted on a distant isle' could have been written by Ondaatje. His sense of the fallen world as violent and chaotic finds its counterpart in Ondaatje's violent characters and scenes and his intuition that life is fundamentally chaotic. Chaos and chaotic occur, often several times, in each of his books. When Ondaatje quotes Muir as saying, 'At its core everything is chaos, and therefore terrible' (22), one can almost feel the author of 'Peter,' *the man with seven toes*, *The Collected Works of Billy the Kid*, and 'King Kong meets Wallace Stevens' nodding in agreement. Even Muir's tendency to depict the chaos in animal images finds an echo in Ondaatje's animal poems or his occasional use of animals, as liminal figures marking the boundary between surface and depth, reason and instinct, order and chaos.

Muir's poems also showed Ondaatje that a poet could find forms and an adequate imaginative language for his experience without resorting to a confessional poetic. Myth was the answer. Ondaatje's own early interest in legend and myth gives an edge to his discussion of Muir's fascination with biblical and Greek myths, journeys, heraldic animals, and mythic figures. His critical commentary on how myths function in Muir's poems can also apply to his own. Though he acknowledges that a poet can use myths to discover both aspects of himself and 'the patterns of the societies we live in' (81), I will emphasize the former here because in his poetry Ondaatje's interest in society will be almost non-existent until *Handwriting*. It may be worth noting at this point that in *Leonard Cohen* Ondaatje distinguishes between social evils and personal ones, and insists that the former, because 'outside us,' 'are capable of being controlled,' while the latter 'never can be' because they are 'one's own recurring nightmare' (21). In his poetry, he is always less interested in the social dimension of our lives than in the personal. This is also true of his interest in myths. Discussing Greek myths in the thesis, for instance, he emphasizes, 'The events and personalities of Thebes, Troy, and Ithaca run parallel to our own lives. We discover ourselves in them, and, at the same time, enlarge and give them meaning, (105). Ondaatje's use of 'we' in the final sentence is suggestive, even if readers may not have enough information to determine how the lives of Paris and Helen or Peter or Billy may run 'parallel' to the author's or our own. Also of interest here is his suggestion that 'in his more personal poems ... [Muir] discovered himself behind a mask' (90). It's a point that Ondaatje will make in later interviews about some of his own poetry. He would agree with Anne Carson's suggestion 'All myth is an enriched pattern, / a two-faced proposition, / allowing its operator to say one thing and mean another, to lead a double life.'[22]

Although he doesn't discuss this aspect in the thesis, Ondaatje might

have mentioned that myths and legends also save a writer the trouble of having to invent a story by providing him with the materials on which he can work. In none of his longer poems or in his fiction has he ever invented *ex nihilo*. He criticizes Muir, however, for his tendency to spend 'nine-tenths of a poem' setting up a scene and for allowing the inherited story or narrative to dominate. He suggests an alternative based on 'Pound's monologues,' which 'instead of following a strict narrative, consist of a string of lyrics which suggest the narrative' (72–3).[23] Ondaatje's stories, whether in verse ('Light,' *Secular Love*) or prose (*Running in the Family*, *Anil's Ghost*), will always be closer to Pound than to Muir's slower and more ponderously unfolding poems.

While he finds Muir's approach to narrative restrictive, he's attracted to what D.H. Lawrence would have called his 'metaphysic' (see 'Study of Thomas Hardy') and what today's critics would call his 'ideology.' Discussing this aspect of Muir's work, Ondaatje quotes a passage with a distinctly contemporary sound: 'To be a perfectly honest writer – a writer, that is, true to his impressions – one thing is essential, one must not have a system. A system of thought is a method of exploiting impressions, of weaving them into a pattern, decided beforehand, and of crushing and distorting them for that end. All that one can honestly begin with is a starting-point; but better still if one have several; it makes for independence' (84).[24] In a 1990 interview with Catherine Bush, this theme reappears in his Bakhtinian preference for 'a form that can have a more cubist or mural voice to capture the variousness of things. Rather than one demonic stare.'[25] For Ondaatje, as for Muir, the fact that life, including human life, is in some deep sense chaotic and therefore meaningless must be enacted in the poem. Should the poem's vision reflect a too obvious metaphysical system or aesthetic pattern, it would falsify reality. Ondaatje's lyrics, as well as his fragmented, temporally discontinuous works such as *Secular Love* and *Handwriting*, go further in this direction than Muir's poems, whose symmetric stanzas offer the reassurance of rhyme, metre, and a temporally sequential narrative in the face of life's inchoate and meaningless violence. Muir is enough of a high modernist to want to use myths as fragments from the past to shore 'against my ruins' (*The Waste Land*, 431) in forming at least an aesthetic totality that will offer, among other things, a substitute for lost religious and philosophical certainties.

By contrast, at least in his most radical poems, Ondaatje resists almost successfully the temptations of pattern and totality. Like Muir, he wants to acknowledge chaos, but he also wants to find aesthetic strategies and forms to enact it while creating the illusion that it isn't being contained. The danger for both, as I pointed out earlier, is that any transfiguration of existential, psychological, or moral chaos into aesthetic form might in the end misrepresent that chaos and inevitably create an unintended sense of meaning. One of the failings of aestheticism – always a temptation for a writer as highly figurative as Ondaatje – is that it gives priority to beauty over truth, if only because the former distracts our attention from the latter. George Bowering, reading the lyrics through Charles Olson's spectacles, thinks that Ondaatje should have abandoned this view of form and turned to the open-field poetics of William Carlos Williams and Black Mountain. He describes the early work as 'well cut and shaped, but not risky,' not 'seeking the unrested form he requires.'[26] Offering a view of Ondaatje's vision that is in fundamental agreement with mine, Bowering nevertheless insists that it can receive its full poetic articulation only in a postmodernist poetics of process such as the one implicit in *The Collected Works of Billy the Kid*. It is worth noting, however, that while that work as a whole is postmodernist in its thrust, several short poems – 'I have seen pictures of great stars,' 'You know hunters,' 'White walls neon on the eye' – have the characteristics of traditional short lyrics.

To return to the thesis, the future author of 'Peter,' *the man with seven toes*, and *The Collected Works of Billy the Kid* must also have found gratifying Muir's occasional appeal to what Ondaatje calls amorality or a higher morality. Discussing Muir's poems about visions, he focuses on those moments when 'Muir leaves moralities and reason behind, removes his own personality from the poem, and allows us a clear glimpse of his insight into the fable. Colour, style and image combine at wonderful moments, and then like Muir, we must believe the image – where Art and the Real "play." These images are more magnificent because of their rarity, and because delight in their amorality or higher morality is delightful only to the fallen' (51). I linger over this passage and the concern with morality primarily because 'moral' (with its cognates) is one of the most slippery terms in Ondaatje's private poetic lexicon. In *The Collected Works of Billy the Kid*, for instance, Billy comments that 'if I had a newsman's brain I'd say / well some morals are physical' (11), and in 'White Dwarfs' the speaker, in a searing couplet, refers to individuals 'who shave their moral so raw / they can tear themselves through the eye of a needle' (RJ, 70). To be moral in Ondaatje's universe is to be free, authentic, more fully human, and,

from the viewpoint of conventional morality, amoral. I'll discuss Ondaatje's uses of the word in some detail in the next chapter; here I simply want to note the attention he pays to it in Muir's work as well as his emphasis on scenes in which the Scots poet's use is co-extensive with his own. For Ondaatje, Muir's poems (and poems in general) fail when they reflect 'the limitations of everyday morality' and become too didactic by allowing questions of social utility, moral purpose, and what we now call identity politics to colour the reader's response. In the following passage, note how quickly he moves from commenting on Muir's poetry to poetry in general:

> The central fault with Muir's war poetry is that it is too didactic. To deal with subjects such as war or violence, a poet should look below the surface of the obvious morality. A poet should discover the subtlety or complexity in an event to such an extent that he will keep the reader or himself unreconciled and uncertain of his attitude towards the event. To do this he must avoid approaching the subject with any preconceived morality. His depiction and judgment must be concerned with the 'right sensation' so that it might even appear inhuman. In Yeats's 'Easter 1916,' we are not conscious of a preconceived morality. The poem is [a] reverie upon the unexpected transformation of violence. In the end there is no resolution, only paradox. (75)

The fragment 'right sensation' is taken from Wallace Stevens's 'The morality of the poet ... is the morality of the right sensation,' (120)[27] the only morality that at his most radical Ondaatje the poet is willing to acknowledge. The various signposts to the poems and fiction of the 1970s and 1980s are obvious. If the discussion's starting point is Muir's poetry, its unstated goal is Ondaatje's own evolving poetic. In it, the objective will be to present characters and events, like life itself, with as few moral, philosophical, and aesthetic preconceptions or mediations as possible, and to leave the reader 'uncertain of his attitudes towards the event.' I suspect that Ondaatje has never reprinted 'Pictures from Vietnam' (1968), one of his rare political poems, because it is too didactic and its morality too obvious.[28]

Ondaatje doesn't mention Muir in any of his poems, essays, or novels, and anyone not aware of the thesis would be hard pressed to see his importance in the writing of Ondaatje's first decade. A study of poetic influence, however, would mention the images that Ondaatje borrows from him – in 'Dragon' and 'White Dwarfs' – and place him drawn to those aspects of Cohen's work that have appeared or will appear in his own. He admires 'Ballad' because 'Cohen sees beauty (gardens, potency, and art) grow out of death and violence' (9); and he praises aspects of Cohen's voice (the wry tone and the ironic understatement) and style (the mixing of modes and styles) that resemble his own; he praises the form of *The Favourite Game* because 'each scene [emerges] as a potent and enigmatic sketch rather than a full blown, detailed narrative. As in a poem, the silences and spaces, what is left unsaid, are essential to the mood of the book' (23). He also pays Cohen the ultimate compliment by borrowing some of his images for his own work. He quotes a passage from *The Favourite Game* that foreshadows a scene in *Coming through Slaughter*: 'He leaped up, ran to the window, smashed his fist through the glass' (34). Another sentence from *Beautiful Losers* – 'I was the tattered billboard for his reality' (50) – may lie behind 'Billboards' (*RJ*, 14). The description of molten brass in *The Favourite Game* (104), not quoted by Ondaatje, may have been on his mind when he wrote, 'I have seen pictures of great stars' and '"The gate in his head."' A line from *The Favourite Game* (17) may have inspired 'Birds for Janet – The Heron' (*DM*, 12): 'A loon went insane in the middle of the lake.' And the fireflies in *Beautiful Losers* (134) reappear in the 'muslin dress / with fireflies' in 'Light.' Other examples are given in the chapters on *The Dainty Monsters* and *Rat Jelly*.

Thinking back to the late 1960s, I can't help wondering whether Cohen represented for Ondaatje a slightly older contemporary writer (he was born in 1934, Ondaatje in 1943) whose work provided a counterweight to the influence of the sometimes more radical, if generally less substantial, writers he met with first at Queen's University and then at Coach House Press. With the publication of *Rat Jelly* in 1973, it must have been obvious to Ondaatje that none of these writers were in his league nor, despite occasional borrowing or quotation, could he learn from any of them. Ralph Gustafson noted in 1970 that Ondaatje owed nothing to Williams or the Black Mountain poets; the comment reminds us that, despite bp Nichol's influence on three poems, he didn't share his fellow Coach House editors' assumptions about poetry.[30] Whatever Cohen's limitations, and Ondaatje is aware of them, he represents a more substantial and original figure. One doesn't have to be Harold Bloom to sense the young poet testing himself against the older one in his judgments on the writing, judgments often made with the vocabulary of Ondaatje's own creative work. Criticism always involves intellectual power, and the criticism of a poet adds creative

among Rossetti, Kafka, Stevens, Yeats, Auden, García Márquez, and Leonard Cohen as one of the authors to whom the young poet is indebted. Ironically, Cohen's place in Ondaatje's career is more widely known, even though he seems to me to have been less influential than Muir on his development. By 1970, when Ondaatje wrote his monograph *Leonard Cohen*, he had published three books, established his reputation as a very promising and original young writer, and won the Governor General's Award for *The Collected Works of Billy the Kid*. He probably agreed to write the book because he still had academic aspirations, what he calls 'the academic stripe up my back.'[29] As an untenured professor of English literature at the University of Western Ontario, he needed to publish a book, no matter how short, to compensate for the fact that he did not have a doctorate. Whatever the reasons – and whatever Ondaatje may have thought of the completed book – it still stands up as a comprehensive, occasionally insightful introduction to Cohen's work by someone who very much admires it. His comment on *Beautiful Losers*, a novel that has not aged well, catches him at his most enthusiastic: 'As it is, *Beautiful Losers* is a gorgeous novel, and is the most vivid, fascinating, and brave modern novel I have read' (45).

But like the Muir thesis, the study is more interesting today for what it tells us about Ondaatje than about its ostensible subject. He's interested in Cohen partly because the latter is exploring situations and an emotional climate similar to his own. Even their poetic lexicons overlap: beautiful losers, wounds, scars, madness, shattered windows, loons, bones, myth, chaos, rats. On Ondaatje's account, Cohen transforms his characters, even those based on real people, into heroes and myths in the sense that he endows them with charisma and shows their archetypal characteristics. Referring to 'Alexander Trocchi, Public Junkie, Priez pour nous,' Ondaatje comments that 'like the narrator, Cohen is left at the end holding a myth in his hands' (42). As in his own work, one of the essential preconditions for heroism or mythic status is being wounded or scarred, and therefore unique and authentic: 'Cohen is making heroes out of these people not because they, like Philoctetes, have brilliant bows, but because they have magnificent wounds' (43). It's as if a wound is a badge of authenticity that removes a character from ordinary time and bestows charisma on him and aura on the event. The reference to the mythic archer reminds us how close Ondaatje's critical writing at this point in his career is to his creative work (see 'The Good Night' [*DM*, 58] and 'Philoctetes on the island' [*RJ*, 34]). He's often power as well. The original writer rewrites his predecessor in his own image, even when praising him. Ondaatje was too young and insufficiently established to be as assertive with Muir, a nearly canonical figure if a minor one.

Cohen, however, represented a different case and opportunity. An established and, in the late 1960s, potentially major writer, he could be the brother-father figure against whom Ondaatje could measure himself. I wonder if there isn't something of him, as well as of Mervyn Ondaatje, in *Coming through Slaughter* in the 'fathers' that Buddy Bolden mentions as having 'put their bodies over barbed wire. For me. To slide over into the region of hell. They showed me their autographed pictures and they told me about their women and they told me of the even bigger names all over the country. My fathers failing. Dead before they hit the wire' (95). This is obviously less a question of literary influence than of presence, and of one writer's profound awareness of another. In this context one can ask whether the poems about poetry in *Rat Jelly* show Ondaatje thinking through some of his responses to Cohen's work, especially his comments on the relationship between violence or suffering and creativity. And if the answer, however tentative, is yes, then is *Coming through Slaughter* on some level a response to *Beautiful Losers*? A historical footnote: the night that Ondaatje launched his novel in Toronto with a reading at A Space, he was almost late because he had attended a Cohen concert that went into three encores.[31]

The important point here is that the monograph was written at a key period in Ondaatje's development. As with Muir, the study of Cohen's work, especially his poetry, helped sharpen his own sense of his vision of life and of what he could and could not do with lyric. Some of Ondaatje's criticisms of Cohen's poems in *Flowers for Hitler* hint at roads he would not take with his own: 'He presents "Pure lists" – which give the skeletons of an emotion or a scene like trailers from a movie, and there are many stray diary-entries or footnotes to emotions. The most obvious fault in these pieces is that they are not self-sufficient. They belong to Leonard Cohen and need him to bolster meaning' (43). A New Critic couldn't have said it better, nor could a former student of George Whalley. This particular passage reminds us that one of the continuing problems or issues in Ondaatje's poetry will be the representation of the self. With both Muir and Cohen he is attentive to their very different strategies of self-representation. At one extreme is Muir's impersonal, if romantic, mythic poetry; at the other is Cohen's

ostensibly confessional approach that nevertheless strives for a mythic dimension. One way of tracing Ondaatje's development as a poet is to note his shift from the first to the second with *Secular Love* and then the retreat into the almost complete impersonality of *Handwriting* (1998), where the self is dissolved and reconstituted in a new and very different mythic poetry. *Secular Love* can be seen as the culmination of the impulse to 'say what happened' and to confront the troubling compulsions of the past and the present.[32] In a manner of speaking, it is implicit in the prose and verse of Ondaatje's first twenty years. Of course, it would not have been written had he not first confronted his father's ghost in *Running in the Family*, a confrontation that had been anticipated during the previous decade by his two elegies for his parents, 'Letters & Other Worlds' (1971) and 'Light' (1975). Having dealt with what happened to his father, he seems to have been able to turn a similarly unsparing eye on himself and his role in the breakup of his own marriage in the late 1970s. Perhaps he could only finally expiate the betrayal and the inevitable guilt involved in telling the father's story by being as ruthless in telling his own in a poetry sequence that is at once a complex act of atonement, an apology, and a love poem.

Since hindsight is always twenty-twenty, it's obvious today that Ondaatje's preface to *The Long Poem Anthology* (1979) was one of the first steps in the writing both of *Secular Love* and *Handwriting*, the two books in which lyrics become part of long, intricate, and relatively open sequences. This brief but important essay marks the turn towards his poetry's last phase. He begins by claiming that 'the most interesting writing being done by poets today can be found within the structure of the long poem' and that our 'best poetry, after we stopped being cocky with narrative, is involved with process and perspective' (11). The emphasis throughout is on poems which 'shift like mercury off the hand' and in which 'stories ... don't matter' because 'what is important' is 'the movement of the mind and language' (12). If we didn't know the author, we might think that he is describing *The Collected Works of Billy the Kid* or the 'Tin Roof' section of *Secular Love*. Even his quotations from the poets included seem like oblique comments on his own subsequent work: 'These poems show a process of knowledge, of discovery during the actual writing of the poem. "You have to go into a serial poem not knowing what the hell you are doing," wrote Jack Spicer. The poets do not fully know what they are trying to hold until they near the end of the poem, and this uncertainty, this lack of professional intent, is what allows them to go deep' (13).

Ondaatje will never be as committed to process poetics as Spicer, John Ashbery, or Frank O'Hara, but there's no doubt that *Secular Love* bears a family resemblance and that *Handwriting* fits Spicer's definition of a serial poem as one that 'deconstruct[s] meanings and compose[s] a wildness of meaning in which the I of the poet is not the centre but a returning and disappearing note' (323). This similarity doesn't make either of these sequences a process poem, but it does seem to indicate that they both owe something, however difficult it might be to define, to Ondaatje's years at Coach House. Considering his strong advocacy of a poetics in which 'stories ... don't matter' because 'the movement of the mind and language is what is important' (12), it may seem at first surprising that his two sequences don't resemble the poems in the anthology more closely in their attitude to language, perception, consciousness, and narration. My hunch is that, however warmly he may respond to process and formlessness in the work of others, Ondaatje is unable to follow them down that poetic road because process, whether epistemological or ontological, is too closely associated in his mind and work with chaos, dissolution, silence, and death. Like Leopardi, he thinks that literary form – the aesthetic structures of the imagination – not only gives life meaning but also makes it bearable. Leopardi puts it this way: 'Works of genius have this in common, that even when they vividly capture the nothingness of things, when they clearly show and make us feel the inevitable unhappiness of life, and when they express the most terrible despair, nonetheless to a great soul – though he find himself in a state of extreme duress, disillusion, nothingness, *noia*, and despair of life, or in the bitterest and *deadliest* misfortunes (caused by deep feelings or whatever) – these works always console and rekindle enthusiasm; and though they treat or represent only death, they give back to him, at least temporarily, that life which he had lost.'33 For a poet haunted by his past and therefore in need of atonement and consolation, a radical poetics is not enough, though he will learn enough from it to make possible his two formally innovative sequences.

From the viewpoint of style, it's interesting to note that Ondaatje's lexis of key terms, idioms, and images remains relatively stable throughout the shifts in his career. Among the privileged words in his private vocabulary are magnets, acrobats, blood, wounds, scars, knives, cuts, moral, ceremony, choreography, ritual, white, chaos, spiders, flies, ants, dogs, herons, the moon, the room, falling, nets, dreams, bones, madness, and boundaries – all of which can be organized under the two headings 'nets' and 'chaos.' Needless to say, at dif-

ferent times in his career different words are foregrounded and emphasized. This diction makes Ondaatje's style almost instantly recognizable, though it might be more accurate to speak of his various styles, since even poems in the same period can sound quite different. In *Rat Jelly*, for instance, the personal or domestic 'Billboards' and the mythic 'Fabulous shadow' could be by different poets. In general, however, it is possible to speak of the poetry in terms of the early Ondaatje (up to and including *Rat Jelly*), middle Ondaatje (culminating in *Secular Love*), and late Ondaatje (*Handwriting*). Though he never completely abandons the habit of bringing a poem to a point or summary with a powerful or resonant ending, there's no doubt that the poems of the middle and late 1970s – *There's a Trick with a Knife I'm Learning to Do* (1979) – are more open-ended and relaxed, with the images untroubled by symbolic compulsions; the syntax and punctuation are more casual; the rhetoric is missing the hard angularity, and the images the burnished quality of the major lyrics in *Rat Jelly*. They also show more examples of what David Shaw calls 'unconsummated symbolism,' in which the images have no fixed or assigned connotation.34 The six poems in *There's a Trick with a Knife I'm Learning to Do* associated with Sri Lanka (I include 'Light') point forward not only to the memoir but also to *Handwriting*. They hint at Ondaatje's turn towards a non-Western poetic that will allow him to immerse and dissolve both his poetry and himself in a past and a culture – an entire way-of-being-in-the-world – that he had left unwillingly nearly half a century earlier. Though the Sri Lankan lyrics in *Handwriting* are still recognizable and discussable *as* lyrics, they are much more fluent than Ondaatje's earlier poems. Their continuity depends less on narrative or the authority of a speaking voice or an underlying symbolic pattern than on what might be called the complex montage between the striking isolated images and stanzas that exist in an almost paratactic relation. As Ondaatje said about Cohen's early poems, 'It is a world where the morals [he means meanings] are imagistic, as they always are in the context of dreams' (14). More than in any of his other books, the poems depend on one another, 'echo and re-echo against one another,'35 to create a pattern of resonant meaning. Yet however different the most recent book may seem, its more open form and discontinuous structure are foreshadowed in Ondaatje's early criticism and in his first two major sequences, *the man with seven toes* and *The Collected Works of Billy the Kid*. Like them, it leaves the reader uncertain and with 'a sense of paradox.'[36] *Handwriting*, however, differs from Ondaatje's earlier books of poetry in seemingly offering little hint about his possible future development as a poet. The only thing that I'm certain of with respect to *Handwriting* is that the trajectory of the major phase of Ondaatje's career as a poet has come to an end.

A year after writing the previous sentence, I ran into the following comment, made by Ondaatje in a recent interview: 'I don't think I can go back to an earlier style, but at the same time, *Handwriting* did feel like a kind of ending to me. It's like the thin end of the wedge that I'd got to.'[37]

## THE TIME AROUND SCARS

A girl whom I've not spoken to
or shared coffee with for several years
writes of an old scar.
On her wrist it sleeps, smooth and white,
the size of a leech.
I gave it to her
brandishing a new Italian penknife.
Look, I said turning,
and blood spat onto her shirt.

My wife has scars like spread raindrops
on knees and ankles,
she talks of broken greenhouse panes
and yet, apart from imagining red feet,
(a nymph out of Chagall)
I bring little to that scene.
We remember the time around scars,
they freeze irrelevant emotions
and divide us from present friends.
I remember this girl's face,
the widening rise of surprise.

And would she
moving with lover or husband
conceal or flaunt it,
or keep it at her wrist
a mysterious watch.
And this scar I then remember
is medallion of no emotion.

I would meet you now
and I would wish this scar
to have been given with
all the love
that never occurred between us.

## APPLICATION FOR A DRIVING LICENCE

Two birds loved
in a flurry of red feathers
like a burst cottonball,
continuing while I drove over them.

I am a good driver, nothing shocks me.

# LETTERS & OTHER WORLDS

*'for there was no more darkness for him and, no doubt like Adam before the fall, he could see in the dark'*

My father's body was a globe of fear
His body was a town we never knew
He hid that he had been where we were going
His letters were a room he seldom lived in
In them the logic of his love could grow

My father's body was a town of fear
He was the only witness to its fear dance
He hid where he had been that we might lose him
His letters were a room his body scarred

He came to death with his mind drowning.
On the last day he enclosed himself
in a room with two bottles of gin, later
fell the length of his body
so that brain blood moved
to new compartments
that never knew the wash of fluid
and he died in minutes of a new equilibrium.

His early life was a terrifying comedy
and my mother divorced him again and again.
He would rush into tunnels magnetized
by the white eye of trains
and once, gaining instant fame,
managed to stop a Perahara in Ceylon
— the whole procession of elephants dancers
local dignitaries — by falling
dead drunk onto the street.

As a semi-official, and semi-white at that,
the act was seen as a crucial
turning point in the Home Rule Movement
and led to Ceylon's independence in 1948.

(My mother had done her share too—
her driving so bad
she was stoned by villagers
whenever her car was recognized)

For 14 years of marriage
each of them claimed he or she
was the injured party.
Once on the Colombo docks
saying goodbye to a recently married couple
my father, jealous
at my mother's articulate emotion,
dove into the waters of the harbour
and swam after the ship waving farewell.
My mother pretending no affiliation
mingled with the crowd back to the hotel.

Once again he made the papers
though this time my mother
with a note to the editor
corrected the report – saying he was drunk
rather than broken hearted at the parting of friends.
The married couple received both editions
of *The Ceylon Times* when their ship reached Aden.

And then in his last years
he was the silent drinker,
the man who once a week
disappeared into his room with bottles
and stayed there until he was drunk
and until he was sober.

There speeches, head dreams, apologies,

the gentle letters, were composed.
With the clarity of architects
he would write of the row of blue flowers
his new wife had planted,
the plans for electricity in the house,
how my half-sister fell near a snake
and it had awakened and not touched her.
Letters in a clear hand of the most complete empathy
his heart widening and widening and widening
to all manner of change in his children and friends
while he himself edged
into the terrible acute hatred
of his own privacy
till he balanced and fell
the length of his body
the blood entering
the empty reservoir of bones
the blood searching in his head without metaphor.

## RAT JELLY

See the rat in the jelly
steaming dirty hair
frozen, bring it out on a glass tray
split the pie four ways and eat
I took great care cooking this treat for you
and tho it looks good
and tho it smells of the Westinghouse still
and tastes of exotic fish or
maybe the expensive arse of a cow
I want you to know it's rat
steaming dirty hair and still alive

(caught him last Sunday
thinking of the fridge, thinking of you.)

## KING KONG MEETS WALLACE STEVENS

Take two photographs—
Wallace Stevens and King Kong
(Is it significant that I eat bananas as I write this?)

Stevens is portly, benign, a white brush cut
striped tie. Businessman but
for the dark thick hands, the naked brain
the thought in him.

Kong is staggering
lost in New York streets again
a spawn of annoyed cars at his toes.
The mind is nowhere.
Fingers are plastic, electric under the skin.
He's at the call of Metro-Goldwyn-Mayer.

Meanwhile W. S. in his suit
is thinking chaos is thinking fences.
In his head – the seeds of fresh pain
his exorcising,
the bellow of locked blood.

The hands drain from his jacket,
pose in the murderer's shadow.

'THE GATE IN HIS HEAD'

*for Victor Coleman*

Victor, the shy mind
revealing the faint scars
coloured strata of the brain,
not clarity but the sense of shift

a few lines, the tracks of thought

Landscape of busted trees
the melted tires in the sun
Stan's fishbowl
with a book inside
turning its pages
like some sea animal
camouflaging itself
the typeface clarity
going slow blonde in the sun full water

My mind is pouring chaos
in nets onto the page.
A blind lover, dont know
what I love till I write it out.
And then from Gibson's your letter
with a blurred photograph of a gull.
Caught vision. The stunning white bird
an unclear stir.

And that is all this writing should be then.
The beautiful formed things caught at the wrong moment
so they are shapeless, awkward
moving to the clear.

38

40

# WHITE DWARFS

This is for people who disappear
for those who descend into the code
and make their room a fridge for Superman
– who exhaust costume and bones that could perform flight,
who shave their moral so raw
they can tear themselves through the eye of a needle
this is for those people
that hover and hover
and die in the ether peripheries

There is my fear
of no words    of
falling without words
over and over    of
mouthing the silence
Why do I love most
among my heroes those
who sail to that perfect edge
where there is no social fuel
Release of sandbags
to understand their altitude—

        that silence of the third cross
        3rd man hung so high and lonely
        we don't hear him say
        say his pain, say his unbrotherhood
        What has he to do with the smell of ladies,
        can they eat off his skeleton of pain?

The Gurkhas in Malaya
cut the tongues of mules
so they were silent beasts of burden
in enemy territories
after such cruelty what could they speak of anyway
And Dashiell Hammett in success

suffered conversation and moved
to the perfect white between the words

This white that can grow
is fridge, bed,
is an egg – most beautiful
when unbroken, where
what we cannot see is growing
in all the colours we cannot see

there are those burned out stars
who implode into silence
after parading in the sky
after such choreography what would they wish to speak of     anyway

'Newly arrived and totally ignorant of the Levantine languages, Marco Polo could express himself only with gestures, leaps, cries of wonder and of horror, animal barkings or hootings, or with objects he took from his knapsacks – ostrich plumes, pea-shooters, quartzes – which he arranged in front of him . . .'

ITALO CALVINO

# PURE MEMORY/CHRIS DEWDNEY

*'Listen, it was so savage and brutal and powerful
that even though it happened out of the blue I
knew there was nothing arbitrary about it'*

CHRISTOPHER DEWDNEY

### 1

On a B.C. radio show the man asked me, coffee half way up to his mouth, what are the books you've liked recently? Christopher Dewdney's *A Palaeozoic Geology of London Ontario.* Only I didn't say that, I started stumbling on the word Palaeozoic . . . Paleo . . . Polio . . . and then it happened on Geology too until it seemed a disease. I sounded like an idiot. Meanwhile I was watching the man's silent gulping of coffee an inch or two away from the microphone. Unconcerned with my sinking 'live' all over the province.

### 2

I can't remember where I first met him. Somewhere I became aware of this giggle. Tan hair, tan face, tan shirt and a giggle-snort as his head staggered back. His arms somewhere.

### 3

The baby. He shows me the revolving globe in the 4-month-old kid's crib. Only it has been unscrewed and the globe turned upside down and rescrewed in that way so Africa and Asia all swivel upside down. This way he says she'll have to come to terms with the shapes all over again when she grows up.

### 4

He comes to dinner, steps out of the car and transforms the 10-year-old suburban garden into ancient history. Is on his knees pointing out the age and race and character of rocks and earth. He loves the Norfolk Pine. I give him a piece of wood 120 million years old from the tar sands and he smokes a bit of it.

### 5

When he was a kid and his parents had guests and he was eventually told to get to bed he liked to embarrass them by - running under a table and screaming out Don't hit me Don't hit me.

### 6

His most embarrassing moment. A poetry reading in Toronto. He was sitting in the front row and he realized that he hated the poetry. He looked around discretely for the exit but it was a long way away. Then to the right, quite near him, he saw another door. As a poem ended he got up and officially walked to the door quickly opened it went out and closed it behind him. He found himself in a dark cupboard about 2 feet by 3 feet. It contained nothing. He waited there for a while, then he started to laugh and giggle. He giggled for 5 minutes and he thinks the audience could probably hear him. When he had collected himself he opened the door, came out, walked to his seat and sat down again.

### 7

Coach House Press, December 1974. I haven't seen him for a long time. His face is tough. Something has left his face. It is not that he is thinner but the face has lost something distinct and it seems like flesh. But he is not thinner. He is busy working on his new book *Fovea Centralis* and I watch him as he sits in the empty back room upstairs all alone with a computer typesetting terminal. I can't get over his face. It is 'tight', as if a stocking were over it and he about to perform a robbery. He plucks at the keys and talks down into the machine. I am relieved when he starts giggling at something. I tell him I'm coming down to London in a week and he says he will show me his butterflies, he has bought two mounted butterflies for a very good price. If I don't tell anyone he will let me know where I could get one. A Chinaman in London Ontario sells them. I start to laugh. He doesn't. This is serious information, important rare information like the history of rocks – these frail wings of almost powder have their genealogies too.

8

His favourite movie is *Earthquake*. He stands in the middle of his apartment very excited telling me all the details. He shows me his beautiful fossils, a small poster of James Dean hitting his brother in *East of Eden*, and the two very impressive mounted butterflies.

9

On the bus going back to Toronto I have a drawing of him by Robert Fones. Wrapped in brown paper it lies above me on the luggage rack. When the bus swerves I put my arm out into the dark aisle ready to catch him if it falls. A strange drawing of him in his cane chair with a plant to the side of him, reading Frank O'Hara with very oriental eyes. It was done in 1973, before the flesh left his face.

10

His wife's brain haemorrhage. I could not cope with that.
He is 23 years old. He does. Africa Asia Australia upside down.
Earthquake.

42

74

## TO A SAD DAUGHTER

All night long the hockey pictures
gaze down at you
sleeping in your tracksuit.
Belligerent goalies are your ideal.
Threats of being traded
cuts and wounds
– all this pleases you.
*O my god!* you say at breakfast
reading the sports page over the Alpen
as another player breaks his ankle
or assaults the coach.

When I thought of daughters
I wasn't expecting this
but I like this more.
I like all your faults
even your purple moods
when you retreat from everyone
to sit in bed under a quilt.
And when I say 'like'
I mean of course 'love'
but that embarrasses you.
You who feel superior to black and white movies
(coaxed for hours to see *Casablanca*)
though you were moved
by *Creature from the Black Lagoon*.

One day I'll come swimming
beside your ship or someone will
and if you hear the siren
listen to it. For if you close your ears
only nothing happens. You will never change.

I don't care if you risk
your life to angry goalies
creatures with webbed feet.
You can enter their caves and castles
their glass laboratories. Just
don't be fooled by anyone but yourself.

This is the first lecture I've given you.
You're 'sweet sixteen' you said.
I'd rather be your closest friend
than your father. I'm not good at advice
you know that, but ride
the ceremonies
until they grow dark.

Sometimes you are so busy
discovering your friends
I ache with a loss
– but that is greed.
And sometimes I've gone
into *my* purple world
and lost you.

One afternoon I stepped
into your room. You were sitting
at the desk where I now write this.
Forsythia outside the window
and sun spilled over you
like a thick yellow miracle
as if another planet
was coaxing you out of the house
– all those possible worlds! –
and you, meanwhile, busy with mathematics.

I cannot look at forsythia now
without loss, or joy for you.
You step delicately
into the wild world
and your real prize will be
the frantic search.
Want everything. If you break
break going out not in.
How you live your life I don't care
but I'll sell my arms for you,
hold your secrets for ever.

If I speak of death
which you fear now, greatly,
it is without answers,
except that each
one we know is
in our blood.
Don't recall graves.
Memory is permanent.
Remember the afternoon's
yellow suburban annunciation.
Your goalie
in his frightening mask
dreams perhaps
of gentleness.

*ESCARPMENT*

He lies in bed, awake, holding her left forearm. It is 4 a.m. He turns, his eyes rough against the night. Through the window he can hear the creek – which has no name. Yesterday at noon he walked along its shallow body overhung with cedar, beside rushes, moss and watercress. A green and grey body whose intricate bones he is learning among which he stumbles and walks through in an old pair of Converse running shoes. She was further upriver investigating for herself and he exploring on his own now crawling under a tree that has uprooted and spilled. Its huge length across a section of the creek. With his left hand he holds onto the massive stump roots and slides beneath it within the white water heaving against him. Shirt wet, he follows the muscle in the water and travels fast under the tree. His dreaming earlier must have involved all this.

In the river he was looking for a wooden bridge which they had crossed the previous day. He walks confidently now, the white shoes stepping casually off logs into deep water, through gravel, and watercress which they eat later in a cheese sandwich. She chews much of it walking back to the cabin. He turns and she freezes, laughing, with watercress in her mouth. There are not many more ways he can tell her he loves her. He shows mock outrage and yells but she cannot hear him over the sound of the stumbling creek.

He loves too, as she knows, the body of rivers. Provide him with a river or a creek and he will walk along it. Will step off and sink to his waist, the sound of water and rock encasing him in solitude. The noise around them insists on silence if they are more than five feet apart. It is only later when they sit in a pool legs against each other that they can talk, their conversation roaming to include relatives, books, best friends, the history of Lewis and Clark, fragments of the past which they piece together. But otherwise this river's noise encases them and now he walks alone with its spirits, the clack and splash, the twig break, hearing only an individual noise if it

occurs less than an arm's length away. He is looking, now, for a name.

It is not a name for a map – he knows the arguments of imperialism. It is a name for them, something temporary for their vocabulary. A code. He slips under the fallen tree holding the cedar root the way he holds her forearm. He hangs a moment, his body being pulled by water going down river. He holds it the same way and for the same reasons. Heart Creek? Arm River? he writes, he mutters to her in the darkness. The body moves from side to side and he hangs with one arm, deliriously out of control, still holding on. Then he plunges down, touches gravel and flakes of wood with his back the water closing over his head like a clap of gloved hands. His eyes are open as the river itself pushes him to his feet and he is already three yards down stream and walking out of the shock and cold stepping into the sun. Sun lays its crossword, litters itself, along the whole turning length of this river so he can step into heat or shadow.

He thinks of where she is, what she is naming. Near her, in the grasses, are Bladder Campion, Devil's Paintbrush, some unknown blue flowers. He stands very still and cold in the shadow of long trees. He has gone far enough to look for a bridge and has not found it. Turns upriver. He holds onto the cedar root the way he holds her forearm.

# "Rumours of Topography": The Cultural Politics of Michael Ondaatje's *Running in the Family*

AJAY HEBLE

IN "GARCÍA MÁRQUEZ AND THE BUS TO ARACATACA," Michael Ondaatje tells us, by way of Vladimir Nabokov, that "Great literature does not tell the truth, it makes it up" (21). While Nabokov's assertion offers Ondaatje a starting point for understanding the impulses that shape and inform Márquez's *One Hundred Years of Solitude* — a text that Ondaatje calls "the bible book of the twentieth century" ("García Márquez" 21) — it also proves useful for testing and illustrating the central preoccupations in Ondaatje's own work. Throughout his long narrative works, Ondaatje, after all, has repeatedly emphasized the value of *imaginative* reconstructions, rejecting factual accuracy in favour of formulations such as the "truth of fiction" (*Coming through Slaughter* acknowledgement page [158]) and the "well-told lie" (*Running in the Family* 206). The primacy of these notions in Ondaatje's oeuvre attests both to the agential function of the imagination and to Ondaatje's willingness to acknowledge — indeed to thematize — the role that one's subjectivity plays in the writing of history. In his account of his own familial history, *Running in the Family*, Ondaatje displays his admiration for, and his ability to traffic in, "Excess caught so surely and dreamily that it becomes real" ("García Márquez" 25). Ondaatje's "excess," however, seems, at least for some recent critics of his work, to be bereft of the real, to be so made up that it refuses "to participate actively in the referential" (Kanaganayakam 40).

Such a critical pronouncement ought, in itself, to be of some interest: what are the implications of such a statement at a time when literary history seems to invite a critique of representationalism? Far from being a critically outmoded plea for a return to traditional mimetic approaches to literature, this response to Ondaatje's work is perhaps best understood if situated within the context not simply of either mimetic realism or even poststructuralism but rather of the emergence of alliances of marginalized or misrepresented groups attempting either to reclaim the past or to map out a space for the possibility of resistance to forms of cultural domination. Indeed, as R. Radhakrishnan points out, "Contemporary theorists of subjugated subject positions (feminists, ethnic theorists, critics of colonialism and imperialism) have contested the necessity to conceive of their positions as 'lacks' and 'absences' within the dominant structure" (64). Seen from within the context of theories of what Michel Foucault calls "subjugated knowledges" (81), the claim that *Running in the Family* fails the test of referentiality thus becomes part of a renewed struggle *for* cultural representation.

"In the realm of culture," writes Patrick Brantlinger in *Crusoe's Footprints*, "crisis occurs when an established system of representation is challenged by increasing numbers of people as *not* representing or as *mis*representing significant aspects of social experience" (128). In *Running in the Family*, representation is fraught with questions that emerge out of a complex network of negotiations between writing, reading, and the maintenance or subversion of power. The text has come under attack recently for its tendency to aestheticize political and cultural issues, for its failure to acknowledge and thematize the conditions of a Sri Lankan writer in Canada. Arun Mukherjee, in particular, argues that "Ondaatje, coming from a Third World country with a colonial past, does not write about his otherness.... [T]here is no trauma of uprooting evident in his poetry; nor is there a need for redefinition in a new context: the subjects that preoccupy so many immigrant writers" (33–34). Criticizing the book and its reviewers for exoticizing (and thus misrepresenting) local culture, Mukherjee is unyielding in her insistence that the book fails to engage with the social and political realities of Sri Lanka.

There are, I think, many ways of responding to these concerns. We might, for instance, ask whether Mukherjee's argument itself, in presupposing the very possibility of representing cultural authenticity, is an essentialist distortion of indigenous culture. Can we speak about Sri Lanka as though its culture offered a unified and unproblematic example of otherness or anticolonial resistance? Need all immigrant writers respond to colonial pasts in the way that Mukherjee envisages? Does her prescriptive argument not run the risk of becoming just another version of the universalist critical methodology that she, elsewhere in her book on cultural domination, criticizes? And is *Running in the Family* as wildly inaccurate in its exoticism as Mukherjee would have it? In a recent article that examines the validity of Mukherjee's charges, Suwanda Sugunasiri argues that the

Eurasian behaviour in *Running in the Family* should be seen as an accurate picture of "the first stage of a post-colonial Sri Lankan culture, the later stages of which can be seen in the increasingly consumer-oriented and westernizing contemporary Sri Lanka under capitalism" (63).[1] Contending also that Mukherjee's criticisms of Ondaatje are invalid because she has generalized her knowledge of Sri Lanka from her own Indian society, Sugunasiri suggests that Mukherjee herself is guilty of the crimes that she pins on Ondaatje: she, too, has "fallen into the trap of being ahistorical and acontextual" (64).

While most of the critics who have recently entered the debate find themselves, justifiably I think, defending the integrity of Ondaatje's text, none, to my mind, has succeeded in articulating the genuinely complex, if problematic, nature of the text's interplay between ethnicity, nationality, and imperialized modes of self-understanding. Furthermore, if we take seriously the text's playful questioning of genres, its *formal* resistance to, and interrogation of, notions of centrality (topics that have received ample consideration), then we also need to recognize that there are other ways of conceptualizing (and resisting) the centre. There are several "ex-centric" dimensions in *Running in the Family*, then, and the relationship between Ondaatje's textual strategies of decentring and the cultural and political contexts out of which the text emerges requires attention.

* * *
*

Ex-centricity is the name that Linda Hutcheon gives to the "minoritarian discourses" that have helped to shape postmodern theory and practice (*Poetics* xi). Put simply, to be ex-centric is to be *outside* the centre in terms of race, nationality, ethnicity, language, gender, sexual orientation, class, or canonization. Although Hutcheon, in an interview in *Other Solitudes*, confronts Ondaatje with some of the cultural criticisms levelled against his work, she goes on (admittedly running the risk of oversimplifying) to suggest that one of his major concerns is the "experience of otherness' and the political consciousness that goes with awareness of racial and ethnic difference." Apparently eschewing the claims of Mukherjee and others, Hutcheon sees Ondaatje as being engaged in an exploration of "the state of being 'different' within a dominant culture" (198). What interests me here is the way in which we negotiate some form of rapprochement between what appear to be contradictory formations: although Hutcheon does not explicitly mention *Running in the Family* in the

context of her comments about "difference" and "otherness," she seems to see in Ondaatje's work precisely those ex-centric dimensions that Mukherjee claims are so conspicuously absent.

Does *Running in the Family* explore the state of being "different" in a dominant culture? On one level, the most obvious ex-centric in the text is Ondaatje himself. In returning to his country of birth, Ondaatje discovers that either "We own the country we grow up in, or we are aliens and invaders" (81). Recognizing the tenuousness of his relationship to Sri Lanka — a tenuousness that is appreciably reflected in Ondaatje's decision to refer to the country as Ceylon — Ondaatje posits himself as both "the foreigner" and "the prodigal who hates the foreigner" (79). This recognition of the impossibility of negotiating a stable sense of belonging, it seems to me, is —despite Mukherjee's claims —roughly akin to the probing of the relationship between self and place that we find in the works of other transcultural writers. I am thinking, for example, of texts such as Rohinton Mistry's *Tales from Firozsha Baag*, John Berger's *And Our Faces, My Heart, Brief as Photos*, Sara Suleri's *Meatless Days*, and Jack Hodgins's *Innocent Cities*. If, as Berger suggests, "to emigrate is always to dismantle the center of the world, and so to move into a lost, disoriented one of fragments" (57), then Ondaatje's text describes an analogous, though very different, kind of decentring. In returning to a place of origin that is *not* home (and, indeed, not even an origin), Ondaatje is not so much trying to rediscover a lost past as perhaps attempting to provide us with a new direction for our reflections on the meaning of postcolonial belonging. What is prompted, in short, by Ondaatje's return visits to Sri Lanka is the recognition that he himself is the other. Indeed, as the critical reception of the text encourages us to recognize, Ondaatje is the prodigal whose relationship to his place of birth is deeply complicated both by relations of accountability to specific, but differing, constituencies of readers and by Sri Lanka's long history of colonial rule.

Equally complex and tenuous in *Running in the Family* are the moorings and the allegiances associated with Ondaatje's forebears:

This was Nuwara Eliya in the twenties and thirties. Everyone was vaguely related and had Sinhalese, Tamil, Dutch, British and Burgher blood in them going back many generations. There was a large social gap between this circle and the Europeans and English who were never part of the Ceylonese community. The English were seen as transients, snobs and racists, and were quite separate from those who had intermarried and who lived here permanently. My father always claimed to be a Ceylon Tamil, though that was probably more valid about three centuries earlier. Emil Daniels summed up the situation for most of them when he was asked by one of the British governors what his nationality was — "God alone knows, your excellency." (41)

Although important essays by Chelva Kanaganayakam and Ernest MacIntyre have helped to situate culturally the community that Ondaatje describes in this passage, I would like, at the risk of reexamining familiar contexts, to reflect further on certain predispositions and emphases in *Running in the Family*. We are told that there was a "large social gap" between, on the one hand, this circle of family and friends and, on the other, the Europeans and English, who, as Ondaatje explains, were never really part of Ceylon. Unlike those who "never grew ancient here, who stepped in and admired the landscape, disliked the 'inquisitive natives' and left" (80), the community to which his family belonged *did* settle permanently in Ceylon. What is particularly interesting is that despite describing this hybrid community in terms of its separateness from the colonizing power — "The English were seen as transients, snobs and racists, and were quite separate from those who had intermarried and who lived here permanently" — Ondaatje, elsewhere in the text, implies that his ancestors "ignored" the indigenous people of the nation (87).

While the Nuwara Eliya passage describes the rootedness of Ondaatje's family, it also alerts us, in Kanaganayakam's words, to "the tenuousness of a community whose strength and its weakness lay in its cultural syncretism" (34). Furthermore, this community, at least in terms of the way that Ondaatje writes about it, seems caught between a universalist mode of representation — "*Everyone* was vaguely related . . ." (emphasis added) — and a desire to reflect a multiplicity of tenuous and heterogeneous histories. Mukherjee argues that words such as *everyone* in the context of Ondaatje's family provide the false impression that all or most Sri Lankans belonged to this group or lived like the Ondaatjes lived (40). I would like to suggest that Ondaatje uses "everyone" as a way of aspiring toward a kind of confidence in reconstructing the belongingness of his family's circle while recognizing, elsewhere in the same passage, the tenuousness of this community, which, as Emil Daniels's response reminds us, is unable to articulate its own national determinations. Moreover, the interplay of confidence and precariousness provides

a structural analogue for the positioning of a community that, as far as cultural integration goes, is at once in *and* out of the running. The deployment of a confidently charged rhetoric to describe the tenuous status of his family's circle enables Ondaatje to preserve a faith in his forebears and, again structurally, to recast the ontological condition of those forebears in terms of what Aijaz Ahmad, writing about Salman Rushdie, calls the "myth of *excess of belongings*" (127). Instead of reading Emil Daniels's response as pointing to the alienation of a community, we can see his inability to declare a national allegiance as a sign of belonging to *too many cultures*. Thus, while a word such as *everyone* may run the risk of taking us away from the referential, its force in *Running in the Family* resides precisely in its ability to compensate for, and recast a condition of, unbelonging through a myth of excess.

Ondaatje's writing is, in fact, saturated with excess, and it is part of his design in *Running in the Family* to encourage us to conflate its repertoire of transgressive practices and exaggerated performances with its cultural politics, to consider Ondaatje's fascination with "rumours of topography" (64) in the context of complex levels of interaction between place, politics, collective identity, and subjectivity. As one way of responding to some of the recent criticisms of *Running in the Family*, it is tempting to argue that Ondaatje's excess is, after the fashion of magic realism, emblematic of a mode of representation that characterizes much postcolonial writing. Postcolonial critics as diverse as Homi Bhabha and Stephen Slemon have theorized a series of affiliations between postcolonial discourse and magic realism. Bhabha, for example, argues that magic realism is "the literary language of the emergent post-colonial world" (7). Slemon, suggesting that magic realism is predicated on a kind of ex-centricity, on a "uniqueness or difference from mainstream culture" (9), speaks, though primarily in a Canadian context (but *not* about Ondaatje), of the usefulness of this category for postcolonial studies. Arguing that "the characteristic manoeuvre of magic realist fiction is that its two separate narrative modes [roughly speaking, realism and fantasy] never manage to arrange themselves into any kind of hierarchy" (11), Slemon explores magic realism's linkages to theories of genre and resistance in order to describe more precisely its destabilizing effects:

As Robert Kroetsch and Linda Kenyon observe, magic realism as a literary practice seems to be closely linked with a perception of "living on the margins," encoding within it, perhaps, a concept of resistance to the massive imperial centre and its totalizing systems. The established systems of generic classification are themselves, in my view, examples of these centralized totalizing systems, for they have been constructed through readings of texts almost exclusively of European or United States provenance. The use of the concept of magic realism, then, can itself signify resistance to central assimilation by more stable generic systems and more monumental theories of literary practice, a way of suggesting that there is something in the nature of the literature it identifies that confounds the capacities of the major genre systems to come to terms with it. (10)

While pronouncements that link magic realism to postcolonial discourse have met with critical resistance from Ahmad, Suleri (in *The Rhetoric of English India*), and others, I have chosen to quote Slemon at length here not because I want to activate the category of magic realism as an easy way of legitimizing the postcoloniality of *Running in the Family* but because I seek ways to read and think through the implications of the relationship between the text's formal decentring strategies and its cultural politics. If *Running in the Family* has been criticized for lacking a politics, then might not the generic disjunctures and resistances that Slemon identifies with magic realism enable us to gain a new perspective on the cultural and political resonances of Ondaatje's text?

Much, of course, has been said about the way in which *Running in the Family* problematizes our understanding of genre. Although both Hutcheon (in *The Canadian Postmodern*) and Smaro Kamboureli have addressed this issue in some detail, there has been little, if any, sustained reflection on the relation between the text's "generic slippages" (see Kamboureli) and its engagement with social and political realities. (It should be quite clear by now that I want to argue that the text *does* engage with social and political realities). Participating in a playful exploration of the site of interaction between the referentiality of its own discourse and a mode of invention and excess, *Running in the Family* seems to me to provide us with the kind of generic resistances that Slemon has in mind. On the one hand, the text locates itself very clearly in terms of specific dates, places, people, and events; at times, lest we dismiss the descriptions as merely "made up," Ondaatje provides us with authenticating details: the dialogue between Lalla and Judge E.W. Jayawardene, for example, "is still in

the judicial records in the Buller's Road Court Museum" (116). On the other hand, however, the text also engages in, and admits to, an exploration of *constructed* moments and histories: Lalla's "magic ride" (129), Ondaatje's father's finding a page from his son's book (189) — the very page that we as readers of *Running in the Family* have reached — and, indeed, its own constructedness, signalled throughout by references to pages, paper, and writing. In light of Slemon's comments, what is particularly interesting here is the impossibility of the text's complete assimilation into either of these discursive modes. Does such an impossibility serve as a sign of political engagement? If we define the text's ex-centricity, at a formal level, on the basis of its refusal to adhere to the central, constraining act of generic categorization, then do we necessarily reach an understanding of its other registers of signification? Does magic realism, in short, enable us to translate Ondaatje's *poetics* of ex-centricity into a *politics* of ex-centricity? Is it enough to counter Mukherjee's allegations with Slemon's argument? The answer to these questions, I think, is no, largely because the establishment of this kind of dialogue between Mukherjee and Slemon fails to account for the complexities and specificities of Ondaatje's text.

I mentioned earlier that there are different ways of conceptualizing (and resisting) the centre, and I would like now to rehearse some of these possibilities. Throughout the text, Ondaatje *does* draw from, and provide us with, a cultural milieu. Mukherjee is correct in pointing out that we hear about important cultural and political events only in passing (39); however, *Running in the Family* demands a more careful reading because of the subtle and telling ways in which its cultural phenomena are encoded. Near the centre of the text (not quite at the half-way mark [85–97]: indeed, the off-centre positioning seems calculated) is a complex textual moment that emblematizes the inseparability of the poetics and the politics of ex-centricity in *Running in the Family*. Ondaatje begins this section by quoting an excerpt of poetry from Lakdasa Wikkramasinha, a Sri Lankan poet whose first collection of poems, *Lustre*, contains the following note:

I have come to realize that I am using the language of the most despicable and loathsome people on earth; I have no wish to extend its life and range or enrich its tonality.

To write in English is a form of cultural treason. I have had for the future to think of a way of circumventing this treason. (qtd. in Gooneratne 199)

Ondaatje, of course, does not mention this comment, but it is nevertheless a useful context for understanding the way in which Wikkramasinha's poetry functions in *Running in the Family*. Here is a poet whose work bespeaks a history of cultural resistance to Sri Lanka's colonial inheritance, whose attempt to assert the indigenous sources of his poetry provides a telling commentary on (to borrow Edward Said's usage) the *contrapuntal* energies in Ondaatje's project: its "simultaneous awareness both of the metropolitan history that is narrated and of those other histories against which (and together with which) the dominating discourse acts" (51). Indeed, the inclusion of an excerpt from Wikkramasinha's poetry constitutes an important ideological moment in Ondaatje's text. Given the ambivalences with which, as we have seen, Ondaatje's family is positioned in terms of both the colonizing power and the indigenous population, the context in which Wikkramasinha was writing, *Running in the Family* reveals itself as an exploration of the clash between cultural syncretism and the desire for a precolonial language.

Defined, in *The Empire Writes Back*, as "the process by which previously distinct linguistic categories, and, by extension, cultural formations, merge into a single new form" (Ashcroft, Griffiths, and Tiffin 15), syncretism finds expression in *Running in the Family* in the "new form" represented by the Burghers, the local descendants of the previous Dutch empire. After Sri Lanka's independence in 1948, and after Sinhala was declared the official language of the nation in 1956, this community, as MacIntyre (316) and Kanaganayakam (34) point out, became increasingly alienated as the nation attempted to revert to precolonial values. A group already "cut off from the indigenous population by ethnicity and culture" (de Silva 17), the Burghers, who had cultivated an association with the ruling power, found themselves in a tenuous position. While Ondaatje seems concerned, for the most part, with an earlier period in Sri Lanka's history, he meditates on the unsustainability of the syncretic model in a multiethnic culture even while celebrating that model.

The mechanism that perhaps best enables us to appreciate the cultural politics of *Running in the Family* is lodged in the complex interplay between three points of orientation: the syncretism of Ondaatje's forebears, the excerpt from a poem by Wikkramasinha (85–86), and the poems that Ondaatje fashions in response. Wikkramasinha's "Don't Talk to Me about Matisse" raises important questions about the politics of cultural representation. Arguing that

acts of cultural appropriation replicate and are, indeed, inseparable from systems of political domination, the poem offers a trenchant critique not only of European representations of non-Western culture but also of a government that is perceived to have ruthlessly suppressed the spirit of a potential revolution: *"to our remote / villages the painters came, and our white-washed / mud-huts were splattered with gunfire"* (86). Painting, here juxtaposed and thus metonymically associated with gunfire, becomes a metaphor for the murder of the indigenous people of Sri Lanka and adds force to an earlier passage, in which Ondaatje speaks of the whitewashing of the imprisoned insurgents' poetry:

> When the government rounded up thousands of suspects during the Insurgency of 1971, the Vidyalankara campus of the University of Ceylon was turned into a prison camp. The police weeded out the guilty, trying to break their spirit. When the university opened again the returning students found hundreds of poems written on walls, ceilings, and in hidden corners of the campus. Quatrains and free verse about the struggle, tortures, the unbroken spirit, love of friends who had died for the cause. The students went around for days transcribing them into their notebooks before they were covered with whitewash and lye. (84)

Countering the act of whitewashing with his own gesture of inclusion, Ondaatje incorporates Wikkramasinha's poetry as part of his own project of reconstructing familial history. This act of inclusion, tantalizingly brief though it may seem, speaks volumes about both the enabling powers and the limitations of *Running in the Family*. Serving as an implicit reminder of the dangers involved in representing cultures other than one's own, the very presence of Wikkramasinha's poetry in Ondaatje's project simultaneously calls attention to the potential for art to effect change through its restorative powers. Quoting Wikkramasinha — a poet who, as we have seen, struggled to come to terms with the indigenous sources of his poetry — is in itself a political act for Ondaatje. It is at once a way of undermining the representational legitimacy of his project (doesn't anything that Ondaatje says about cultural and political phenomena in Sri Lanka inevitably run the risk of playing into the grid of Western thought and representation so sharply invoked and criticized by Wikkramasinha?) and of declaring his faith in acts of imaginative understanding.

Let me be more precise about what I have in mind. Ondaatje has always recognized (and, in fact, foregrounded) the partial nature of historical truths, but his recognition has paradoxically been accompanied by his insistence on the ability of the imaginative writer to create alternative histories, to get us, in effect, *inside* history better than writers of history or biography can.[2] In ways that I have already touched on, *Running in the Family* continues to interrogate this site of interaction. Its combination of factual/historical material with a rhetoric of excess, and its mingling of (auto)biographical facts with "*rumours* of topography" (64; emphasis added), alert us to Ondaatje's ongoing interest in probing the relationship between history, story, and autobiography. What is new in *Running in the Family* — the culmination of a series of narrative works that, by stages, have become more explicitly autobiographical — is the manner in which the text negotiates the cultural conditions of its representability.

If the force of Wikkramasinha's poem resides, at least in part, in its evocation of the way in which an entire trajectory of Sri Lankan history was, in effect, wiped out by a centralizing force, then the poems that Ondaatje fashions by way of response constitute a rough approximation of another kind of insurrection, of what Foucault calls an *"insurrection of subjugated knowledges"* (81). Foucault, of course, has a number of things in mind when he speaks of such knowledges, but one definition seems particularly appropriate in the present context: it is the phrase that he uses to describe "a whole set of knowledges that have been disqualified as inadequate to their task or insufficiently elaborated" (82). "High Flowers" (*Running in the Family* 87–89) seems to me to be a poem that explicitly addresses such an insufficiency. Indeed, it not only acknowledges "The woman [whom Ondaatje's] ancestors ignored" (87) but also offers a kind of restoration through the agency of its own imaginative capacities. I am not arguing that Ondaatje's poem seeks, by a simple act of imaginative inclusion, to redress the injustices of centuries of colonial domination; rather, I am suggesting that, given its positioning in *Running in the Family* and the context in which it appears, "High Flowers" achieves something of an interventionary effect.

As an artistic intervention in the process of hegemonic consolidation, the poem recasts modes of relation between differing but overlapping cultural topographies. By writing about the indigenous Sri Lankans who were ignored by his ancestors, Ondaatje, at least on a structural level, manifests a confidence in the ability of the imaginative writer to reclaim the past, to restore to history what has

been suppressed or marginalized. Such an insistence on the agential function of the imagination is not new to Ondaatje's work; what I would like to signal here specifically is the imbrication of representational practices with acts of cultural intervention. The poem itself demonstrates and, in fact, enacts the enabling power of imaginative discovery. By focusing on two figures, "the toddy tapper" (88) who "... moves / in the air between trees," and his wife who, on ground level, "sits at the doorway chopping coconut / cleaning rice" (87), Ondaatje redefines our understanding of networks of exchange between shadow and light, severance and continuity, and silence and conversation. In its exploration of the commerce between "up there" (89) and "[d]own here" (88), between the "darkness among high flowers" and the light that "storms through branches / and boils the street" (88), the poem opens a space for the possibility of complex and magical acts of cultural negotiation. Just as the toddy tapper's

"... dreams of walking / from tree to tree without ropes" (88) seem to become actualized when, as a result of his wife's seemingly unconnected movements below, "shadows eliminate / the path he moves along" (89), so Ondaatje's dialogue with Wikkramasinha (and, indeed, with his ancestors) similarly enables a magical accomplishment. Ondaatje's achievement, of course, is an imaginative act of cultural recuperation, but the force of the poem, I think, resides primarily in its meditation on the difficulty, if not the impossibility, of having such recuperation without the agency of imaginative intervention. Clearly an actual restoration of the precolonial past is impossible. Instead, what "High Flowers" adumbrates is a political frame of reference for Ondaatje's imaginative retellings, a context that enables us to generate new ways of reading and understanding his penchant for the "well-told lie" (*Running in the Family* 206).

Once again we find ourselves stumbling over the problem of referentiality. How are we to adjudicate the poem's demonstration of the difficulty of disentangling imaginative relations from historical understanding? If the impossible occurrence (walking without ropes) functions in Ondaatje's text as a kind of metaphor for the possibilities of reclaiming history, then what are the implications for our understanding of Ondaatje's accountability to social and political frames of reference?[3] *Is* Ondaatje, to replay Mukherjee's criticism, simply aestheticizing key cultural issues? And does the fact that Ondaatje is of European-Sri Lankan descent not leave him open to the charge that, though perhaps in spite of himself, he is ultimately participating in yet another attempt to assert the values of European culture (in the guise of reclaiming indigenous history)? Can only European-Sri Lankans remedy the silence of indigenous voices in the writing of Sri Lanka's cultural and political history? *Running in the Family* does not offer easy answers to these sorts of questions. While it does acknowledge that Ondaatje's forebears ignored members of the indigenous population of Sri Lanka, it also advances the idea that it may be possible to reclaim indigenous history, even within the context of cultural syncretism. The movement in Ondaatje's text from Wikramasinha's poetry to Ondaatje's own poetry about the indigenous people of Sri Lanka makes possible a dialogic relation between precolonial values and postcolonial cultural syncretism. The dialogic mode is what "High Flowers," in particular, adumbrates, and it is primarily through acts of imaginative understanding that the cultural force of this mode is most incisively registered.

Another act of imaginative understanding takes place in "The Cinnamon Peeler," the final poem in this section of *Running in the Family* (95–97). Given the autobiographical nature of the book and, more generally, the rearrangement of the traditional proximity between author and narrator/speaker that we find in much of Ondaatje's writing, my inclination is to see Ondaatje himself as the poem's first-person speaker. If this is the case, then the poem, unlike the others in this section, does not, in the first instance, concern itself with the indigenous people of Sri Lanka. Although the title, especially if combined with a later reference in the text to a Tamil cinnamon peeler to whom Ondaatje's father gave a lift (187), leads us to expect a poem about the people of the land, the conditional construction with which the poem begins suggests the possibility of an outsider's perspective:

> If I were a cinnamon peeler
> I would ride your bed
> and leave the yellow bark dust
> on your pillow. (95)

Announcing at the outset its involvement with hypothetical spheres of experience, the poem implicitly identifies itself as the product of a culture other than the one being described. If "High Flowers" (to adapt Foucault's terminology) creates a space for the possibility of an insurrection of subjugated local knowledges, then "The Cinnamon Peeler," insofar as it begins with a conditional formulation, reminds us of the impossibility of disentangling the context of

production from *Running in the Family*'s apprehension of ignored or marginalized indigenous histories. Put more simply, "The Cinnamon Peeler" begins by signalling Ondaatje's own role in the production of knowledge about the people of Sri Lanka.

To read Ondaatje as the speaker of the poem, a speaker hypothetically constructing an other history, is, perhaps, one way of forestalling the kinds of objections broached earlier, of sidestepping the hotly contested issue of the relationship between epistemology and cultural appropriation. By acknowledging the conditionality of his project and recognizing the tenuousness of his own position in relation to a figure who is ontologically and epistemologically remote from his domain of experience, Ondaatje invites us to recognize the extent to which the poem is about himself as much as it is about a Sri Lankan cinnamon peeler.

As we read on, however, we become aware of important modulations in Ondaatje's use of language. In shifting from the conditional to the future tense — "You will be known among strangers / as the cinnamon peeler's wife" (96) — Ondaatje, by the end of the third stanza, appears to be tempering his understanding of the conditional situation, which he describes in the opening stanza, with a marked alteration in the dynamics of operation. Even as he recognizes the gap between cultures, he articulates the possibility of circumventing that gap through the process of imaginative understanding. Indeed, after providing a structural break indicated by an asterisk, he further retreats from his acknowledged zone of speculation into a more confident mode:

> When we swam once
> I touched you in water
> and our bodies remained free,
> you could hold me and be blind of smell. (96)

The past tense here suggests that this event actually took place; gone is the tentative status of the opening lines. What is operative in these lines, and in the stanzas that follow, is a declaration of solidarity with a figure who, at the outset, is figured conditionally. Now the implication seems to be that the "I" of the poem *is* a cinnamon peeler rather than Michael Ondaatje. Or, to use a different if more problematic formulation, we might read the "I" as *both* a cinnamon peeler *and* Michael Ondaatje.[4] Is he thus evading the issue of cultural appropriation only to invite us to recognize the extent to which his poem is inevitably vulnerable and accountable to the criticisms that it seeks to forestall? Is the poem's ultimate confidence in the ability of its speaker to imagine the other at odds with the kinds of contexts signalled by its hypothetical opening? Exemplary insofar as its interplay between precariousness and confidence in *Running in the Family*, the shifting registers of presentation in *Running in the Family*, the poem celebrates the necessity of cultural interaction, not so much alerting us to the power of the centre to recuperate — and hence dominate — the margins as, I think, foregrounding the ability of poetry to negotiate a space for the apprehension of subjugated histories or knowledges. More than simply one of the many manifestations of generic slippages or resistances in Ondaatje's prose-dominated text, poetry — to paraphrase T.S. Eliot by way of C.L.R. James and Edward Said (see Said 281) — becomes a place where the impossible union of very distinct spheres of experience becomes actual. In a move that recalls the ending of "High Flowers" and, in fact, replicates the discursive configuration of the text as a whole, Ondaatje demonstrates his involvement in an exploration of the ways in which "made-up" situations achieve a kind of resonance that enables them to participate in a newly articulated mode of referentiality.

This kind of reformulated understanding of referentiality is, of course, part of the reason that Ondaatje is so drawn to Márquez's *One Hundred Years of Solitude*. "How," asks Ondaatje, "do you make the hyperbolic sentences which make up about ninety-seven per cent of the book *normal*? Believable?" ("García Márquez" 24). I have tried, in some measure, to indicate the ways in which we might raise analogous questions about *Running in the Family* and to attend to the importance of these questions for our understanding of its cultural politics. Acknowledging both the powers and the limits of its representational activity, the proximity and the distance of Ondaatje's relationship with Sri Lankan culture, *Running in the Family* presents the dialogic mode as a way of modulating from the condition of cultural displacement into a declaration of the possibilities of solidarity. Only by exhibiting a willingness to enter into the imaginative realm, by hypothesizing, can texts — *this* text seems to say — address other cultures and histories in a critically sensitive manner. If, as Hayden White argues, "history as a discipline is in bad shape today because it has lost sight of its origins in the literary imagination" (99), then Ondaatje's text is sensitive not only to the imaginative ways in which "history is organized" (*Running in the Family* 26) but also to both the transformational possibilities engendered by the

processes of dialogue and the sort of commerce that imaginative environments make possible.

## NOTES

[1] Ernest MacIntyre also suggests that the Eurasian behaviour dramatized in the text is not as divorced from actual circumstances as it might at first appear: "Those who react to Michael Ondaatje's *Running in the Family* as fantastic and exaggerated should only bother to go into the details of how these people [the Burghers] careered madly into a midnight 'manoeuvre' to topple and replace the government of Mrs. Sivimavo Bandaranaike in 1961. Then they will see that the attempted coup of 1961 has been running in the family from as far back as the decades of the 20s, 30s and 40s as Mervyn Ondaatje (the author's father) soaked in gin but thinly clothed in the uniform of the Ceylon Light Infantry runs riot in the Colombo Trinco train, loaded revolver and all, as he senses an imminent Japanese invasion" (316–17).

[2] For a fuller discussion of this site of interaction in Ondaatje's writing, see Heble.

[3] On the complex question of Ondaatje's accountability to society, see Bök: "While the early Ondaatje appears to believe that great literature must be sociopolitically indifferent, the later Ondaatje appears to express a burgeoning tension between two conflicting, artistic impulses: the will to social retreat and the will to social contact" (112).

[4] That Ondaatje's volume of selected poems bears the title *The Cinnamon Peeler* may well indicate the centrality of the poem both to his self-definition and to the subject of his writing.

## WORKS CITED

Ahmad, Aijaz. *In Theory: Classes, Nations, Literatures*. London: Verso, 1992.

Ashcroft, Bill, Gareth Griffiths, and Helen Tiffin. *The Empire Writes Back: Theory and Practice in Post-Colonial Literatures*. New Accents. London: Routledge, 1989.

Berger, John. *And Our Faces, My Heart, Brief as Photos*. New York: Pantheon, 1984.

Bhabha, Homi K. "Introduction: Narrating the Nation." *Nation and Narration*. Ed. Bhabha. London: Routledge, 1990. 1–7.

Bök, Christian. "Destructive Creation: The Politicization of Violence in the Works of Michael Ondaatje." *Canadian Literature* 132 (1992): 109–24.

Brantlinger, Patrick. *Crusoe's Footprints: Cultural Studies in Britain and America*. New York: Routledge, 1990.

de Silva, K.M. *Managing Ethnic Tensions in Multi-Ethnic Societies: Sri Lanka 1880–1985*. Lanham, MD: UP of America, 1986.

Foucault, Michel. *Power/Knowledge: Selected Interviews and Other Writings, 1972–1977*. Ed. Colin Gordon. Trans. Gordon et al. New York: Pantheon, 1980.

Gooneratne, Yasmine. "Cultural Interaction in Modern Sri Lankan Poetry Written in English." *Only Connect: Literary Perspectives East and West*. Ed. Guy Amirthanayagam and S.C. Harrex. Adelaide: Centre for Research in the New Literatures in English; Honolulu: East-West Center, 1981. 186–208.

Heble, Ajay. "Michael Ondaatje and the Problem of History." *Clio* 19.2 (1990): 97–110.

Hodgins, Jack. *Innocent Cities*. Toronto: McClelland, 1990.

Hutcheon, Linda. *The Canadian Postmodern: A Study of Contemporary English-Canadian Fiction*. Toronto: Oxford UP, 1988.

———. "Michael Ondaatje" [interview]. *Other Solitudes: Canadian Multicultural Fictions*. Ed. Hutcheon and Marion Richmond. Toronto: Oxford UP, 1990. 179–202.

———. *A Poetics of Postmodernism: History, Theory, Fiction*. New York: Routledge, 1988.

Kamboureli, Smaro. "The Alphabet of the Self: Generic and Other Slippages in Michael Ondaatje's *Running in the Family*." *Reflections: Autobiography and Canadian Literature*. Ed. K.P. Stich. Reappraisals: Canadian Writers. Ottawa: U of Ottawa P, 1988. 79–91.

Kanaganayakam, Chelva. "A Trick with a Glass: Michael Ondaatje's South Asian Connection." *Canadian Literature* 132 (1992): 33–42.

MacIntyre, Ernest. "Outside of Time: *Running in the Family*." *Spider Blues: Essays on Michael Ondaatje*. Ed. Sam Solecki. Montreal: Véhicule, 1985. 315–19.

Mistry, Rohinton. *Tales from Firozsha Baag*. Penguin Short Fiction series. Markham, ON: Penguin, 1987.

Mukherjee, Arun. *Towards an Aesthetic of Opposition: Essays on Literature Criticism and Cultural Imperialism*. Stratford, ON: Williams-Wallace, 1988.

Ondaatje, Michael. *The Cinnamon Peeler: Selected Poems*. 1989. Toronto: McClelland, 1992.

———. *Coming through Slaughter*. Toronto: Anansi, 1976.

———. "García Márquez and the Bus to Aracataca." *Figures in a Ground: Canadian Essays on Modern Literature Collected in Honor of Sheila Watson*. Ed. Diane Bessai and David Jackel. Saskatoon: Western Producer Prairie, 1978. 19–31.

———. *Running in the Family*. Toronto: McClelland, 1982.

Radhakrishnan, R. "Toward an Effective Intellectual: Foucault or Gramsci?" *Intellectuals: Aesthetics Politics Academics*. Ed. Bruce Robbins. Cultural Politics 2. Minneapolis: U of Minnesota P, 1990. 57–99.

Said, Edward W. *Culture and Imperialism*. New York: Knopf, 1993.

Slemon, Stephen. "Magic Realism as Post-Colonial Discourse." *Canadian Literature* 116 (1988): 9–24.

Sugunasiri, Suwanda H.J. "'Sri Lankan' Canadian Poets: The Bourgeoisie That Fled the Revolution." *Canadian Literature* 132 (1992): 60–79.

Suleri, Sara. *Meatless Days*. Chicago: U of Chicago P, 1989.

———. *The Rhetoric of English India*. Chicago: U of Chicago P, 1992.

White, Hayden. *Tropics of Discourse: Essays in Cultural Criticism*. Baltimore: Johns Hopkins UP, 1978.

# PATRICK'S QUEST: NARRATION AND SUBJECTIVITY IN MICHAEL ONDAATJE'S *IN THE SKIN OF A LION*

## Rod Schumacher

My discussion of Michael Ondaatje's *In the Skin of a Lion* is intent on seeking a correspondence between narration and the acquisition of subjectivity. To achieve this correspondence I centre my argument specifically on Patrick Lewis in order to illustrate how his incremental movement from private to communal symbolic registers facilitates his quest to subjectify himself within society. This approach is dependent upon understanding the role narration plays in the framing of personal and collective experience, and also how narration functions as a medium for desire. The theoretical foundation of my discussion borrows heavily from Lacanian poststructural theory. Here again, I am attempting to gain a fuller understanding, not only of the relationship between language and subjectivity, but also the important roles that community (or collective discourse) and narrative play in the development of subjectivity.

In addition to my analysis of Patrick, I also intend to situate the reader as a subject who gains knowledge through narration by identifying his/her own position within textual discourse. My reading necessitates viewing Patrick as the pivotal agent through whom the reader is encouraged to enter the fictional realm, seek and discover knowledge, and finally, carry that knowledge into the real world. In this regard my discussion is very much in the service of the social and political aims of Ondaatje's text. However, before dealing directly with the novel it is necessary to present a fairly broad understanding of how I will be employing the term *narration* in the contexts of reading and framing experience.

Poststructural theorists such as Jacques Lacan and the later Roland Barthes have continually reminded us that we are always involved, consciously and unconsciously, in reading the world and narrating our experience. As Barthes states: "narrative begins with the very history of humanity; there is not, there has never been, any people anywhere without narrative" (*Semiotic 95*). Reading the world constitutes a narrative act, a continual placing and displacing of signifiers, the goal of which, on a conscious level, is to gather experience into a coherent pattern. Our memories, conclusions, dreams, fantasies, careers and our projected visions of our futures appear most coherent to us when we can consciously situate them within narratives.

According to Lacan, narration is motivated by the unconscious search to reinstate the unity of the self that is imagined to have existed prior to the acquisition of language. For Lacan, our need to speak our experience and to attend to stories is driven by our desire to be (what V.A. Miller calls) sutured to a symbolic representational code, to unite the speaking subject with the "whole structure of language" (Cohen 156). In other words, language is both a representational substitute for the absence of a whole self, and the source of the self. Likewise Barthes views narration as a process motivated by the desire to bond with language: "reading is a conductor of the Desire to write . . . we desire the desire the author had for the reader when he was writing, we desire the *love-me* which is in all writing" (*Rustle* 40-41). However, despite the implied promise of wholeness, language "does not unify subjectivity . . . but, on the contrary, continually manifests the division of the subject" (Cohen 156). That is, we can imagine there is meaning in language, we can be inscribed by discourse and situate ourselves within a community, but we can never become the being of our speech or the subject of speech. Signification is always a process of "sliding . . . [of] no fixed binding of signifier to signified in the mental life of the subject" (Cohen 157).

My point in presenting this brief excursus into poststructuralism is to emphasize how discourse—and by extension narrative—is always falling short of unifying the speaking subject with the subject of speech; we are always subjects of, and subjected to, the representational system of language and, as Cohen and Shires assert, the subject "cannot mean independently of it" (153). And because we are unable to step outside this symbolic realm, we strive to attach meaning to it in order to mediate our lives. Language, applied in all of its possible forms, remains the primary means by which we attempt what might be called *self-closure* (the contentment of being). However, as listening and speaking agents, as nominal producers and subjects of narrative, we constantly grant "some full meaning to the words we speak" and hear, only to be "surprised to find them determined by relations outside our control" (Cohen 161). Every discursive community is always already formed prior to our entrance into its representational codes and, according to Lacan, our status as subjects within these representational codes begins when we are initiated into the established structures of discourse.

In their explanation of Lacanian theory, Cohen and Shires note that "a narrative representation of subjectivity functions similarly as a signifier with which a reader or viewer identifies" (149). By extrapolation, a narrative such as Ondaatje's, with its focus on acquiring identity through language, functions as a sort of surrogate world in which the reader, by becoming entangled in the hero's desires, imaginatively joins in the quest for subjectivity. According to Lacan, the reader is motivated by the unconscious desire to pursue narrative as a means to construct an image of him/herself that will hopefully resolve the separation that occurred when the symbolic register of language fractured the coherent relationship between the mother and the pre-linguistic child. The reader's desire is the unconscious Other, the buried aspect of the human psyche that, like a hungry infant, is always craving contentment. The desire of the reader is an attempt to resolve the lack of the mother. As Barry Cameron states in his article "Lacan: Implications of Psychoanalysis and Canadian Discourse," "For Lacan, narrative is an effort to catch up retrospectively on the traumatic primordial separation from the self and mother with the entry into language" (Moss 148). In other words, the text activates the reader's unconscious desire to be sutured to its symbolic code, the hoped-for result of which is to enable the reader to share Patrick's desire to be signified as a coherent subject. (Of course, not all novels provide the same level of subjective coherence, and may seek to resist signifying a coherent subject; however, this is not the case in Ondaatje's text.) Because the reader is always positioned outside the text s/he has to enter into a very personal relationship with the work in order to discover how s/he can become signified within it. This is one of the reasons Barthes refers to the act of reading as "a work and a game"

(*Rustle* 41). When we commit ourselves to a text—and here as throughout this paper I am referring to a literary text—we enter into a process that allows us to play the fictional text against our own personal texts. In doing so, we test the competence of our personal experience against that of the text's. This interaction is, in essence, founded on the reader's desire to continually search for alternative modes of representation that will provide a more stable self-image. In addition, the reader also gains pleasure in imagining him/herself as an active and desiring subject within a discursive field that is distanced from the turbulence of everyday life. In other words, literature offers a safe outlet for the desire of the unconscious Other.

*

As I have stated, Patrick Lewis is the pivotal figure in Ondaatje's novel, and for a number of reasons. First of all, Ondaatje intended the reader to seek to identify with Patrick and to use him as a guide throughout the text. There are many other important characters in the novel but Patrick is the only one whose process of self-discovery is intimately related. The narrative is dependent upon Patrick's ever increasing awareness of the world, and more importantly, the actions which stem from what he learns. If we desire to read and learn this world we will seek to identify with Patrick, because he, like us, and in the manner of the Bildungsroman, is also being introduced to it. In other words, Patrick and the reader share in the activity of cultural initiation, and as we shall see, Ondaatje has made certain that the ground on which we begin our journey is as barren as possible.

The novel begins with Patrick looking out at the world, trying to situate himself in the "pale green and nameless" backwoods of northern Ontario. Because there is very little knowledge of the world available to him, Patrick uses the few resources he has to feed his imagination and give voice to his thoughts. He studies the moths and insects attracted by the kitchen light, giving them fictional names and recording their visits in a notebook. He opens his geography book and whispers the exotic names of "Caspian, Nepal. Durango" (9). This very rigorous display of writing, reading, whispering, and imagining are in direct conflict with what Christian Bök has termed Patrick's "deliberate aphasia" (119). Any feelings of alienation that Patrick experiences, either in the wilderness or in Toronto, arise not from some calculated withdrawal from the world, but rather from his inability to use language effectively. His desire is not to seek silence, but to break out of it. The names he creates and reads from maps serve his desire to frame his private experience in language, and this begins the naming motif that runs throughout the text. By naming the world, even if only in whispers and in his imagination, Patrick displays his desire to create his own private narrative.

Patrick's textualizing of his life is presented as a concealed act, something he does not do in the presence of his father. He waits until his father is asleep, and this furthers the isolation of his desire to narrate his experience. Hazen Lewis, being an "abashed man, withdrawn from the world . . . uninterested in the habits of civilization" (15), is clearly of no help to Patrick's quest. There is very little conversation between Patrick and his father; in fact, there are only two moments in the novel in which there is dialogue between them, and even these instances amount to a scant thirteen words (12,14). Hazen's first words to Patrick, "I'm going under now" (12), are significant in that they imply that the end result of remaining silent is to be left in obscurity, and this is exactly what happens to Patrick's father. Hazen's silence denies Patrick the opportunity to vocalize his experience, and this in turn forbids him to test his own competence with language. As the text points out, "he wants conversation" in his life; only by sharing language with others will he be able to "leap . . . over the wall of this place" (10). By being restricted to a concealed and monologic articulation of experience, Patrick's desire to situate himself in the world is severely hampered.

The isolation and silence of Patrick's early years serve a very specific function in the novel. As we know from the first epigraph, and from Gordon Gamlin's comparative analysis, Ondaatje framed much of the narrative around *The Epic of Gilgamesh*. There are many approaches to a comparative study of the two narratives—Gamlin, for example, discusses the corresponding oral implications. Many of my predecessors (Beddoes, Beran, Duffy, Sarris) have also offered comparative readings of the two texts, and a general consensus exists in viewing Patrick in the image of the ancient hero Gilgamesh.[1] However, there is more than a passing likeness of Enkidu, the beloved friend of Gilgamesh, in Ondaatje's hero, Patrick Lewis, in that both have been raised outside a highly-developed cultural setting. In addition to this, both narratives tell the story of how these two characters respond when encountering a civilization wherein a majority of the inhabitants is oppressed by a dominant figure of power. And finally, both Enkidu and Patrick, by managing to remain on the periphery of culture, are positioned as having a perspective that I will generalize as being aloof from ideological constructs. By comparing Patrick's character to Enkidu's, it becomes possible to view Patrick as a culturally uninscribed figure who carries within him some sort of instinctive ability to separate justice from injustice. This instinctive aspect is very central to both narratives; and although it would not be in the interests of most poststructuralists to allow for it, I will, nevertheless, refer to it on occasion. Suffice it to say, that where Enkidu's "primeval" nature (Kluger 31) acts as a positive and active force in *Gilgamesh*, Patrick's marginalized cultural inscription—he has, after all, gone to school, and has at least a fragmented history—functions as a means to defamiliarize, or, better yet, disassociate the reader from his/her own cultural/ideological perspective. In other words, the beginning of the novel details a world so personal that the reader's imaginative entrance into Patrick's life is more a sensual initiation than a social and cultural introduction. We would not be far off the mark to consider Patrick as representing *l'enfant sauvage* popularized in Europe in the 1970s, the feral child of folklore, or any one of the similar romantic figures who have surfaced since Rousseau's era. By initiating our identification with Patrick outside of a highly structured discursive community, we become dependent on his ability to provide us with the knowledge of the text. And because so much of his boyhood experience is founded on his instinctive relationship with nature, we are encouraged to trust in our own ability to sense our way through the text, rather than trying to bend it into a predisposed coherent pattern. In short, the reader, as subject, is seduced by Patrick's lack of identity into privileging an emotional response over a cognitive one. Ondaatje is attempting to loosen our attachment to established centres of discourse in order to intensify our desire to assume a subject position similar to Patrick's. Ondaatje wants the reader to *feel* the experience of being displaced.

When we meet up with Patrick again, he is twenty-one years old and has just been "dropped under the vast arches of Union Station" in Toronto (53). We quickly realize that during the nine years since we first met him he has made very little progress in giving voice to his experience. His documented past is reduced to nothing more than "letters frozen inside mailboxes (53), a figure that once again echoes his desire to share language and also foreshadows a time—a spring—when he will be able to. Once again, his most significant memories arise from sensual experience: "What he remembered was loving only things to do with colour . . . the warm brown universe of barns, the breath and steam of cattle" (53). There is still no sign of his having acquired the vocabulary necessary to signify his subjectivity. His past is still predominantly couched in private images of the natural world of his early years. Patrick's attachment to nature, when considered in the context of Lacan's theory, suggests that he has cultivated an imaginary relationship with nature in order to mediate the silence in his life. This point will be developed further when I discuss the important role Clara plays in preparing Patrick's full entrance into the symbolic register of language; suffice it to say that even the fragmented, private narrative of his youth has been lost: "He spoke out his name and it struggled up in a hollow echo and was lost in the high air of Union Station" (54).

After this very brief reintroduction the novel leaps through time and Patrick is now employed as a searcher. There is a specific irony in his trying to discover the whereabouts of Ambrose Small in that, unlike Patrick who desires to name and situate himself within a community, Small has purposely fashioned a network of false names in order to become invisible. It is also ironic that while searching for someone so determined to erase himself from history, Patrick should find the very person who initiates his self-identity.

When we consider the components of Patrick's private narrative it is easy to understand why he becomes infatuated with Clara. In less than two paragraphs the text of his introduction to Clara calls forward all of the signifiers of his concealed narrative. Her body not only provokes his sexual desire, it also affects him like a sensual wound. She is "rare" and "perfect" (61) like the exotic names of far away countries. Her elegant clothes remind him of "a damsel fly" and his boyhood fascination with moths and insects. Furthermore, there is no coincidence in our being told of their destined lovemaking in the "silence of the reading room" at the library (62)—a site which evokes both the silence and the textual basis of his boyhood desire to know the world. Patrick is also drawn to her because he senses that by "not turning around to talk to him properly," Clara may live in a silence similar to his own. In this brief and evocative passage, Clara textualizes the whole repertoire of Patrick's concealed narrative; his personal signifiers have, for the first time, been validated beyond his private sphere. Her body has become a text of his desire for wholeness. Clara's impact on Patrick is a necessary step in his subjective quest, but it does not, in itself, bring him fully into the realm of collective discourse. What Clara does is provide him access to a coherent personal history.

As we read the novel, we are aware that Patrick's narrative is destined to encounter the other narratives that have been interlaced with his. His contact with Clara can be understood as a necessary step in preparing his entrance into the whole context of the novel. There is a pattern represented here, in which the stories that weave around Patrick's narrative correspond to his desire to fill the absence in his own life. In this regard, the Lacanian notion of suture has been incorporated within the very structure of the novel. As the novel progresses Patrick's narrative becomes more and more imbricated with the other narratives—he and the reader are gradually moving from a private and isolated space to an interpersonal relationship with Clara, which in turn will lead to the collective site of the immigrant community. Clara's function is to bridge the space between personal and social narrative. The origins of Patrick's infatuation, at least from the point of view of narrative, stem from her ability to articulate and educate Patrick in the intimate details of personal history:

> He loved the eroticism of her history, the knowledge of where she sat in the classroom, her favourite brand of pencil at the age of nine. Details flooded his heart. . .he found he had become interested only in her, her childhood, her radio work, this landscape in which she had grown up. (69)

By listening to Clara narrate her past, Patrick learns a valuable and practical lesson regarding the importance of maintaining personal history. By becoming an engaged listener—an activity that corresponds to the reader's entanglement with narrative—Patrick begins to understand that his own history has significance, and that there are forces outside of himself that have shaped his life. However, when encouraged to narrate his own life, he is still incapable of speech:

> He defended himself for most of the time with a habit of
> vagueness. . .There was a wall in him that no one reached. . .
> A tiny stone swallowed years back that had grown with him
> and which he carried around because he could not shed it. . .
> Patrick and his small unimportant stone. It had entered him
> at the wrong time in his life. (71)

The isolation of his youth and the silence of his father are obstacles which even Clara's history cannot overcome. There is, however, a reason why Patrick's relationship with Clara fails to immediately bring him into the realm of language.

What is of particular significance vis-à-vis a Lacanian reading of Patrick's youth is the mystery of the mother-figure. Ondaatje's text carefully avoids any mention of a feminine presence in Patrick's early years. We are left to assume that the dynamic Oedipal moment, so necessary in psychoanalytic theory, has somehow not taken place, and therefore his acquisition of language and the subsequent identification outside of the mother have yet to be completed. This lack of mother is further evidence of his entering the social realm as a marginally inscribed subject, but it does not necessarily imply that the mother-figure is absent during his upbringing.

As I have already stated, Patrick's attachment to nature represents an imaginary relationship through which he attempts to situate himself in the world. In other words, he has adopted the natural world as an imaginary referent for the absent mother. The manner in which the text describes his bond with nature is similar to the kind of protective relationship a young boy would have with his mother. Patrick's maternal bond with nature is obvious in his response to the Finnish skaters. This scene also serves to intimate the increasing degree of conflict he will encounter as he becomes more and more subjectified within language.

In Lacanian terms, Patrick's fascination with the skaters represents his unconscious desire for the phallic authority of language symbolized by the light cast from the burning cattails. In fact, the whole motif of fire and light that runs throughout the novel can be read as a symbol of Patrick's search for the authority of language. Just as the moths are attracted to the *man-made* glow of his kitchen light, so too is Patrick attracted to the "fire" of the symbolic register. However, when he approaches the river he senses the authority of the *male* skaters and hides the lamp he is carrying behind a tree so he will remain hidden from view—a gesture similar to a timid child clinging to the hem of a mother's skirt. He is afraid to contact "these strangers of another language" (22) because their "light" threatens his bond with the mother-figure which is troped as nature. The skaters remind him of "a coven, or one of those strange druidic rituals" he had read about. And even though he is fascinated by their joyful energy, and wishes he could "hold their hands and skate the length of the creek," he still refuses to step from the safety of the bushes. He cannot compete against the light of this strange language which gives these men the confidence to move "like a wedge into the blackness" (22). The encounter has awakened his desire to enter the authoritative realm of language, but it has also made him aware that these men are his rivals; that is, they are in possession of "*his* shore, *his* river." In other words, he senses that the phallic authority of language is a threat to his maternal bond with nature. By remaining in the darkness of the trees, by concealing himself from view, he is safe from confronting what Lacan calls "The Law of the Father": the masculine authority inscribed in the symbolic register which prohibits the child's desire for and access to the intimacy of the mother. According to Lacan, "The Law of the Father" manifests itself in language by renouncing desire for the mother, and substituting and/or compensating this loss by seeking dominion over the feminine (mother/nature) through the possessive act of naming. This capacity to authorize existence, to situate himself and gain some form of control in the world, is exactly what Patrick is striving for. However, because he is unable to articulate an appropriate response, some kind of self-empowering statement, retreat "back through the trees and fields" (22), is his only option. His withdrawal to the safety of the mother-figure is an unconscious acknowledgement of his inability to defend his subjective status. However, as the title of the chapter suggests, the incident has given him the "Little Seeds" that eventually bring about his full entry into the symbolic register.

It is important then to view Clara (and to a lesser extent Alice) as representing, in a very literal though non-biological sense, Patrick's absent mother(s). By transferring his maternal bond from the natural world to a genuine female presence he has achieved another incremental step in his quest. Through Clara, he seeks to establish contact with the mother who lives solely for him and is the object of all his desires. The reason he is still unable to speak his own narrative in the presence of Clara is because he is fully contented with being the object of her attention; and the reason he becomes attracted and distressed when in contact with the phallic "light" of the Finnish skaters is because he has yet to move from the imaginary to the symbolic registry. In terms of a Lacanian reading, Patrick, although nearly thirty years old, has yet to find the means to mediate his separation for the mother-figure. As long as Clara remains in his life he will be content to simply be in her presence, and this in itself will furnish him with all the meaning he requires. It is only after Clara disappears, like an actress having fulfilled her part, and leaves Patrick to suffer the absence, or the lack, of the mother-figure, that language begins to function as a substitute for his loss. With Clara no longer present, he finally rehearses the "Oedipal crisis, which is the inauguration of full entry into the symbolic register" (Cohen 159). His brief and passionate relationship with Clara is a belated yet necessary step in his quest for subjectivity.

Patrick's next attempt to position himself within the symbolic register begins with his entry into the labour class. However, the representational register through with he comes to identify himself is not based on language, but on the visual markings that distinguish the various jobs of the immigrant workers. When we consider the important role that the natural or sensual worlds play in both his life and in the novel as a whole, it seems appropriate that Patrick should first come to situate himself according to visual or tactile inscription. The stained skin of the dye workers, the stiff clothing of the tunnellers and the signifying hole in the back of their shirts are like the tribal body inscription of "primitive" societies. Again, this manner of seeking identity is another incremental step toward the more sophisticated register of language.[2]

After two years of living in almost total silence, Patrick finally becomes situated within Toronto's Macedonian community. It is important to note that his initiation into this cultural site is precipitated by his having learned and employed the Macedonian word for iguana: "A living creature, a gooshter" (112). Once again we see how the phallic authority invested in naming, and therefore codifying and possessing the feminized natural world, serves as an attraction to the symbolic register. Furthermore, this one new word leads to a vast network of "new words" (113) that "he must now remember" (114). At this point in the novel Patrick's acceptance into the Macedonian community is dependent upon his ability to articulate some aspect of his character that aligns him with the cultural expectations of the community. In order for him to become a trusted member of this society, and, more importantly, for him to feel he truly belongs within their ranks, he needs to prove his competence, as much to himself as to the community at large. There is a correspondence here that I wish to develop between Patrick's inscription into the Macedonian community and Lacan's interpretation of the *fort/da* game played by Freud's grandson.

The relationship between language and community is similar to the *fort/da* game in that, just as the child gains control over his separation from his mother by staging the disappearance and return of the lost object, so too does Patrick come to position himself by testing his personal text against the social text of the community. In a sense, Patrick must cast his personal narrative outward in order to test whether or not it will be accepted by the greater community. If he has acquired a representational code that corresponds with, or is sympathetic to, the ideological concerns of the immigrant labour classes, he will then be able to enter a community that will permit him to vocalize, and therefore situate himself, as a subject. Just as Freud's grandson transferred his anxiety to a referent outside the mother, so too does Patrick employ language as a referent to seek a fuller sense of control within a greater field of discourse. This sense of control can only be obtained by testing his personal experience against the customary knowledge of the community. Customary knowledge, to borrow Jean-Francois Lyotard's explanation, "includes notions of 'know-how,' 'knowing how to live,' how to listen" (18). Patrick must test his lived experience, his personal narrative, and his ability to articulate, in order to prove his right to become subjectified within a larger social narrative. If his personal narrative is deemed competent, it is because it "conform[s] to the relevant criteria of justice, beauty, truth, and efficiency respectively accepted in the social circle of the 'knower's' interlocutors" (Lyotard 19). Of course Patrick's admittance into the Macedonian community is easily achieved since both parties share the common narrative of displacement.

By being accepted within the Macedonian community Patrick is given access to a vast history of cultural experience. This is the first time he has come in contact with a collective narrative that is older than any living individual. There are roots here that he has never imagined before, and he begins to love the historicity of culture. It should be noted that Macedonia and *Epic of Gilgamesh*—which, like Ondaatje's novel, is also a narrative of tribal solidarity—are culturally and geographically inseparable, and by using them as referents in the novel Ondaatje is explicitly drawing attention to narrative as the primal structure for making meaning and, perhaps more importantly, sustaining culture.[3] Material referents of culture—bridges, water stations—have always been subject to decay, but narrative, travelling through time from subject to subject, has always been able to carry cultural identity to future generations. As Fredric Jameson states:

> [P]ersonal identity is itself the effect of a certain temporal unification of past and future with one's present; and. . .such active temporal unification is itself a function of language, or better still of the sentence. . . If we are unable to unify the past, present, and future of the sentence, then we are similarly unable to unify. . .our own biographical experience. (324)

Patrick's newly-acquired social register also unites his narrative with the inner-narratives that have woven their separate paths throughout the novel. We have anticipated the merging of these narratives to be a sort of joyful reunion for Patrick, and also for ourselves as readers. The fragmented linearity of the text has encouraged us to desire that Patrick's narrative become sutured into the whole structure of the novel. Although this wholeness is achieved, the joy that we have anticipated is only temporary. I suggest that Patrick's growing attachment to Alice and Hana, and the regularization of his life within immigrant culture, represent the kind of imaginative celebration of wholeness that we seek as readers. However, Alice's role—to "veer" Patrick "to some reality" (88)—is clearly meant to foil the celebration that we wish for Patrick and ourselves. Her primary function is to activate the political implications that are always already attached to all discourse. It is Alice who bursts Patrick's bubble by educating him—

as Clara, though in a different capacity, has done earlier—in the
hard world of political expediency. "I'll tell you about the rich"
(132), she says to him, and Patrick stubbornly begins to realize
that language is also a powerful political weapon, and that the
power in Alice's words is dangerous and necessary. By becoming
a subject within the discourse of the marginalized, he has un-
knowingly and unavoidably situated himself in opposition to
dominant culture. In a particularly parodic move, Patrick begins
to conceal his identity from his employers so he can join Alice in
bringing down the authority of the elite. Like Ambrose Small, Temelcoff, and his father, Patrick begins to make himself as invisible
as possible. Just as Enkidu in the Gilgamesh narrative struggles to
correct the abuse of authority, so too must Patrick attempt to bring
justice to his world.

Although Alice initiates Patrick into the politics of signification, it is through the printed word that he becomes fully acquainted with the barbaric treatment of immigrant workers.
By reading Cato's letters, and the "official histories" (145)
wherein only the elite are credited with the construction of
*their* cultural monuments, Patrick realizes that the vibrant history
and the contributions of the immigrants has not been, and will not
be, properly documented for prosperity; the depth and warmth of
the very community in which he has become a subject will be
erased from history—its narratives will become invisible. When
Alice is accidentally killed by a bomb that has likely been made
by Patrick, his anger with himself is displaced to the rich. His im-
mediate response is to retreat into silence—an attempt to cast off
the irresolvable turmoil which surrounds him and to reclaim
the wonderment and innocence of his youth. But his entrance
into immigrant society has altered him; he can never return to his
past, and he can never step outside of the realm of language. It is
important to note that from the time of Alice's death and Patrick's
encounter with Harris, Patrick never expresses remorse. And it is
during this time that he becomes personally involved in destructive activities. Judy Beddoes likens Patrick at this point in the
novel  to "a child playing with matches" (211), and Sarris goes
even further by viewing him as a "purely sensual, unthinking
savage" (197). The word "feral" surfaces both in the novel (172)
and in Sarris's essay (197), but nowhere is there any sense of the

innocence that was so much apart of Patrick's early years of isolation in the Ontario wilderness. His romanticized attachment to nature has been shattered by the ideological implications inscribed in language and his indoctrination into the constant turmoil of civilization. As in all encounters where innocence is defeated by experience, there is no way to retrieve the past.

His militant activism is largely due to his inability to speak of his involvement in Alice's death. Silence and violence have become the only channels through which he can attempt to mediate his loss. In short, Patrick is literally tongue-tied because he has yet to assume responsibility for the creation of his own narrative. By this, I mean that his entrance into the symbolic register has been achieved by borrowing from Alice's discursive schema. We recall how, unlike Clara's open and detailed history, Alice's past "remains sourceless" (74), and her body is filled with "suppressed energy" (75). By relying on Alice to indoctrinate him into language, Patrick has become an extension of her militant story. He has yet to find his own vocabulary, or the kind of *skin* that will grant him the means to express his own subjectivity.

What Patrick has unwittingly been attempting to achieve in his search for Small, and also in his encounter with Harris, is to finally confront the father-figure who left him "at the wrong time in his life" (71). Figuratively speaking, Patrick's ultimate quest is to steal the "fire"—the phallic authority—that resides in language. According to Lacan, gaining the authority of language requires some form of violent psychological struggle, a castration or "self-mutilation" (Cohen 159). We can now understand why Patrick, as a boy of only eleven, was so intimidated by the Finnish skaters. If he is to find "his own time zone, his own lamp" (143), he must first accept the wounding by the father-figure; only then will he be able to detach himself from the imaginary realm represented by Clara and nature, and move toward the symbolic register. The *burns* (read: the wound) he receives from Small's attack are yet another step toward spitting out the "small unimportant stone" (71) that has kept him from accessing his own narrative voice—a voice he eventually discovers to be quite different from the one he has borrowed from Alice, who, in turn, had borrowed it from her husband, the self-named Cato.

Patrick's encounter with Harris in the water plant can be viewed as his ultimate confrontation with the authority of language, and I would like to take two discrete yet corresponding approaches to the scene. First of all, the encounter creates a wonderful sense of the unifying potential of narrative. There is a distinct archetypal pattern here as first Harris, and then Patrick, reveal their intimate narratives in the dark and cave-like space that surrounds them—a setting that is also a Father-space, made to control nature (water). Even the moon-shaped windows suggest Harris and Patrick are removed from the time frame of the novel and are acting out the most fundamental social activity known to humankind. Harris begins defending himself by narrating the visions he had in dreams. He tells Patrick that "We need excess, something to live up to" (236), and that the only reason the elite exist is because people like Patrick reject the responsibility of power, and therefore allow "bland fools" to speak for them. He tells Patrick that what he is "looking for is a villain" (237), and because Harris's narrative is not founded on political power, but on a personal vision of beauty, Patrick is unable to view Harris as a figure of evil. Patrick then turns on the light—a significant gesture in Lacan's lexicon—to confirm Harris's sincerity:

> Patrick turned the light on and saw Harris' eyes looking directly into his.
> — Have you decided?
> — Not yet.
> He switched off the light. Again they disappeared from each other. (238)

The material world is the point of contact, but the world of narrative is where we wrestle with ourselves, and with each other.

It is now Patrick's turn to tell his private narrative, but, as with Clara, he is still reluctant to speak. Again another ironic shift occurs as Harris, who we might have supposed to symbolize the authority of dominant culture, becomes the agent who insists that Patrick not remain silent. When Patrick balks at speaking of Alice's death—"I don't want to talk about this anymore" (239)—Harris tells him his life will "always be a nightmare" (238) if he refuses to speak. Giving voice to private experience, and sharing it within a community of listeners—even if that community is made of only a speaking subject and a single listener—provides both Patrick and Harris the opportunity to be heard, understood, and also to frame experience into a coherent narrative pattern. The darkness of the scene shuts out the real world, and we are left with two individuals struggling with language, trying to find some common ground. Beran claims that "[I]n acknowledging his own role in the accident that killed Alice Gull, Patrick ends his defiance and denial" (78). I agree with Beran, but I would place less emphasis on Patrick acknowledging his role—he was undoubtably aware of it from the very moment the bomb went off— than I would on the actual act of speaking about it. The theme of breaking silence, of giving voice to what lies beneath the surface of events, is too important an issue in the novel, and Patrick's silence is much less an act of denial than an inability to articulate grief.

Patrick, after finally voicing his distress, falls asleep on Harris's bed. Sarris takes a Rip Van Winkle approach to Patrick's sleep by interpreting it as a "withdrawal from the world . . . a forfeit[ing] of moral responsibility" (200). In contrast to Sarris's appraisal, this sleep scene is also one of the most powerful and affirming moments in the novel, in that it further asserts the unifying potential of narrative while at time same time providing a figurative reunion of the earlier image of Patrick and his father sharing the same bed after rescuing the cow from the river. It would be difficult to imagine a more complete gesture of trust than falling asleep in the presence of a potential persecutor. When Harris realizes the danger in Patrick's incredible entry into the building— "My God, he swam here . . . What vision, what dream was that?" (241)—he is stunned by Patrick's selfless devotion to his ideals. By listening to each other they have become obligated to the common ground expressed in their personal narratives. If Harris hands Patrick over to the authorities, he knows he is also rejecting the vision that has guided his own life.

The second interpretation of this scene involves recognizing it as Patrick's final confrontation with the Lacanian father-figure. Patrick, although believing he has entered the water station to destroy it, is really motivated by his subconscious desire to gain or at least challenge the phallic authority that it symbolizes. His encounter with Harris defuses his urge to destroy the building because Harris, the holder of phallic power, becomes actively involved in helping Patrick identify his role within the symbolic register. In short, Harris becomes the benevolent father-figure who passes phallic knowledge to the younger male. Patrick's underwater journey, his subsequent wounds, and his meeting with Harris in the womb-like atmosphere of the temple, symbolize his acceptance of "The Name of the Father," a crucial and final step in his entrance into the whole context of language. He has, in effect, suffered the pains of rebirth and fully entered the symbolic realm. He now knows his role is not that of an anarchist, and his life is "no longer a single story but part of a mural . . . a wondrous web" (145) that must be preserved. And finally, he has come to the point of taking responsibility for his own narrative. He is now able to interpret Alice's favourite quotation from Joseph Conrad—"Let me re-emphasize the extreme looseness of the structure of all objects" (135)—on his own. He no longer believes, as Alice did, that Conrad is calling for the destruction of the centres of authority. He now realizes that what Conrad is really stating is that all ideological structures are inherently vulnerable, and they will all be replaced by other structures that are similarly flawed. And the only cultural objects that can withstand the rise and fall of these loose ideological objects are the narratives of its history. As Dennis Duffy states, the novel "makes use of ancient, durable monuments and thereby demonstrates the power of the fragile medium of paper finally to encompass them" (132). These "durable monuments" are in ironic juxtaposition to the seemingly fleeting and unstable nature of language.

As the novel closes we realize the entire story has been told by Patrick while he and Hana are driving to reunite with Clara. Patrick will never be silent again, and by sharing his narrative with Hana his story and the stories of the immigrant workers will be carried into the future. Sarris, after acknowledging that most critics agree the novel's point of view belongs to Patrick, makes an important and, for the purpose of this paper, a very significant claim that "perhaps that point of view might more accurately be seen as that of Hana, Alice's daughter" (189). Sarris argues for this shift because in the novel Hana is the actual recipient of Patrick's story. Hana's role, as stated in the prologue, is to "gather" Patrick's story, a gesture which, when placed within a Lacanian reading, is an attempt to unify the mediating realm of language/ narrative with the wholeness that is associated with the female/

mother realm. Patrick remains the focus of the novel, but on a figurative level Hana, at the age of sixteen, can be seen as a sort of mythic regenerator of narrative, whose role is to gather, incubate, and safeguard what she hears. If this story had been a fairy tale we would have no difficulty viewing Hana as the embodiment of an ideal similar to Snow White, Cinderella, and Sleeping Beauty. Her gender, age, purity, and fecundity make her an idyllic figure for the safeguarding and regeneration of language, and the fantasized site of the longed-for resolution of the lost mother.[4] What Patrick passes on to her is not an "official history," and there are no statistics attached to it; and it is only one of the living narratives Hana will use to position herself in the world. The closing image of Patrick and Hana driving toward the rising sun once again opens readers' imaginations to the possibility that the wholeness we desire in narrative may still be achieved.

*

By joining in Patrick's quest we gain a fuller understanding of what it means to be an attentive listener, and we also become better acquainted with the importance attached to sharing our experiences in an intimate atmosphere. In fact, every time we become entangled in narrative we are, in a sense, reenacting Patrick's and Harris' intimate struggles to be heard and understood: we read, pay attention, ask questions—we feel the life within the pages. Literature constantly reminds us who we are, who we were, and who we might become. As Robert Kroetsch states, "we haven't got an identity until somebody tells our story. The fiction makes us real" (63).

If we place any significance in Barthes statement that "literature and language are in the process of recognizing each other" (*Rustle* 11), then we have already begun to acknowledge that when we speak we are calling forward the text of our experiences. And even though this text is only a symbolic register of experience, and has already been coded with meaning, it is still the primary medium for mediating our lives. In the case of Ondaatje's novel, the text draws our attention to the role narration plays in inscribing and sustaining meaning. In other words, the novel calls attention to the value of narration, and specifically, it reminds us that stories are the fundamental mode of transferring cultural knowledge. On this point I conclude by recalling Lyotard's assertion that narration "is the quintessential form of customary knowledge" (75).

## NOTES

[1] Although my focus throughout is on Patrick, it is interesting to note a similar correspondence exists between Enkidu and Ondaatje, as both arrive in a civilization of which they have no previous knowledge, yet both step boldly forward to address existing injustice. Enkidu, perhaps the oldest example of what we now refer to as Rousseau's noble savage; Ondaatje, the contemporary writer from the margins. Carol L. Beran also views Commissioner Harris as "one of the most surprising alter egos" for Ondaatje, as both imagine "wonderful structures and then bring them into being" (72).

[2] In fact, Patrick's movement from the wilderness to Macedonian society can be read as a retelling of humanity's emergence as linguistic beings.

[3] *The Epic of Gilgamesh* is also the oldest narrative known to the west, and considered by many scholars to be a founding text of western civilization. See Kluger.

[4] Furthermore, Hana, like the fairy-tale characters mentioned, also lacks a living mother.

## WORKS CITED

Barthes, Roland. *The Rustle of Language*. Trans. Richard Howard. Toronto: Collins, 1986.

_____. *The Semiotic Challenge*. Trans. Richard Howard. Toronto: Collins, 1988.

Beddoes, Julie. "Which Side Is It On? Form, Class, and Politics in *In the Skin of a Lion*." *Essays on Canadian Writing* 53 (1994): 204-215.

Beran, Carol L. "Ex-centricity: Michael Ondaatje's *In the Skin of a Lion* and Hugh MacLennan's *Barometer Rising*." *Studies in Canadian Literature* 18.1 (1993): 71-84.

Bök, Christian. "Destructive Creation: The Politicization of Violence in the Works of Michael Ondaatje." *Canadian Literature* 132 (1992): 109-124.

Cohen, Steven and Linda M. Shires. *Telling Stories: A Theoretical Analysis of Narrative Fiction*. New York: Routledge, 1988.

Duffy, Dennis. "A Wrench in Time: A Sub-Sub-Librarian Looks beneath the Skin of a Lion." *Essays on Canadian Writing* 53 (1994): 125-140.

Gamlin, Gordon. "Michael Ondaatje's *In the Skin of a Lion* and the Oral Narrative." *Canadian Literature* 135 (1992): 68-77.

Kluger, Rivkah Scharf. *The Archetypal Significance of Gilgamesh: A Modern Ancient Hero*. Einsiedeln: Daimon Verlag, 1991.

Jameson, Fredric. "Excerpts from Postmodernism, Or the Cultural Logic of Late Capitalism." *A Postmodern Reader*. Ed. Joseph Natoli and Linda Hutcheon. Albany: SUNY of New York, 1993. 312-32.

Kroetsch, Robert, James Bacque and Pierre Gravel. *Creation*. Toronto: New Press, 1970.

Lyotard, Jean-Francois. *The Postmodern Condition: A Report on Knowledge*. Minneapolis: U of Minnesota P, 1984.

Moss, John, ed. *Future Indicative: Literary Theory and Canadian Literature*. Reappraisals, Canadian Writers 13, Ottawa: University of Ottawa, 1987.

Ondaatje, Michael. *In the Skin of a Lion*. Toronto: Penguin, 1988.

Sarris, Fotios. "*In the Skin of a Lion*: Michael Ondaatje's Tenebristic Narrative." *Essays on Canadian Writing* 44 (1991): 183-201.

# The Representation of "Race" in Ondaatje's *In the Skin of a Lion*

## *Glen Lowry*

With a few notable exceptions, Ondaatje's depiction of racialized subjects has received only limited attention (see, e.g., Turcotte; Mukherjee; Rundle; Lowry). While his identity as a Singhalese emigrant or Canadian immigrant is often noted (see, e.g., Kamboureli; Richler; Wachtel; Young), critics tend to ignore the political implications of "race" in relation to that of other writers of colour, effectively eliding "race" as an element of his writing. The elision has meant that the difficult questions of critical positioning, or what I, following Judith Butler, would term the "performative" aspect of his texts *qua* "racialized" writing, have fallen from view. Within the dominant post-modern discourse, i.e., a discourse focused on formalist readings of his texts, Ondaatje's writing becomes abstracted from the colonial and post-colonial contexts with which it engages. In an examination of Ondaatje's writing, up to and including *Running in the Family*, Arun Mukherjee has criticized an apparent lack of "cultural baggage … brought with him when he came to Canada" (114); she argues that because Ondaatje "does not write about his otherness" and his writing shows "no trauma of uprooting" (114), critics have been allowed to oversimplify the issue of Ondaatje's identity. Although it has become dated by Ondaatje's later writing, particularly his overt engagements in the issues of "trauma" and "otherness" at the heart of *The English Patient* and *Anil's Ghost*, both of which deal with (neo)colonialism and complex questions of social justice, Mukherjee's concern about the critical reception of his work is still relevant. Prioritizing social realism and intentionality, her contention that Ondaatje has "simply refused to address himself to the particular needs of his community" (132) is problematic; however, it does locate the matter of "race" blindness in responses to Ondaatje's writing: "The question, then, is whether Ondaatje's work contains more than 'the heat and the mountains and the jungle' of Sri Lanka that the white critics are unable to see in their ethnocentrism. For surely, Sri Lanka has more to it than the three things mentioned above. It consists of seven million human beings who ostensibly must have a world view unique to them" (Mukherjee 114).

Inasmuch as a dearth of "third world" (Mukherjee's term) references in the writing, wariness around giving interviews (Fagan 115; Finkle 90), and lack of public identification with writers of color, all seem to be instrumental in the continued construction of Ondaatje as an un-hyphenated—i.e., non-"racialized"—Canadian writer by predominantly "white" readers, Mukherjee's question remains vital. In raising the issue of representing "racialized" alterity, which is very different from marginality, Mukherjee's critique foregrounds an aporia in the critical discourse that I hope to address with this paper. Although it is, perhaps, less obviously so in this novel than in the two most recent novels, "race" is, nevertheless, a central concern in *In the Skin of a Lion*. Instead of

taking issue with an apparent lack of "racialized" subjects (as Mukherjee might do) or assuming that the absence of non-"white" subjects is tantamount to a lack of interest in "race" (as the majority of critics seem to have done), I contend that Ondaatje's writing, from *In the Skin of a Lion* on, represents "race" as a complex problem of representation that not only puts into play the interpolated identities of so-called "racialized" subjects but of "white" subjects as well. Rather than fixating on Ondaatje's actual identity and becoming caught in a trap of racial positivism, we might think through the way his "passing" as a "white" writer, not to mention the appropriation of "racialized" difference upon which it depends, performs and undoes the dominant "race" codes of CanLit ("Canadian literature," here with reference to the field of scholarly discipline). Reading *In the Skin of a Lion* as a statement on the problematic construction of "whiteness" rather than "color," enables us to re-situate Ondaatje's work, and/or our interpretative performances of it, within a much more contradictory and contentious conception of CanLit as a space of "race." I propose, therefore, to return to this novel to help develop thinking about Ondaatje's writing as writing about "race." Focusing on his depiction of Toronto in terms of a complex history of shifting social spaces and the ethnic and racial identities of the novel's two central characters, Patrick and Caravaggio, this paper looks forward to a more thorough discussion of Ondaatje's critique of nationalism and multiculturalism. Focusing on the issue of "race" *In the Skin of a Lion*, I am arguing that this novel is a precursor to *The English Patient* and *Anil's Ghost* and, as such, that it offers insight into a multivalent development of racialized writing, both in terms of Ondaatje's work and CanLit as a whole.

I begin with a quote from *In the Skin of a Lion*: "Patrick Lewis arrived in the city of Toronto as if it were land after years at sea…. at twenty-one, he had been drawn out from that small town like a piece of metal dropped under the vast arches of Union Station to begin his life once more…. He was an immigrant to the city" (53). For Patrick, "the searcher," whose life and actions knit together the characters and plot of the novel, entering the city means arriving in modernity, in a space of contradiction, alienation and possibility: "Now, in the city, he was new even to himself.… He saw his image in the glass of telephone booths. He ran his hands over the smooth pink marble pillars that reached into the rotunda. The train station was a palace, its riches and caverns an intimate city. He could be shaved, eat a meal, or have his shoes coloured" (54). In the station, Patrick notices "a man well-dressed with three suitcases, shouting out in another language" (54). Two days later, "He saw the man again, still unable to move from his safe zone, in a different suit, as if one step away was the quicksand of the new world" (54). The juxtaposition of these two migrants suggests both Patrick's reluctance to move into this spectacular "new world" and the importance of the city in his reconstruction of self. Sitting on a nearby bench and watching the "tides of movement," Patrick feels the powerful "reverberations of trade" (54). When he speaks out his name," however, it becomes "lost in the high air of Union Station. No one turned. They were in the belly of a whale" (54). The use of the third person plural articulates an affinity between the Canadian-born Patrick and this figure of the well-dressed "foreigner," both of whom transform and are transformed by the city.

Ondaatje's narrative blurs the recognized order of originary identities. Overlapping the trauma of immigration with the alienation of urbanization, it refigures the expansion of Toronto, the modern industrial core of an emergent nation state, within an international flow of bodies and cultures. Imagining voices for marginalized individuals and/or their forgotten communities, *In the Skin of a Lion* re-maps Toronto in terms of class struggle; in so doing, it depicts a city under construction, returning readers to key sites in the social development of the nation. Ondaatje's representation of the building of the Viaduct and the Waterworks spatializes the city's historic development; these key sites become representations of complex, contradictory drives to control not only physical spaces but also their conception. Symbolically, the novel reminds readers that the monuments of the modern city bear traces of divergent social meanings and purposes. Thus, *In the Skin of a Lion* destabilizes a linear historical view of Canadian society as a top down initiative orchestrated by a predominantly Anglo ruling, or managerial class. The city Patrick enters is a space of linguistic and cultural diversity beyond the purview of Franco-Anglo biculturalism or Anglo-imperialism, but coterminous with it. If metaphorically, Patrick "begins his life once more" (53) searching for the lost millionaire, Ambrose Small, a heroic figure of prosperity in this depressed city, he ultimately establishes himself in the nexus of Toronto's working-class communities. His identity develops in relation to a host of other, not quite "white" subjects—Greek, Macedonian, Russian, and Italian. His actions and the kindness of others, rather than his name or his country birth, become the determining factors in his self development.

While this idealized conception of social being coincides with the ideological precepts of official multiculturalism, Ondaatje's engagement with the historical elision of class difference offers an important point of entrance into critiques of what has been referred to as "song and dance" Multiculturalism. Spatializing and historicizing ethnic development within an urban setting, this novel helps to reframe government policy and the ideology of its utopic pluralism. Put another way, Ondaatje's exploration of Patrick's working-class experience challenges notions of Canadian identity as a racially neutral basis upon which a "just" multicultural society is built. Patrick's cultural displacement is negotiated rather than static. At times, his cultural background allows him access to spaces of privilege—the Muskoka Hotel, Harris's office; however, in general Patrick moves through a complex social network in which cultural differences between any us (Canadian) and them (foreign) are seen in terms of class us (the labourers) and them (the rich):

"I'll tell you about the rich," Alice would say, "the rich are always laughing. They keep saying the same things on their boats and lawns: *Isn't this grand! We're having a good time!* And whenever the rich get drunk and maudlin about humanity you have to listen for hours. But they keep you in the tunnels and stockyards. They do not toil or spin. Remember that.... There are a hundred

fences and lawns between the rich and you. You've got to know these things, Patrick, before you ever go near them—the way a dog rolls in the shit of the enemy." (132)

Patrick is happiest amongst people with whom he shares little ethnic affinity. His personal growth is predicated on movement away from his Anglo-Irish roots; rather than the inculcation of a kind of parochial Englishness, it points toward a more extensive sense of cultural awareness and identity. Significantly, Cato's letters teach Patrick the identity of the Finnish loggers with whom he shared his childhood landscape. In the city, as a worker, he learns that the separation between himself and the itinerant loggers is more apparent than real. Listening to Alice and reading Hana's archive, he deciphers the unacknowledged social-networks, and fundamental material relations, that have, in part, structured his life.

When Patrick learns *goosher*, the Macedonian word for *iguana*, he bridges the divide between himself and those around him, and he is suddenly overwhelmed by their "friendship," concern." Crying openly in their midst, exposing his loneliness, Patrick draws an invitation to "The waterworks at eight, Sunday night. A gathering." This breakthrough leads to a remarkable scene in which Ondaatje depicts the Waterworks, not as an empty Mausoleum or new high-tech sanitized filtration plant, but as an inhabited space in which the workers perform and create their own counter-histories. Re-inscribing the monumental site of the R.C. Harris Filtration Plant—Toronto's official tribute to its own Boulevard Haussmann—as a social space, re-imagining it as a zone of class conflict, the novel challenges us to revisit the official history and rethink our conceptions of the city's spaces.

In an essay examining the archival basis for *In the Skin of the Lion*, Dennis Duffy unearths documentary evidence for the kind of cultural linguistic conflicts depicted in the novel. In terms of this scene at the Waterworks, Duffy's discovery of a pamphlet protesting the intrusion of "foreign," non-English speaking workers into the Beach (the neighbourhood housing the plant) provides an interesting example of historical archive with which Ondaatje engages. Duffy feels that Ondaatje's novel might have included an episode in which "local strollers" take issue with a security guard who blocks them from entering the Waterworks. In fact, the apparent discrepancy between the archival record of the conflict and the events depicted by Ondaatje presents readers with an important impasse. However, Ondaatje's choice to represent imagined events realistically allows the novel to resist the primacy of the archival fact and to refigure agency in a complex manner. In final analysis, the assumed similitude between historical fact and the fiction upon which Duffy's conception of the novel's political potential rests is grounded in a problematic reading of power relations. To put it simply, this assumption relies on a conception of class conflict in which the aggressor is all powerful and the victim completely disenfranchised. Ondaatje's text, on the other hand, presents readers with the problem of having to construct a historical narrative against which to read the complex interplay... the event does not appear in the novel because it oversimplifies the complexity of linguistic, cultural, and political relations represented, and therefore contradicts the story Ondaatje is telling.

Read from the perspective of counter-hegemonic historiography—Marxist, feminist, queer, and postcolonial—Ondaatje's "fictional history" provides more than a positivist attempt to add the stories of the disenfranchised to the history. More than simply expanding the parameters of Canadian literature to include writing about the working class and ethnic minorities forgotten in the "Official histories and news stories" of Toronto's metropolitan expansion, the novel challenges a dominant discourse which is "always as soft as rhetoric, like that of a politician making a speech after a bridge is built, a man who does not even cut the grass on his own lawn" (145). As others have pointed out, Ondaatje's writing crosses the line between fact and fiction, history and literature (see Bowering). However, rather than attacking the one (fact/history) from within the bounds of the other (fiction/literature), this novel performs a critical intervention within the emergence of the postmodern or multicultural canon/s to which it is ascribed—an intervention that draws attention to the historical function of CanLit as cultural praxis, rather than cultural expression. The forgotten stories from the building of Toronto, which have caught most critics' attention, are offset by quotations from popular song, art criticism, and Canadian literature. In his acknowledgments, Ondaatje specifies that he has had permission to print lyrics for "Up Jumped You with Love" and "I Can't Get Started," lines from the *Epic of Gilgamesh*, sentences from Judith Mara Gutman's essay "Lewis Hine and the American Social Conscience," two sentences from the journals of Anne Wilkinson, and lines from Martha Ostenso's novel *Wild Geese*. In addition to these few re-cycled fragments of text, Ondaatje's text gestures toward a young Al Purdy, Anne Wilkinson, and Judge Sheard of *Judge Sheard's Jokes* (grandfather of Sarah Sheard, to whom the novel is dedicated). The novel's revision of the historical account of Toronto's modern development embroils itself in a fanciful depiction of CanLit as social space or geography through which Caravaggio, steals his way back to the city.

To this end, Ondaatje borrows "two sentences" from Wilkinson's journals: "Let me now re-emphasize the extreme looseness of the structure of things" (163) and "Demarcation.... That is all we need to remember" (179). Paradoxically, the text does not attribute either of the sentences to Wilkinson or her character, but rather ascribes the former to Alice and the latter to Caravaggio. Without an intimate knowledge of Wilkinson's writing one might pass over the sentences; only the *demarcation* of the text, the fact both sentences are in italics, draws attention to the gesture. In both cases, however, Alice's utterance of "Let me now re-emphasize the extreme looseness of the structure of things" is powerfully ironic. Coming to Patrick as a reminder of Patrick's shattered dream of their growing old together: "There was always, he thought, this pleasure ahead of him, an ace up his sleeve so he could say you can do anything to me, take everything away, put me in prison, but I will know Alice Gull when we are old" (164). The sentence also conjures up the chain of loosely related, seemingly coin-

cidental events that brought Alice and Patrick together: her spectacular fall from the Bridge, Temelcoff's miraculous catch, an ensuing friendship with Clara, and Patrick's decision to abandon pursuit of Ambrose Small. As a counter-point to Patrick's searching, Alice's death is a thread which ties together key elements of the plot. The explosion that wrenches her from Patrick solidifies his connection with Temelcoff, Caravaggio, Hana, and in the end R.C. Harris while cementing his fate.

The second sentence—"Demarcation, that is what we all need to remember"—functions like a refrain in the last section of the novel and, as such, is crucial to the unfolding of its final episode. Much as the character of Alice becomes a realization of the first sentence, the figure of Caravaggio is firmly connected to this second one. Again, Patrick recalls this statement; he remembers Caravaggio uttering it while he and Patrick were painting of the penitentiary roof, just prior to Caravaggio's escape. Again, the statement is ironic. On the surface, it is a comment on the problem of painting an "intentional blue roof," which made "the three men working on it [become] uncertain of the clear boundaries" between roof and sky. It also speaks to Caravaggio's genius. We might say that in fooling the guards by painting himself into the scene, i.e., painting himself blue, Caravaggio flaunts the line between himself and his environment. Furthermore, the notion of "demarcation" resonates with Caravaggio's somewhat tenuous identity; it is connected with both colonial history and class politics. Historically, the demarcation line of 1496 was the historical line dividing the New World between Spanish and Portuguese interests or lands. The word is inflected with issues of ownership and proprietary relations between competing economic units. This particular term, particularly in the context of the phrase in which it surfaces, functions to further establish Caravaggio as a "racialized" figure.

A conventional reading of this indirect quotation might suggest that, through the voice of Caravaggio, Ondaatje has appropriated Wilkinson's writing. As literary scholars, we ascribe ownership to the individual from whose journal the words appear to be lifted; however, within the logic of the novel itself, the reverse might also be said to be true: Wilkinson has stolen Caravaggio's language. In fact, this phrase is ascribed to Caravaggio and it has provided the abstract basis for his plan. Realizing as he does that demarcation makes visible, he realizes also that it can be used to render himself invisible. In having himself painted the conspicuous blue of the prison roof, Caravaggio escapes by vanishing from sight. This is the story Caravaggio tells Anne when he meets her. We are told that "She sits across from him laughing at the story of his escape, not fully believing it" (201). We might extrapolate from this that Caravaggio has repeated this phrase—after all, it is the cornerstone of his masterly plan—and that later it comes to appear in Wilkinson's journal. Again, Ondaatje undermines the originary moment of the very material; his novel appropriates and rewrites literary history within the frame of fiction.

To develop the significance of this meeting with Wilkinson, it is useful to consider Caravaggio's encounter with another figure of Canadian literature. During his escape, Caravaggio turns up in Trenton, where he meets a young boy who helps him to remove the blue paint. As Caravaggio is preparing to leave, the boy gives him a note with his name, Alfred, written on it. When Caravaggio apologizes for having nothing to give the boy in return, "The kid grimed, very happy. 'I know,' he said. 'Remember my name'" (182). This puzzling exchange does not appear to have a direct bearing on the plot itself: while the young Al is helpful in cleaning the paint off Caravaggio, he recedes into the fabric of the novel after Caravaggio goes on his way. For readers versed in the localism of Canadian poetry, the boy's name and that he is in Trenton suggest homage to Al Purdy. This fits with the Anne Wilkinson scene discussed above to establish a kind of literary map of his escape root. From Trenton to Bobcaygen, Purdy to Wilkinson, Caravaggio moves through a geography of literary reference. As a counterpoint to the historical archive out of which the urban events of the novel are collected, Caravaggio's escape takes place within the sanctified spaces of an agrarian literary tradition.

At the risk of undervaluing the complexity of Ondaatje's literary sleight of hand, one might argue that this figure of the thief moving through the landscapes of Canadian literature can be read as an imaginative reflection of Ondaatje's own presence within the centralist tradition of Canadian letters. The fact that Caravaggio speaks Ondaatje's re-appropriation of Wilkinson's journal entries and shares Purdy's slightly skewed sense of landscape suggests an affinity between writer and character. This affinity is heightened by Ondaatje's description of Caravaggio's gentle teachers, "the company of thieves ... who looked refined and wore half-moon glasses" (191). This passage depicts Caravaggio as an acolyte or devoted craftsman rather than as a common criminal: "Caravaggio was welcomed into their midst and lectured with great conservatism on the art of robbery.... They were protective of their style and area of interest. They tried to persuade the young man that *they* did was the most significant but at the same time they did not wish to encourage competition.... He was in awe of them, wanted to be all of them in their moments of extreme crisis. He hung around them not so much to learn their craft but to study the way they lived when they stepped back into the world of order ... he was fascinated only by character" (191). Thus, he learns his way into the art of thievery by shadowing these men "in order to watch their performances." He learns to be comfortable in other people's houses, at home in their absence, "high up on the bookcases ... as still as a gargoyle against Trollope and H.G. Wells" (198). Like Patrick who is "always comfortable in someone else's landscape" and who enjoys "being taught the customs of a place" (138), Caravaggio learns to inhabit a space to which he makes no claim of ownership.

The racialization of Caravaggio is a much more explicit enactment of the ambivalence underlying Patrick identity. His escape through the imaginary landscape of Canadian literature on his way back to the city follows Ondaatje's description of his attack at the hands of the bigots, "smug without race." Within the thematic tropology of 1970s Canadian literature, Caravaggio's escape fits the Atwoodian model. On one level, Caravaggio's "survival" is based on his ability to escape through the wilds. His borrowing of a paragraph from Martha Ostenso's *Wild Geese*, with which the description of

the prison attack begins, further suggests Ondaatje's indebtedness to this tradition. However, in reading Caravaggio's journey in terms of this more mainstream sense of Canadian literature, there is a danger of losing sight of the "racism" that precipitates it. The discursive layering, in fact the highly allusive nature of this section of the novel, points to a kind of double inscription—by which the character of Caravaggio both articulates and disavows the hegemonic subject of literary nationalism.

Rehearsing a common theme in the critical discourse, Smaro Kamboureli's introduction to Ondaatje in her recent anthology of multicultural writing in Canada, *Making a Difference: Canadian Multicultural Literature*, foregrounds the writer's identity as an immigrant of Ceylonese or Sri Lankan descent, without explicitly mentioning the subject of "race" or identifying Ondaatje with other writers of colour. Kamboureli does note Ondaatje's identification with "a generation of writers that "was the first real migrant tradition ... of writers of our time—Rushdie, Ishiguro, Ben Okri, Rohinton Mistry" (Kamboureli 194), which, in the context of this anthology and its somewhat problematic mixture of white and non-white writers under a generalized rubric of difference and immigration, suggests an important shift in the discourse. While there is no suggestion how the excerpted fragment from *In the Skin of a Lion* speaks to this tradition of Asian writers Ondaatje sees himself fitting into, it fore grounds the question at the centre of my paper. How do we begin to read this novelistic depiction of class struggle amongst various European ethnic communities in relation to Ondaatje's implicit self-identification with this particular group of writers? How do we read the construction of a "white" identity in relation to the various interpelated, racialized subjectivities, against which it is constructed and over which it asserts power? In the context of contemporary CanLit and/or the emergence of multiculturalism in general, how does the appearance of a "white" subject presuppose an elision of particular class differences or the re-appropriation of racialized histories and experiences

In resisting the essential binaries of identity by which much of the critical understanding of Canadian literature is figured, centre/margin, "white"/non-"white," immigrant/"native," *In the Skin of a Lion* offers readers a highly complex site by which to theorize the function of "race" in the development of a "white" subjectivity as it is figured against the backdrop of European ethnic communities. One might say that Ondaatje's novel "reverses the *gaze*" and throws the question of "race" back on the readers. If working backwards, contemporary critics tend to think of "whiteness" (when it is thought about at all) in terms of a kind of homogenous Western or European subjectivity, this novel points towards the history of this emergent racial identity. As a number of postcolonial critics have suggested the assumption that "whiteness" signifies some kind of neutral position in opposition to various "racialized" identities is itself one of the master tropes of modern "racist" thought. As "race" theorists have made clear, the tendency to assume that racism is solely concerned with the construction of others, people of color and First Nations, obfuscates or again naturalizes the fact that "whiteness" is itself a construct. In "returning the gaze," cultural theorists have argued that the formation of a "white subject" and the attendant system of social value to which it is connected is dependent on a series of differences in which "race" functions. As such, "whiteness" is part of the complex and violent history of Western racism; it is a social construct with which divisions of labour and social values are controlled (on this, see Stoler; Razack). A common suggestion made within the circles of anti-racist activism and pedagogy is that more work needs to be done understanding this historical fact. The argument that "race" is only an issue in texts that deal specifically with a "racialized" subject or character or conversely which articulate overt racism depends on the facile conflation of "whiteness" with an absence of "racial" significance, or more precisely recognizable signifiers of "race" or "racialized" identity.

If, as George Eliot Clarke argues, "The general incoherence of color-based identity in Canada permits Canadian whiteness to exist… as an ethereal force… a kind of ideal whiteness, ready for export" (100), then the question left open is how does this floating identity, the ethereal force of whiteness, come to depend on the hegemonic control of "race" discourse? By what means does the assumption of "whiteness" as a neutral position, something that simply is rather than something that comes into being (in place and time), effect that construction of a "racialized" other. According to Clarke, the popular conception of Canada as a nation that has developed free from a US-style history of "race" conflict is in itself a particular kind of racism. The oft rehearsed notion that Canada is or has been a predominantly "white country" that came to be peopled by the descendants of European settlers is but part of a recurrent struggle for self-creation, which pits a national identity off against various non-European immigrants and First Nations people ("First Nations" is the Canadian term for the Indigenous Indian population). With the emergence of state-sponsored Canadian Multiculturalism and a revamped notion of citizen articulated in the new Charter of Rights and Freedoms, which provide the historical context into which this novel is published, "racial" difference comes to be re-conceived in terms of immigration and arrival. In the dominant discourses of cultural production, "racialized" identities are taken to be extrinsic to the emerging multi-ethnic "Canadian," a residue of histories and conflicts beyond the borders of this (post) modern nation-state. Thus, in the popular histories Canada's multicultural literature, "race" continues to have a silent function. In the Skin of a Lion, does more than legitimize the notion of Toronto as a "white" city. It brings to light a complex set of discourses and identity formations that continue to shape the development of multiculturalism in Toronto specifically and Canada in general. In spite of the fact, that both geographically and historically the city comes into being through the expropriation of First Nations land and culture, that it is illegal for people of Chinese ancestry to vote, that there are restrictions placed on the hiring of "white" women in "Chinese businesses," that neighbourhoods and a number of high profile institutions—the University of Toronto, the Granite Club, the Royal Canadian Yacht Club—have by-laws barring "Jews" and "Catholics," that night clubs were paying different rates for Black performers, there is a complacency amongst readers of Ondaatje's novel in acknowledging the ethnic and racial reality of Toronto during the 1930s.

As I have suggested elsewhere (Lowry 2001), the space or neighbourhood in which much of the action in the novel takes place is the spawning ground for a group of fascist sympathizers who walked the streets wearing black arm bands and who were to instigate the Christie Pits riot of 1933. In reading In the Skin of a Lion as a novel about the working class without paying some heed to the manner in which labour politics and ethnic identity are connected, without acknowledging the racism rampant within the closed social circles of the ruling class but also in various labour movements, critics perpetuate the idea that Toronto, like the nation of which it would come to be the social and economic centre, developed outside racism. The question that needs to be addressed in the discussion of this novel is how it is that critics have come to see discontinuity, rather than continuity, between the ethnic divisions depicted in it and the systematic creation of "race"-based privilege that we now recognize as the downside of national politics. In adding the figures of Patrick and Caravaggio to the writing of the city, Ondaatje's novel does more than simply expand the scope and texture of what has become Toronto. The struggle these two characters undergo suggests a re-conception of the multicultural citizen that has been emerging in and through the development of Canadian cultural politics during the 1970s and 1980s. The question that I have attempted to open in my reading of this novel is the relationship between the development of "racialized" subject positions and the emergence of "whiteness" as a historically contingent position of privilege—the invisible identity in the cultural mosaic of a new Canadian Multiculturalism.

## WORKS CITED

Bowering, George, and Michael Ondaatje, eds. An H in the Heart: A Reader. Toronto: McClelland and Stewart, 1994.

Clarke, George Elliott. "White Like Canada." Transition: An International Review 73.1 (1998): 98–109.

Duffy, Dennis. "A Wrench in Time: A Sub-Sub-Librarian Looks beneath the Skin of a Lion." Essays on Canadian Writing 53 (1994): 125–40.

Fagan, Cary. "Where the Personal and Historical Meet: Michael Ondaatje." The Power to Bend Spoons: Interviews with Canadian Novelists. Ed. Beverley Daurio. Toronto: The Mercury P, 1998. 115–21.

Finkle, Derek. "Vow of Silence: Michael Ondaatje…" Saturday Night 3.9 (November 1999): 90–94, 96.

Kamboureli, Smaro. "Introduction." Making a Difference: Canadian Multicultural Literature. Ed. Smaro Kamboureli. Toronto: Oxford UP, 1996. 1–16.

Lowry, Glen. After the End/s: CanLit and the Unravelling of Nation, "Race," and Space in the Writing of Michael Ondaatje, Daphne Marlatt, and Roy Kiyooka. Ph.D. Dissertation. Burnaby: Simon Fraser U, 2001.

Lowry, Glen. "Between *The English Patients*: 'Race' and the Cultural Politics of Adapting CanLit." *Essays on Canadian Writing* 76 (2002): 216–46.

Mukherjee, Arun. "The Poetry of Michael Ondaatje and Cyril Dabydeen: Two Responses to Otherness." 1985. *Oppositional Aesthetic: Readings from a Hyphenated Space*. By Arun Mukherjee. Toronto: TSAR Books, 1994. 112–32.

Ondaatje, Michael. *Anil's Ghost*. New York: Knopf, 2000.

Ondaatje, Michael. *The English Patient*. Toronto: Random House of Canada, 1992.

Ondaatje, Michael. *In the Skin of a Lion*. Toronto: McClelland and Stewart, 1987.

Ondaatje, Michael, ed. *The Long Poem Anthology*. Toronto: Coach House Press, 1979.

Ondaatje, Michael, ed. *From Ink Lake: An Anthology of Canadian Short Stories*. 1990. Toronto: Vintage Canada, 1995.

McClintock, Anne. *Imperial Leather: Race, Gender, and Sexuality in Colonial Contest*. New York: Routledge, 1995.

Razack, Sherene H. *Looking White People in the Eye: Gender, Race and Culture in Courtrooms and Classrooms*. Toronto: U of Toronto P, 1998.

Richler, Noah. "Ondaatje on Writing." Review of Michael Ondaatje, *Anil's Ghost. National Post* (1 April 2000): B1, B2–B3.

Rundle, Lisa. "From Novel to Film: *The English Patient* Distorted." *Borderlines* 43 (1997): 9–13.

Stoler, Ann Laura. *Race and the Education of Desire: Foucault's History of Sexuality and the Colonial Order of Things*. Durham: Duke UP, 1995.

Tötösy de Zepetnek, Steven. "Social Discourse and Cultural Participation in a Multicultural Society." *Canadian Culture and Literatures*. Ed. Steven Tötösy de Zepetnek and Yiu-nam Leung. Edmonton: Research Institute for Comparative Literature, U of Alberta, 1998. 57–69.

Turcotte, Gerry. "'Fears of Primitive Otherness': 'Race' in Michael Ondaatje's *The Man with Seven Toes*." *Constructions of Colonialism: Perspectives on Eliza Fraser's Shipwreck*. Ed. Ian McNiven, L. Russell, and K. Schaffer. London: Leicester UP, 1998. vi, 192.

Wachtel, Eleanor. "An Interview with Michael Ondaatje." *Canadian Literature* 53 (1994): 250–61.

Young, David. "An Ondaatje for the Ages." Rev. of Michael Ondaatje's *Anil's Ghost. The Globe and Mail* (1 April 2000): D2, D16.

# DROPPING THE BOMB ?
## ON CRITICAL AND CINEMATIC REACTIONS TO
## MICHAEL ONDAATJE'S *THE ENGLISH PATIENT*

## Josef PESCH

*Abstract*

This paper analyses Anthony Minghella's film adaptation of Michael Ondaatje's *The English Patient*. It aims at establishing patterns of transformation and strategies of adaptation. Not only the nostalgic romanticisation, but also the de-politicisation of the novel is critically scrutinized. As dropping all reference to the atomic bomb from the film is the most blatant example of deviation from the novel, critical and political background is provided which may explain this act of self-censorship. Although Minghella and Ondaatje admit omissions and disagreements, their statements do not clarify the decision making process.

*Résumé*

Cette communication analyse l'adaptation filmique du roman de Michael Ondaatje, *Le Patient anglais*. Son but est de tenter de définir des structures de transformation et des stratégies d'adaptation. Il s'agit d'analyser non seulement la romancisation nostalgique mais aussi la dépolitisation du roman. Comme le fait d'avoir omis dans le film toute référence à la bombe atomique est l'exemple le plus évident de déviance par rapport au roman, on rappelera l'arrière plan critique et politique susceptible d'expliquer cet acte d'auto-censure. Bien que Minghella et Ondaatje reconnaissent omissions et désaccords, leurs déclaration ne permettent pas de clarifier le processus de prise de position.

*Criticism of the highest kind [...] treats the work of art simply as a starting-point for new creation. It does not confine itself [...] to discovering the real intention of the artist and accepting that as final. [...] To the critic the work of art is simply a suggestion for a new work of his own, that need not bear any obvious resemblance to the thing it criticises. (Wilde 1966: 1029-1030)*

Translating a novel into film may not be what Oscar Wilde had in mind. Nonetheless, by necessity any writer of screenplays will treat the work of fiction on which his idea is based as a starting-point for a new work. If that starting-point is a complex work of art, the transformation cannot but change, alter, adapt that work into something it is not, and this fact has long since been accepted in film studies (Beja 1979: 80-88). To expect fidelity of a film to the novel on which it is based is as absurd as expecting a faithful translation - faithful to what standard? imposed by whom? (McFarlane 1996: 8-10).[1] Any attempt at a line-by-line comparison and critique of an adaptation does not make much sense, for it would be asking the film to do what the novel has done already, almost like Borges 'ideal' translator of *Don Quixote* (see Bassnett 1997). What is intended here is a critical reading of Anthony Minghella's grandiose film in search of patterns of transformation and strategies of adaptation. This necessitates an occasional re-reading of Ondaatje's novel as well as critical reactions to it.

The film begins with a magic flight over the desert of a woman and a pilot (EP-SP: 3).[2] Their plane is shot down by a German anti-aircraft gun

---

1. Ondaatje agrees in his comments on the screenplay (EP-SP: xv-xvi).
2. Special thanks to Patrick Hilt (Universität Frankfurt/M.) on a research scholarship in Toronto in autumn 1997. He helped me obtain a copy of the screenplay and the video.

(EP-SP: 4) in a most dramatic opening scene which contrasts the peaceful lightness of flight (and song) with the horror of war and gunfire. A few scenes situated in Italy are cut in before we return to the desert: "THE PILOT HAS BEEN RESCUED BY BEDUIN TRIBESMEN" (EP-SP: 6). This is absurd: a plane shot down would immediately be inspected by the anti-aircraft gunners, especially if there was a parachute. If this is so, why is the burnt man picked up by beduin tribesmen? The logic of the scene has been sacrificed for a cinematic effect. In the novel, the pilot "is flying a rotted plane, the canvas sheetings on the wing ripping open in the speed" (EP: 175), and crashes into the middle of nowhere, where Beduins are the only ones likely to find him. A scene that is logical, coherent, and poetic in the novel has here been adapted into confused scenes that quote action cinema and its stereotypes.[3]

Cinematic licence may be involved in turning Hana and Caravaggio into strangers, and then make up for it in an awkward introduction: "CARAVAGGIO: 'I met your friend Mary. She said I should stop and see if you were alright. Apparently, we're neighbors - my house is two blocks from yours in Montreal. Cabot, north of Laurier'" (EP-SP: 36). This decision

---

3. The critique of the geographer and Sahara specialist Stefan Kröpelin is much more down to earth: he has listed a number of inaccuracies in the locations used in the film. No dunes of the type shown in the film exist in the Gilf Kebir. Furthermore, he ridicules the scene in which companions have to be dug out of the sand that has covered their car in one night's sandstorm: on the one hand he has not experienced such a thing in 20 years of research in the area, on the other hand, no one has *ever seen wet* sand in the region (1997: 35) - and of course this scene is not in the novel. More significantly, the cave of swimmers is nothing like the cave in the film, but a half open structure formed by overhanging rock (Almásy 1997: photos following 192). Such things may be minor and in part due to financial and logistical problems - or cinematic licence; after all, even Shakespeare is not unknown to have made the occasional geographical blunder.

makes the special relationship between Hana and Caravaggio in the rest of the film hard to understand. Minghella seems to want to see Caravaggio motivated solely by revenge, an age-old theatrical device that streamlines the plot and allows for stronger contrast, even antagonism, between Almásy, the 'bad' count and Nazi collaborator, and Caravaggio, the post-war vigilante and victim of Almásy's conspiracy with the Germans.[4] In the novel, Caravaggio stumbles across the Patient by accident while looking for Hana. His interaction with the Patient is not driven by revenge, but by a desire to comprehend what has happened to him and his world in this war. The telling of stories is an integral part of coming to terms with the many losses of world for Caravaggio as well as for the Patient (see Pesch 1997a: 120-124). It is a talking-through the apocalyptic traumas they have experienced.[5] For both, the antagonism of war is history; they have arrived at that "strange time, [at] the end of a war, [... the] period of adjustment" (EP: 54). As in so many simplistic war movies, Minghella uses antagonism between enemies to create a completely different kind of tension.

The following scene is more revealing. After having been caught by the Germans, Caravaggio is interrogated by Muller, a German officer:

*I'll tell you what I'm going to do. This is your nurse, by the way. She's a Moslem, so she'll understand all of this. What's the punishment for adultery? Let's leave it at that. You're married and you were fucking*

---

4. There is no doubt at all in the film that the Patient is Almásy - as there is in the book (Pesch 1997a: 120-121).

5. As Simpson puts it, "the advent of the nuclear age, blasting nations and people on all points of the imperial map past time and space, past a limit in the historical imaginary, renders such forgetting impossible precisely because its apocalypse enflames a rage for mourning" (1994: 229).

*another woman, so that's - is it the hands are cut off? Or is that for stealing? (EP-SL: 114)*

This short passage suggests that Moslems are on one level with the Nazis. It associates Moslem legal practices (on which I am not commenting here) with Nazi atrocities. The German officer forces this nurse to cut off Caravaggio's thumbs. In this scene Minghella confirms a religious and racial stereotype of Muslims which has become politically popular in the USA particularly since the end of the Cold War.[6] What is Minghella adapting here? There is no precedent anywhere in Ondaatje's works for this: on the contrary, Ondaatje persistently questions and scrupulously avoids stereotypes like this; nowhere does he ever confirm such views (see Pesch 1997a; 1997b; 1997c). My suggestion is that Minghella[7] is all too obviously catering for the political tastes of his American audience here. Ondaatje has constructed this episode very carefully: in the novel it takes place in Italy and the order to cut off Caravaggio's thumbs is given by someone with an Italian name: "Ranuccio Tommasoni" (EP: 55; 59). As Caravaggio relates, the nurse was "an innocent, knew nothing about me, my name or nationality or what I may have done" (EP: 55). Neither her nationality nor her faith are mentioned.

---

6. To the point of trying to stylize Sadam Hussein into a latter day Hitler. An absurd notion as the Second Gulf War revealed: the Iraqis had not been able to defeat the badly armed Iranians in the First Gulf War - and never had the slightest chance to win against the military might of the Allies. After the end of the Cold War the search for a new enemy seems to have begun as Huntington's "The Clash of Civilizations?" indicates (cf. Pesch 1997<b>).

7. When I write 'Minghella' here, I am identifying him as the writer of the screenplay. I am fully aware of the fact that he is not the only one responsible for what appeared on screen. It would be of great interest to inspect the records of all involved in the decision making, but that was beyond the scope of this paper.

Clearly Ondaatje does not need stereotypes of Muslims - or Germans - to show the brutality of Fascist Christians during World War II.

One of the climactic scenes in the film is the defusing of the big "2,000 pounds" (EP-SL: 134) bomb, dramatically set near a viaduct and at what appears to be the end of the war in Europe (see EP-SL: 138-139). The scene shows tanks with celebrating "citizens and soldiers, and children" (EP-SL: 135) waving "their flags - Stars and Stripes, Union Jacks" (EP-SL: 137), towering high above Kip who is trying to defuse that bomb. The tanks completely ignore Kip and the fact that they are putting him (and themselves) in mortal danger.8 A victory celebration which threatens the life of an Asian from up high is interesting for what it does - and for what it does not show.

That scene is more significant than anyone watching the film can know, for Anthony Minghella has moved back an episode from the novel and substituted the big bomb Kip did defuse for the even bigger nuclear bombs which explode his calm and control in the novel (Pesch 1997a: 127-128). These bombs, thrown from up high on Hiroshima and Nagasaki in August 1945, ended the Second World War. This incident relating the dropping of the bombs is pivotal in the novel (EP: 284). These bombs mark the climax in the development of ever more powerful and dangerous bombs that Kip had been defusing all the war. Yet this time the destructive weapons were used by his side, and he is exploded by 'friendly' fire. Furthermore, in the novel the nuclear bombs take up the image of fire falling from heaven, and of burning humans that the English Patient introduced into the novel. Or is the burnt

---

8. Again: any team of sappers worth their money would have made sure that no one would get anywhere near the defusing of a bomb this size.

man not to be read as a reminder of all those burnt in this war of whom no trace, no cinder remains?

On a very private level, the bombs generate Kip's emotional outburst that ends his romantic relationship with Hana. This relationship is also developed in the film, albeit on a lesser scale, in scenes preceding Kip's defusing of the bomb (EP-SP: 131-134). In the film the split-up between Kip and Hana follows Hardy's death by a hidden German mine (EP-SP: 143). But as the bombs were dropped from the film script, the end of the relationship is a rather sombre, rational affair. Kip asks Hana whether she will accompany him to India; when she does not reply immediately, he says, "here I am always a brown man, there you would always be a white woman" (EP-SP: 145). This statement not only lacks psychological depth and motivation, it implies that because of their race, they cannot live as a couple, neither in Canada nor in India. Although not motivated by the book,9 such positions are well in line with unofficial Hollywood policies on showing mixed-race relationships - and again confirm a stereotype cherished by some on both sides of the racial fence. However, this scripted ending apparently was too awkward, potentially controversial, and disharmonious. So the film here departs from the script and provides a more open, hopeful, harmonious ending of their relationship: both want to return to the church they had visited together earlier, and express the hope that they will meet again in this church someday (see EP-film). This ending confirms the strategy of romanticisation that dominates the adaptation of this post-romantic novel.

---

9. Minghella may have been trying to transfer something of Kip's racial outburst here, but without anything momentous enough to generate such an outburst, the statement utterly lacks motivation.

What takes Kip out of his relationship with Hana in the novel is much more momentous, much less romantic, for his world and belief system are shattered when the atomic bombs are dropped - "this tremor of Western wisdom" (EP: 284). He feels betrayed by the side he has been fighting and dismantling bombs for. He resents "the smell of celebration" (EP: 285) and breaks his relationship with all Europeans and North Americans when he screams: "American, French, I don't care. When you start bombing the brown races of the world, you're an Englishman" (EP: 288). It is this sense of outrage and betrayal that makes impossible any further relationship with such people.

Kip may be right or wrong about this, but the scene in the book clearly marks the end of his service as a colonial in the British Army. It bodes ill for colonial/post-colonial relations and inter-cultural understanding after the war. Despite the presence of a burnt man, and all the stories of death and dying, Kip's imaginative evocation of "the streets of Asia full of fire [...] the hurricane of heat withering bodies as it meets them, the shadow of humans suddenly in the air" (EP: 284; also 286-7) are the most harrowing scenes in the novel (see Pesch 1997a). Caravaggio re-emphasizes the racial aspect of the nuclear bombs in a mental comment: "They would never have dropped such a bomb on a white nation" (EP: 288).

The reason why Minghella dropped the bombs from his script may be related to Kip's outburst and Caravaggio's mental comment, for these generated the most pronounced attack on Ondaatje in US-American reviews which challenged the historical accuracy and balance of his novel. In The New Republic Craig Seligman attacks Ondaatje and his novel because of what is said about the nuclear bombs:

[...] beyond the blandness and the psychological thinness, there's also a serious political confusion. [...] Kip [...] goes to pieces at the news of Hiroshima and Nagasaki. [...] when the bomb - 'this tremor of western wisdom' - drops on Japan, he freaks out. [...] Caravaggio agrees: They would never have dropped such a bomb on a white nation', and no doubt he is right. [...] Ondaatje [...] here proudly allies himself with the Asians. [...] And though there's no dismissing the elements of racism in the bombing, only a sentimentalist would feel comfortable lumping Japan with 'the brown races of the world'. (1993: 41)

Seligman seems not to remember Kip's words to his brother that although Japan is part of Asia, "the Sikhs have been brutalized by the Japanese in Malaya" (EP: 217), and ignores that Kip is not looking at the imperial army, but at burning humans on the ground in Hiroshima and Nagasaki.

Hilary Mantel's review in The New York Review of Books takes the moral onslaught against The English Patient even further. She concludes that

the feuds of the world are not all the same. There is an artist's sentimentality which encourages evil by seeking to disengage. Ondaatje ... wins ... [no admiration] ... when he sneaks from responsibility - as a storyteller, as a thinker, one who cleaves always to what is private, hidden, ambiguous; who slips away from statement. This is a hard thing to say, because in Ondaatje's books there is the powerful pulse of human sympathy, a pull towards benevolence. Puls, pull - it's not enough. Sometimes ambivalence is immoral. When souls burn, the quietist stinks with the rest. (1993: 23)

Both statements not only ignore entirely the literary facts of Ondaatje's novel, but also, in a move more Victorian than postmodern, hold the author responsible for political statements of his characters. Particularly Mantel is blind to the historical facts (Pesch 1997b: 103-105), for the war in the Pacific had its racist aspects. As the Prime Minister of Canada, Mackenzie King, confided to his diary: "It is fortunate that the use of the bomb should have been on the Japanese rather than on the white races of Europe" (rpt. in Granatstein & Neary 1995: 337). Even an outspoken defender of the bomb with a book entitled *Thank God for the Atom Bomb*, Paul Fussell, who served both in Europe and the Pacific theatres of war, acknowledges and documents the wide-spread racism in the Pacific war (1990: 13-37 & 45-50).[10]

Clearly, Ondaatje's novel had touched a very raw nerve in the USA (cf. Lifton & Mitchell 1996). How raw that nerve still is, became apparent between the publication of the novel and the making of the film when the Smithsonian Institution planned an exhibition commemorating the 50th anniversary of Hiroshima and Nagasaki at the National Air and Space Museum. This exhibition was to show not only the heroic development of the bomb, but also the consequences of its use for human beings on the ground. The script for this exhibition came under vociferous attack by the Air Force Association, a veterans' organization and lobby group for the Air Force, and by Republican members of congress. The controversy was so public, and historically biased, that the exhibition had to be reduced to showing just the *Enola Gay* and not a single photo of victims (cf. Linenthal & Engelhardt 1996). While the triumph of American science and technology symbolized in

10. The otherwise identical British edition of this book is entitled *Killing in Prose and Verse*. But the essay "Thank God for the Atom Bomb" in this collection keeps its original title.

the bombs and the *Enola Gay* were shown, photos of the destruction and human suffering on the ground were not.[11]

Looked at from this background, dropping the nuclear bomb scene from the film is both a political and a cultural statement: where the book faces the issue, the film looks the other way, and shows how effective self-censorship is in the industry. With the references to the bomb left in, the film would have been more honest and coherent, but it would also have attracted criticism of the type Seligman and Mantel addressed at the novel.[12] What is more: it is unlikely that a film touching such a politically controversial issue would have been awarded 9 Oscars. It might not even have found a producer or distribution in the U.S.A.

Ondaatje's novel is "historiographical metafiction" (Hutcheon 1987) in the best sense of the word: it presents the problems of writing history and counters official History with its stories recording the memories of suffering - even on the side of the victors (Pesch 1997). Minghella is much less courageous: he repeatedly falls back on racial and national stereotypes and does not deeply explore the implications of his material. Where the novel attempts to present the difficulties of coming out of a war, even if you are on the winning side, the film decides to present nostalgia, romance, and exoticism. I believe this is not just a matter of medium, but a matter of choice, for technically the nuclear bombs could have been incorporated as

11. In a large study on *Mystic Chords of Memory: The Transformation of Tradition in American Culture* (800 pages), American historian Michael Kammen analyses all kinds of historic amnesia in American history from the times Europeans arrived to Vietnam, but does not mention Hiroshima and Nagasaki (1991).

12. Especially when long disproved mis-information was still published in all the media during the *Enola Gay* controversy as Alperovitz remarks with some bitterness (1995: 627 ff.)

easily as the sandstorm scenes in the desert. Admittedly, this would have made a more political, a very different film.

Dropping the bomb had other implications for the film as a whole. Looking away from the explosive end of the war and the start of the Nuclear Age, Minghella's script concentrates on nostalgic flashbacks relating Katherine's and Almásy's romance. This is safe territory, before all the mines, all the bombing, before Auschwitz and Hiroshima - and all the burnt bodies of this war which the Patient embodies and keeps reminding us of. The film allows us to forget that the world of the international desert explorers, "desert Europeans" (EP: 135), was itself a fallen world, peopled by survivors of the Great War to End all Wars who had withdrawn to the end of the world, off the maps of history into the prehistoric, remote, and uninviting North African desert. The Patient's hate of nations, of possessions, of being forced into taking sides, is a consequence of experiences and lessons learnt during the First World War. How were these men to know that all the fighting and destruction, and uniformed nationalism, was to catch up with them even where "there was supposedly no water [... and where] the world ended" (EP: 135)?

It is significant that the script comes into its own in the flashbacks describing the love affair of two upper-class individuals in an exotic setting in the North African desert or in Cairo's bazaars and diplomatic circles. Is is just an accident that the film produced and showered with honours in the new empire pushes into the background the post-colonials from Canada and India, and instead focuses on two representatives of old empires: Katherine, British, and Almásy, Austro-Hungarian?[13] Or is it just that this story of a love that is

13. Victor Ramraj, editor of *Ariel*, first pointed this out to me in an email (1997).

not to be fulfilled because of the circumstances of war, recalls another film classic, *Cassablanca*?

At any rate, just as the film omits references that may challenge the perceived and nostalgic view of the heroic History of the end of World War II, after which everyone was to go home and live happily ever after, it disregards to look at the reality of Hana and Kip, for whom the war and the Nuclear Age was a world not of their making into which they were thrown. The Patient and Caravaggio share memories of a world before it all came apart - for the Patient in the holocaust of a burning plane, and for Caravaggio after his escape from his captors when he lay on a mined bridge that "exploded and he was flung upwards and then down as part of the end of the world" (60).

For Hana and Kip, the postcolonials, that end comes where their life should have started. They are blown apart and into the Nuclear Age by the atomic blasts. Where the film and the Patient's life end with reading Katherine's letter from the distant past, the book ends with Hana's letter to her mother about her post-apocalyptic present - and future. She writes: "[It is] *One day after we heard the bombs were dropped in Japan, so it feels like the end of the world. [...] If we can rationalize this we can rationalize anything*" (EP: 292). Hana and Kip may have survived this apocalyptic moment unscathed physically, but their world is no longer the same. Kip is re-baptised Kirpal when he falls into a river (EP: 296). He returns to his old world and becomes a doctor, thus taking up the profession that the old tradition of his family prescribed for him (EP: 182). The apocalypse has literally blown him into the past,[14] back into the tradition he had emerged from, but it has not

14. see footnote 5.

turned him into a hater or fanatic. He has become a doctor, a professional healer, someone who still is a saver of lives. Hana has no such tradition to draw on. She returns to the new world, but cannot go back to business as usual. Years later, at the age of thirty-four, she "has not found her own company, the ones she wanted" (EP: 301). Her experience of apocalypse has left her unmarked physically,[15] but it has deeply affected her mentally. She has not been socialized back into "her" society. As "she is a woman of honour and smartness" (EP: 301), she may have resisted the easy accommodation of World War II into popular and official history and we do not "know what her profession is or what her circumstances are" (EP: 300). None of this makes in into a film that is clearly not interested in facing the beginning of life in the post-apocalypse.[16]

Minghella has adapted Michael Ondaatje's novel and presented it as something it is not, thereby turning it into a new creation. As the prizes and the commercial success show, this new creation works very well within the parameters and strategies, the norms and conventions of the American film industry. These are not of Minghella's making, yet the choice to adapt a novel that is neither sentimental nor nostalgic, and even anti-romantic at times, into a film focussed on nostalgic flashbacks and sentimental romance was his. The decision to drop the bomb and to focus on the pre-war and war history in

---

15. Hana is one of those nurses with "hardly a world around them" (EP: 40) who "began to believe in nothing, trusted nothing. They broke the way a man dismantling a mine broke the second his geography exploded" (EP: 41).

16. A moment that, as Baudrillard says, and as the debates about the effect of the bombs on humans in the U.S. reveal, many seem indeed to have passed unawares (Baudrillard 1989: 33-34).

effect meant de-politicising the film, rather than reflect on all the unexploded mines and bombs left as a legacy of the war, both physical and political.[17]

To be fair, Minghella was the first to admit "sins of omission and commission [...] misjudgments and betrayals" that, as he pointed out, "were all made in the spirit of translating his beautiful novel to the screen" (EP-SP: xii). He also hints at the controversies between producer, director, and the author of the novel: "in Saul[Zaentz]'s home in Tuscany [...] there were memorable discussions held in the cool, aquamarine pool, [...] punctuated by bouts of what we called water polo but which was essentially a form of licensed violence to work off all our various pent-up hostilities, and at which Michael proved to be the master" (EP-SP: xi) - which may not be too surprising for someone who learnt to do *A Trick with a Knife*.

As most public statements about his work, Ondaatje's preface to the film script is very philosophical and diplomatic. Familiar with scripting and shooting film, he is fully aware of the restrictions and limitations involved in adaptation, and so he is fair enough to maintain that "What we have now are two stories, one with the intimate pace and detail of a three-hundred-page novel, and one that is the length of a vivid and subtle film. Each has its own organic structure" (EP-SP: xvii). He praises Minghella's film as "a community story made by many hands" (EP-SP: xviii).[18] Despite the diplomatic tone, Ondaatje is fairly straight forward about the omissions which matter most to him. He first mentions the cutting of "Anthony's scenes

---

17. Such as American exhibitions of nuclear air raids, gold in Swiss bank vaults, chapters in German companies' histories, or belated trials of French high officials.

18. "A literary work is a communal act. And this book could not have been *imagined*, let alone conceived, without the help of many people" (RF: 205), Ondaatje had written in the "Acknowledgements" to *Running in the Family*.

of Kip in England" (EP-SP: xvi), then continues quite frankly: "For me, the long roots of Hana's and Caravaggio's psyches, Kip's training in England, his reaction to the atomic bomb, and his eventual fate, will always remain in the original country of the book" (EP-SP: xvii). He may have been successfully working off his anger in water polo, but I feel that he did not want to attract attention to himself in a public row with a script writer, director, and producer he had been cooperating with. After all, it does not happen that often that a Canadian novel is turned into a film by a major American production company. Perhaps he was hoping for a "Trojan Horse" effect, for any success of the film was likely to generate a new readership for the novel, and thus introduce the writer and his works to some who might otherwise never have heard of neither. If that effect re-directs attention to The English Patient and Ondaatje's other work, there would be cunning in his silence in the best Joycean tradition.[19] This volume (and the conference that generated it) may be an indication of the effectiveness of this strategy.

19. As Joyce's artist hero, Stephen Dedalus, puts it in A Portrait of the Artist as a Young Man: "I will [... be] using for my defence the only arms I allow myself to use - silence, exile, and cunning" (Joyce 1988: 251).

---

## Works Cited

Michael Ondaatje. The English Patient. Toronto: McClelland & Stewart, 1992. [= EP]

Anthony Minghella. The English Patient: A Screenplay. New York: Hyperion, 1996. [= EP-SP]

The English Patient. Dir. Anthony Minghella. Prod. Saul Zaentz. Miramax, 1996. [= EP-film]

* *

Almásy, Ladislaus E. Schwimmer in der Wüste. Auf der Suche nach der Oase Zarzura. Innsbruck: Haymon, 1997.

Alperovitz, Gar. The Decision to Use the Atomic Bomb. London: HarperCollins, 1995.

Barbour, Douglas. Michael Ondaatje. New York: Twayne; Toronto: Macmillan, 1993.

Bassnett, Susan. "Intricate Pathways: Observations on Translation and Literature." Translating Literature. Ed. Susan Bassnett. Cambridge: Brewer, 1997. 1-13.

Baudrillard, Jean. "The Anorexic Ruins." Looking Back on the End of the World. Eds. Dietmar Kamper & Christoph Wulf. New York: Semiotext(e), 1989. 29-45.

Beja, Morris. Film & Literature. New York & London: Longman, 1979.

Joyce, James. A Portrait of the Artist as a Young Man. London: Paladin, 1988.

Linenthal, Edward T. & Tom Engelhadt. Eds. History Wars. The Enola Gay and other Battles for the American Past. New York: Metropolitan Books, 1996.

Fussell, Paul. "Thank God for the Atom Bomb." Killing in Verse and Prose and Other Essays. London: Bellew, 1990. 13-37.

---. "Postscript (1987) on Japanese Skulls." Killing in Verse and Prose and Other Essays. London: Bellew, 1990. 45-50.

Huntington, Samuel P. "The Clash of Civilizations?" The Clash of Civilizations: The Debate. A Foreign Affairs Reader. New York: Foreign Affairs & Council on Foreign Relations, 1993. 22-49.

Hutcheon, Linda. "The Pastime of Past Time': Fiction, History, Historiographic Metafiction." Genre 20.3-4 (1987): 285-305.

Kammen, Michael. *Mystic Chords of Memory. The Transformation of Tradition in American Culture.* New York: Knopf, 1991.

Kröpelin, Stefan. "Die Wüste des Englischen Patienten." *Die Zeit* 17 (18. April 1997): 35.

Lifton, Robert Jay & Greg Mitchell. *Hiroshima in America. A Half Century of Denial.* New York: Avon, 1996.

Mantel, Hilary. "Wraith's Progress." Rev. of *The English Patient* by Michael Ondaatje. *The New York Review of Books* 40.1/2 (1993): 22-23.

McFarlane, Brian. *Novel to Film. An Introduction to Adaptation.* Oxford: Clarendon, 1996.

Ondaatje, Michael. *There's A Trick With a Knife I'm Learning To Do.* Toronto: McClelland & Stewart, 1979.

---. *Running in the Family.* Toronto: McClelland & Stewart, 1989.

Pesch, Josef. "Post-Apocalyptic War Histories: Michael Ondaatje's *The English Patient.*" *Ariel* 28.2 (1997): 117-139. <a>

---. "Globalized Nationalisms: Michael Ondaatje's Novels and (Post)Colonial Correctness." *Zeitschrift für Kanada-Studien.* 31 (1997): 96-109. <b>

---. "Mediation, Memory and a Search for the Father: Michael Ondaatje's *Running in the Family.*" *Zeitschrift für Anglistik und Amerikanistik* 45.1 (1997): 56-71. <c>

---. "Mediating Memories: Michael Ondaatje's (Auto?)Biography *Running in the Family.*" *La Création Biographique - Biographical Creation.* Ed. Marta Dvorak. Rennes: Association Française d'Études Canadiennes & Presses Universitaires de Rennes, 1997. 111-117. <d>

Ramraj, Victor. Email of 26 March 1997.

Schrott, Raoul & Michael Farin. "Schwimmer in der Wüste." Vorwort zu *Schwimmer in der Wüste. Auf der Suche nach der Oase Zarzura.* Ladislaus E. Almásy. Innsbruck: Haymon, 1997. 7-22.

Seligman, Craig. "Sentimental Wounds." Rev. of *The English Patient* by Michael Ondaatje. *The New Republic* March 15, 1993. 38-41.

Simpson, D. Mark. "Minefield Readings: The Postcolonial *English Patient.*" *Essays on Canadian Writing* 53 (1994): 216-237.

Wilde, Oscar. "The Critic as Artist." *Complete Works of Oscar Wilde.* London & Glasgow: Collins, 1966. 1009-1059.

## Lit: Literature Interpretation Theory

Publication details, including instructions for
authors and subscription information:
http://www.tandfonline.com/loi/glit20

# WILL THE 'UN-TRUTH' SET YOU FREE? A CRITICAL LOOK AT GLOBAL HUMAN RIGHTS DISCOURSE IN MICHAEL ONDAATJE'S ANIL'S GHOST

Teresa Derrickson

Version of record first published: 12 Aug 2010.

To cite this article: Teresa Derrickson (2004): WILL THE 'UN-TRUTH' SET YOU FREE? A
CRITICAL LOOK AT GLOBAL HUMAN RIGHTS DISCOURSE IN MICHAEL ONDAATJE'S ANIL'S
GHOST , Lit: Literature Interpretation Theory, 15:2, 131-152

To link to this article: http://dx.doi.org/10.1080/10436920490452092

whatsoever or howsoever caused arising directly or indirectly in connection
with or arising out of the use of this material.

*Literature Interpretation Theory*, 15: 131–152, 2004
Copyright © Taylor & Francis Inc.
ISSN: 1043-6928 print/1545-5866 online
DOI: 10.1080/10436920490452092

# WILL THE 'UN-TRUTH' SET YOU FREE? A CRITICAL LOOK AT GLOBAL HUMAN RIGHTS DISCOURSE IN MICHAEL ONDAATJE'S *ANIL'S GHOST*

## Teresa Derrickson

Teresa Derrickson is Assistant Professor of English at Gonzaga University. Her research interests involve examining class-based structures in contemporary novels, with a particular emphasis on the intersections between globalization and literature. Most recently, she has published essays in *MELUS*, *International Fiction Review*, and *American Transcendental Quarterly*.

Initial book reviews of Michael Ondaatje's novel *Anil's Ghost* (2000) were not altogether favorable. Some critics, like Tom LeClair of *The Nation*, were especially scathing on the subject of the author's seemingly disinterested approach to the civil strife that takes center stage in this narrative about Sri Lanka's devastating internal conflict. LeClair writes that Ondaatje's "apolitical gaze seems irresponsible" (31) and that his overwhelming "silence on class and religion and ethnic prejudice" is apt to "retaliate somewhere" (31). Others are less acerbic but equally insistent on the author's turn from politics. Paul Gray notes the "neutrality of Ondaatje's language" and observes that the novel, as a result, features "no clear demarcations between opposing forces, allies and enemies" (75). In a more dramatic account, *The Economist* initiates its review with the title "Brrrr!" and concludes that "there is a certain coldness about the book altogether," something too "easy, tidy, and literary" in the way the story unfolds.

Claims that Ondaatje's novel holds its political views at arm's length are not altogether unfounded. After all, the novel famously repeats the assertion throughout that *"The reason for war was war,"* a statement that conveniently takes the author off the hook from having to offer a less simplistic analysis of why the two major ethnic groups of Ondaatje's homeland are locked in a gruesome political dispute that involves daily disappearances, mass graves, torture, fear, and cover up. That having been said, *Anil's Ghost* does in fact promote a political stance, and a sophisticated one at that. As subtle as it may be, the text self-consciously engages in an extended discussion about one of the most highly contested topics to be raised in the wake of

131

94

economic globalization: the United Nations' universal mandate on human rights.

Of concern in *Anil's Ghost* is not so much the issue of whether or not global human rights should be stipulated, but the approach by which those rights are legislated through means of international intervention. Specifically, *Anil's Ghost* troubles the idea that the "truth" of human rights violations is both, on the one hand, *discoverable*, and, on the other hand, *desirable*. Without condoning the violence that characterizes the Sri Lankan civil war, Ondaatje demonstrates that the search for justice in such situations is not unproblematic. On the contrary, to the extent that international human rights investigations invariably take sides, to the extent that such investigations often occur without a proper contextual understanding of the domestic situation at hand, to the extent that they often impose Western[1] philosophies of justice in non-Western settings, and to the extent that they broadcast an arrogance that is culturally belittling, they provide us, according to Ondaatje's novel, with ample reason to rethink methods of adjudicating human rights violations.

Far from being heavy-handed in his approach, and far from indicting the United Nations and other NGOs (nongovernmental organizations) for human rights work that is both good-intentioned and terribly needed,[2] Ondaatje's goal is focused on underscoring the fact that there are indeed politics at work behind the function of the United Nations. According to the novel, both the UN organization itself and the work it conducts as the guardian of international human rights bear out Michael Ignatieff's assertion that "human rights is nothing other than a politics, one that must reconcile moral ends to concrete situations and must be prepared to make painful compromises not only between means and ends, but between ends themselves" (21–22). *Anil's Ghost* makes apparent these compromises and, in doing so, contributes to a larger political discussion about the viability of a universal human rights discourse and the viability of a global operative to legislate those rights.

Debate about such questions has raged since the passage of the Universal Declaration of Human Rights in 1948. In an effort to prevent a repeat of the atrocities of World War II, the newly-formed United Nations fought for broad approval on the language of a document that articulated a common set of rights for all people, regardless of national affiliation. The declaration states in part that "All human beings are born free and equal in dignity and rights" and that "no distinction [in the respect of these rights] shall be made on the basis of the political, jurisdictional or international status of the country or territory to which a person belongs..." (qtd. in Alves 480). The significance of this declaration and the significance of its formal reassertion by more than 170 countries at the World Conference on Human Rights in Vienna in 1993 was to globalize the juridical system of human rights (Alves 478). In other words, the statement undercut (and continues to undercut) the Westphalian claim that the nation-state wields exclusive authority over the rights and freedoms of its citizenry. In its place, it posits the notion that people are governed (additionally) by the legal standards of a broader political group, namely the international community at large. Mary Robinson, President of Ireland, summarizes the weight of this outcome in the following terms: "[T]oday countries can no longer say that how they treat their inhabitants is their own business. The state's duty to protect human rights is not only owed to individuals within its jurisdiction but to the international community as a whole" (630).

Although the Universal Declaration of Human Rights has gained significant authority since its debut fifty years ago,[3] initial complaints about the Western bias underscoring the "universal" values reflected in the document have yet to go away. Even those who strive to steer clear of foundationalist and constructivist arguments about the Western hegemonic roots of current human rights discourse conclude that there is much to worry about in this regard. Henry Rosemont summarizes those worries in the following way:

> Our concept of human rights is closely related to our view of human beings as freely choosing autonomous individuals, a view at least as old as Descartes and which is reaffirmed in the 1948 United Nations Declaration of Human Rights. But this concept is overwhelmingly drawn from the culture of the Western industrial democracies and is concerned to propose a particular moral and political perspective, an ideal, appropriate to that culture. (167–68)

Rosemont goes on to claim that while the codes of conduct promoted by the West may not be at odds with codes of conduct supported by other cultures, the underlying philosophies of such codes are inherently different, and in a way that matters. To illustrate this point, he examines the classical Chinese language in which Confucian thinkers expressed their beliefs, noting that within such a language, no lexicon equivalents exist for the terms "freedom, liberty, autonomy, individual, utility, principles, rationality, rational agent, action, objective, subjective, choice, dilemma, duty, or rights" (Rosemont 173). The conclusion he draws from this partial analysis is that a consensus for human rights discourse cannot be based on a philosophy that is exclusionary in its privileging of the individual over the collective—something this linguistic discrepancy points out. Charles Taylor emerges with similar conclusions in his comparative analysis of the disparate legal cultures maintained within the Western tradition and Thai Buddhism. As the following quotation indicates, there are real concerns to be heard about the charge that current human rights rhetoric fails to promote value systems that are non-EuroAmerican:

> [Some Easterners] are certainly ready, even eager, to espouse some universal norms, but they are made uneasy by the underlying philosophy of the human person in society. This seems to give pride of place to autonomous individuals, determined to demand their rights, even (indeed especially) in the face of widespread social consensus. . . . Can people who imbibe the full Western human rights ethos, which (on one version anyway) reaches its highest expression in the lone courageous individual fighting against all the forces of social conformity for his rights, ever be good members of a "Confucian" society? (17)

It is easy to see from such evidence how human rights advocates in the West—and even the United Nations organization itself—have been left to defend themselves against implications of cultural imperialism. Other critics refuse to stop there and maintain that in addition to supporting a non-inclusive world view, international human rights law is flagrantly tailored to privilege civil and political rights over economic and social rights, a condition that proves favorable to the proliferation of economic capitalism and the legitimization of unequal distributions of wealth and power around the world (Evans 415). Taken as a whole, such realizations have led Slovenian professor of sociology Sergej Flere to assert cynically, "The meaning of human rights as a concept in political discourse has passed from an emancipatory stage to one where it legitimates the existing global order and, at best, partly limits the use and abuse of political power" (59).

It is within the context of these complaints that Ondaatje writes a novel in which questions about the possibility of achieving justice through UN-sponsored human rights investigations are posed. Michael Ondaatje's *Anil's Ghost* is a narrative in which a 33-year-old forensic anthropologist, working under the auspices of the United Nations, travels from the United States to present-day Sri Lanka to investigate the mass civilian murders occurring in conjunction with the country's ongoing civil war. The anthropologist, a woman named Anil, is teamed up with a local Sri Lankan archeologist, 49-year-old Sarath, to determine whether or not a recently exhumed skeleton can indeed provide evidence that the Sri Lankan government has been systematically killing and torturing its own people in the campaign of murder that consumes the country. Although there are at least two other political factions involved in the country's mass killings aside from the Sri Lankan government,[4] Anil's task is to investigate state-sponsored murders, and so when she and Sarath find a relatively new body buried among the excavations of a sixth-century archeological preserve on government-access-only property, Anil decides that this is the case she will investigate: "We can prove this, don't you see?" she tells Sarath, "This is an opportunity, it's traceable. We found him in a place that only a government official could get into" (52). Sarath, aware of the fact that such a politically charged probe could cost them their lives, reluctantly agrees to go along with Anil. And so the pair, working in makeshift laboratories as far from the penetrating eye of the government as possible, begin their dangerous investigation by taking protective custody of the skeleton they dub "Sailor" and by using soil samples, pollen samples, and bone distortion patterns to reconstruct the identity of the murdered man as well as the circumstances of his death.

Of assistance in their investigation is Gamini, Sarath's younger brother and one of the few medical surgeons left on the island; a blind epigraphist named Palipana, who serves as a professional mentor to Sarath; and a Buddhist statue-painter named Ananda, an artist commissioned to fashion a sculpture of Sailor's face so that the skeleton may be identified. After weeks of furtive research, Anil and Sarath successfully establish Sailor's name, profession, and date of abduction. Their teamwork falls apart, however, when Anil's underlying distrust of Sarath's political motives prompts her to take matters into her own hands. Panicked at the thought that her colleague has sold her out to the Sri Lankan government, Anil rushes to Colombo to present their evidence to a group of military and police personnel on her own. During the hearing, she is confronted by a hostile Sarath, who interrogates her from his position in the audience because he is able to see what she cannot: that their investigation is far too incriminating for the government to tolerate and that Anil's own life depends upon his ability to discredit her as well as the entire investigation. Sarath has seen this happen before in other cases where civilian informants have been brutally retaliated against for attempting to expose the government's illegal actions (42). His careful strategy, while angering his colleague, ultimately works, and the naïve Anil is allowed to leave the hearing alive. That their joint discoveries come at a price foreseen by Sarath all along, however, is confirmed only days later when Gamini's routine inspection of the day's tally of political victims turns up a photo of his older brother's tortured body. Sarath, it would appear, has been killed for his part in the investigation, while Anil has presumably escaped the country with their condemning report intact—a fact the novel leads us to conclude but never fully confirms.

Just as critics call into question the "universality" and "objectivity" of a system of international law that is founded on Western philosophies and Western capitalist gains, Ondaatje's novel invites us to question the brand of justice offered to the people of Sri Lanka by a Western-dominated legal institution, the United Nations. Central to Ondaatje's critique of UN-sponsored human rights violation investigations is the extent to which such an institution appears to wield significant control over the narrative of justice that will be told about the Sri Lankan conflict. The following excerpt from the end of *Anil's Ghost* serves as a metatextual comment on the book in this regard, summarizing the essence of Ondaatje's concern over what is at stake in the globalization of human rights standards:

> "American movies, English books—remember how they all end?" Gamini asked that night. "The American or the Englishman gets on a plane and leaves. That's it. The camera leaves with him. He looks out of the window at Mombasa or Vietnam or Jakarta, someplace now he can look through at the clouds. The tired hero. A couple of words to the girl beside him. He's going home. So the war, to all purposes, is over. That's enough reality for the West. It's probably the history of the last two hundred years of Western political writing. Go home. Write a book. Hit the circuit." (285–86)

It is no secret that the kind of stories we tell ourselves matter. This fact is made plain by the details of the foregoing passage, where Gamini's insights prompt us to understand that the story Anil will ultimately tell about the "truth" of Sri Lanka is a Western story. She, like the "tired [American/British] hero" who "gets on a plane and leaves" will escape back to the West where her accounts will invariably reflect "enough reality" for that part of the world, that is to say, a *distorted* reality, a reality commensurate with the narrative of "Mombasa or Vietnam or Jakarta" that the West repeatedly constructs—to its own liking—through books and the magic of Hollywood. Where is the justice in this kind of telling? the passage implicitly asks. And how can the West, which has been involved in such distortions for "the last two hundred years" be entrusted with its continued narration? Both questions, of course, are purely rhetorical. That the "truths" Anil will take back are ultimately ones that serve the interests of the parties by whom she has been commissioned is suggested in the comment that the information she bears might be used to "Write a book. Hit the circuit." The statement "Hit the circuit" implies that there is a capitalist venture underscoring her mission after all.

Justice, it would seem from Gamini's account, is fully situational. It is decided by the West, and it is meant to serve the West.

This conclusion is echoed by Susan Silbey, whose essay "Globalization, Postmodern Colonialism, and the Possibilities of Justice" discounts claims that justice is achievable in a global society. Arguing that current legal practice is shaped to do the bidding of economic liberalization, Silbey reminds us that "justice is not eternal and universal but is a culturally and historically constructed ideal whose values and approximate performance simultaneously share and are shaped by local and variable social organization" (209). Ondaatje's novel presents us with a similar reality, opening with the observation that "here [in Sri Lanka] it was a more complicated world morally. The streets were still streets, the citizens remained citizens. They shopped, changed jobs, laughed. Yet the darkest of Greek tragedies were innocent compared to what was happening here" (11). By invoking the Greek tradition from which Western law and politics takes its cue, and by asserting that Sri Lanka's case is "more complicated morally" than that tradition, Ondaatje frames his text with the suggestion that justice for the Sri Lankan people may not be obtainable through a human rights mandate that is governed by cultural outsiders.

And yet that is precisely what occurs in his novel. The narrative of justice at stake in *Anil's Ghost* is fought over by two characters, Anil and Sarath, and there is little doubt from the onset who holds the upper hand. While both are technically native Sri Lankans, Anil stands in as the novel's "Western hero." A woman who left the island when she was eighteen and never looked back until a "halfhearted" application to the Center for Human Rights in Geneva sent her home as an investigating forensic anthropologist (15), Anil now arrives in Sri Lanka as a formal Westerner, bearing "a British passport" to signal her new national affiliation (16). Years of medical school in Great Britain and years of field work in the American Southwest have left her identifying more with the West in less formal ways as well: "In her years abroad, during her European and North American education, Anil had courted foreignness, was at ease whether on the Bakerloo line or the highways of Santa Fe. She felt completed abroad. (Even now her brain held the area codes of Denver and Portland)" (54).

Anil's mission is a simple one. Charged with the authority of the UN's Office of the High Commissioner for Human Rights, her job is to investigate the complaints of government-sponsored murder that have been filed by Amnesty International and other civil rights groups on behalf of the people of Sri Lanka (16). As the novel reveals, there is much to investigate. Anil encounters the brutality of the island's violence on her very first day, volunteering to offer a group of students an impromptu lesson in the use of forensics to determine a body's cause of death. The first corpse she examines presents a bit of a conundrum, as Anil wonders aloud how the murdered man's arms could have been broken without damaging the hands that would have gone up in a gesture of defense. One of the students offers an explanation that takes Anil aback by revealing the stoic brutality of the island's war: "Maybe he was praying" the student offers quietly (14). The second body tells an equally disturbing tale. Ondaatje writes, "The next corpse brought in had flail fractures on the rib cage. It meant he had fallen from a great height—at least five hundred feet—before hitting the water belly down. The air knocked out of the body. It meant a helicopter" (14).

Anil's introduction to the horrors of the Sri Lankan civil war is only the first of many incidents in which we learn of the gruesome atrocities that have plagued the island. On a night drive back to Colombo, for example, Anil and Sarath come upon a man spread-eagled on the quiet highway, taking a snooze in front of his truck, as was common practice in those parts (109). Miles down the road and yet increasingly suspicious of the scene they had just passed, Anil and Sarath return to the truck only to discover that the "sleeping" driver is very much awake, his palms hammered to the pavement with the spikes of two large bridge nails—a live crucifixion in the middle of a desolate stretch of road (111).

The fate of the truck driver, it turns out, is far less horrific than a scene witnessed by Ananda's wife several years earlier as she makes her way down a dusty path toward the village school in which she works. Arriving at the bridge where she generally encounters a group of gawking teenage boys, the young schoolteacher is met with a different sight altogether on this ordinary weekday morning: "*She is about ten yards from the bridge when she sees the heads of the two students on stakes, on either side of the bridge, facing each other. Seventeen, eighteen, nineteen years old…she doesn't know or care. She sees two more heads on the far side of the bridge and can tell even from here that she recognizes one of them*" (174–75). Later in the novel, we learn that the teacher herself and forty-six of her students are picked up in the schoolyard by trucks with no license plates, a mass abduction executed by the government to purge rebel supporters and other political insurgents from Sri Lanka's rural villages (185). They are never heard from again. As Sarath informs Anil, both the heads on stakes and the abductions are a national commonplace:

"We have seen so many heads stuck on poles here, these last few years. It was at its worst a couple years ago. You'd see them in the early mornings, somebody's night work, before the families heard about them and came and removed them and took them home. Wrapping them in their shirts or just cradling them. Someone's son. These were blows to the heart. There was only one thing worse. That was when a family member simply disappeared and there was no sighting or evidence of his existence or his death." (184)

Sarath points out in this passage that the brazen civilian murders on the island are just as numerous as the open abductions. Rarely are either crimes reported, however. As Sarath tells his partner, "Everyone's scared, Anil. It's a national disease" (53). Ondaatje elaborates on this comment, writing, "In a fearful nation, public sorrow was stamped down by the climate of uncertainty. If a father protested a son's death, it was feared another family member would be killed. ...This was the scarring psychosis in the country" (56). No one experiences this psychosis more deeply than Sarath's brother, Gamini, a surgeon who is forced to witness the war's casualities on a daily basis, confronting human burns, scars, shrapnel lacerations, limb contortions, flesh carvings, and orifice mutilations in the patients who stream into Colombo's main hospital. His own response to such daily horrors is to retreat from the world altogether through an immersion in drugs and a ruthless twenty-four-hour work schedule. Others choose similarly destructive means of escape, Sarath turning his back on social relationships, Ananda turning to alcohol, and Sarath's wife taking her own life. Thus, even the physically unscathed become casualties in a war where, as Ondaatje states, terror has become an incomprehensible normalcy of everyday life: "The country existed in a rocking, self-burying motion. The disappearance of schoolboys, the death of lawyers by torture, the abduction of bodies from the Hokandara mass grave...You thought, What did they do to deserve this, and then, What did they do to survive this?" (157, 242).

Anil is thrown into the middle of this complexity with a directive to find evidence of government wrong-doing in a place where nearly everything is wrong and where nearly everyone is implicated in its doing. Her orders on the surface, however, appear to be objective enough. Even she is convinced of her own political impartiality, emphasizing during her climactic hearing before the Sri Lankan government that she works for "an *independent* organization" and that she "makes *independent* reports" (274, emphasis added). Her investigative colleague, Sarath, however, is not so convinced. The fact that Anil's mission is focused on gathering the truth about a specific kind of atrocity—that is, a state-sponsored one—signals to him a mission that is both partial and subjective. His attempts to rectify the perceived bias in her orders are reflected in the following brief he gives Anil during their first meeting together:

The bodies turn up weekly now. The height of the terror was, eighty-eight and, eighty-nine, but of course it was going on long before that. Every side was killing and hiding the evidence. *Every side . . .* The government was not the only one doing the killing. You had, and still have, three camps of enemies—one in the north, two in the south . . . There's no hope of affixing blame . . . What we've got here is unknown extrajudicial executions mostly. Perhaps by the insurgents, or by the government or the guerrilla separatists. Murders committed by all sides. (17–18)

The point Sarath repeats so emphatically in this speech is that everyone has blood on their hands in Sri Lanka, not just the government. In other words, the truth of the situation may be far more complicated than Anil and her orders allow. For Ondaatje, this is a significant problem. He questions the Western assumption that the truth is patently discoverable (i.e., clean and uncomplicated), just as he casts doubt on the related assumption that justice is a binary affair that offers up a tidy victim and villain. If "murders [are] committed by all sides," he suggests, then no objective assessment of the situation can lead to the "affixing [of] blame."

The question of whether or not truth is discoverable is asked and re-asked throughout the novel, starting with one of the opening scenes in which Anil's enthusiasm about finding evidence that might link the Sri Lankan government to the murder of the body they have dubbed "Sailor" is juxtaposed to a chilling train scene in which a young man—a man who could very well be a living version of Sailor himself—takes advantage of a three-minute tunnel blackout to strangle a government official and force his body through the opening of a howling window. The train incident is meant to pose the same question Anil is asked during her formal interrogation at the hands of the Sri Lankan government, "Why do you not investigate the killing of government officers?" (275). The question she is asked is one we know to be ludicrous in the sense that one form of murder does not justify another. And yet at the same time, the total exclusion of any other possible outcome in Anil's search for truth in Sri Lanka is somewhat troubling, as many of the characters point out. Gamini, for example, warns Anil to keep in mind that when it comes to the Sri Lankan civil war, "Nobody's perfect. Nobody's right" (132). The epigraphist Palipana shares similar insights, confiding to Anil that even in ancient times, "there was nothing to believe in with certainty. They still didn't know what the truth was. We have never had the truth. Not even with your work on bones . . . Most of the time in our world, truth is just opinion" (102). Palipana's assertion that truth cannot be known because truth is "just opinion" is a belief that Sarath appears to subscribe to as well: "I'd believe your arguments more," he tells Anil, "if you lived here... You can't just slip in, make a discovery and leave" (44). In other words, the novel suggests that the facts of the domestic and political situation Anil is asked to assess are not so easily discerned, and certainly not easily discerned without a proper understanding of the context in which such facts are situated. Sarath continues to emphasize this point, instructing Anil, "I want you to understand the archeological surround of a fact. Or you'll be like one of those journalists who file reports about flies and scabs while staying at the Galle Face Hotel. That false empathy and blame... That's how we get seen in the West" (44).

Unfortunately, Sarath's warning to Anil to avoid easy conclusions about the situation in Sri Lanka (conclusions that would invariably involve "false empathy and blame") are not fully internalized by his eager colleague. When he later tells Anil of an archeological find in which an ancient ruler's tomb is interred with the bodies of twenty female musicians, Anil seizes upon the only "fact" of the situation that is available to her from her limited cultural perspective: "Twenty murdered women," she scoffs, ignoring Sarath's suggestion to keep in mind that "It was another world with its own value system" (261). Sarath's desperate attempt to get Anil to understand the complex nature of truth in this exchange parallels his message in yet another interaction. In this third discussion, Sarath explains to Anil that things were so bad in the early days of the country's civil war that the illegal murder of civilian insurgents by the Sri Lankan government was a desperate and necessary measure to try to control the bloodshed: "the law [was] abandoned by everyone... We wouldn't have survived with your rules of Westminster then," he states with conviction (154).

The fact that Sarath discounts the applicability of "Westminster rules" to the situation in Sri Lanka does not mean that the novel argues for cultural relativism when it comes to global human rights. On the contrary, the text's ongoing conversation about the possibility of discovering "the truth" is merely meant to invite questions about the seemingly apolitical nature of international-sponsored human rights investigations. The role of forensic science in the identification of the Sailor skeleton is an especially compelling indication of this last point. The Untied Nations' use of forensic scientists in an investigative capacity effectively obscures the relations of power that underwrite UN-sponsored human rights operations by invoking truths that are practically unassailable. The ideological power of science emerges from the common belief that science deals with "irrefutable" facts, facts that are seemingly beyond history, culture, and politics. The novel confirms for us the potency of this myth by describing Anil's lab work in the following way: "She began to examine the skeleton again under sulphur light, summarizing the facts of his death so far, the permanent truths, same for Colombo as for Troy. One forearm broken. Partial burning. Vertebrae damage in the neck" (65). Anil's scientific probing of these bones is said to reveal "permanent truths," truths that hold no political bias because of their overarching applicability to both Western and Eastern culture: "same for Colombo as for Troy."

The problem with these "permanent truths," however, is that they necessarily become conflated with the "truths" about the situation of Sri Lanka as a whole. Recorded in the formal papers of a UN inquiry, they become part of the metaphoric "American movie" or "British book" that Gamini speaks so vehemently against, a text that uses only part of the story to speak for history in full. In other words, the move from scientific objectivity to rationales for political neutrality is undercut and revealed as ideologically charged. The use of science to bolster human rights claims in such a politically inflected way has important consequences. In the novel, the forensic truth about Sailor's death is parlayed into a political truth about Sri Lanka's human rights record, and not even Anil can tell the difference. When Sarath expresses hesitation about the advisability of their investigation, Anil appeals to the scientist in him, saying "You're an archeologist. Truth comes finally to the light. It's in the bones and sediment" (259). In this passage, Anil is no longer talking about the truth of Sailor's death; she is talking about the truth of the broader situation in which Sri Lankans find themselves, extrapolating the former from that latter, just as others will do with the information she takes back to Geneva. Sarath's quiet reply that "[Truth is] in character and nuance and mood" offers an alternative perspective, and yet it is flatly denied by Anil, whose faith in science remains resolute: "That is what governs us in our lives, [but] that's not the truth," she tells Sarath (259).

The UN, by relying on the "objectivity" of science to impute a similar objectivity to its own strategies and practices, conceals the political nature of its work while promoting a narrative of justice about Sri Lanka that is alarmingly devoid of unvarnished politics. Lost in this account, for example, is a summary of the foreign agenda that is served by initiating a human rights investigation on the island to begin with. As the novel tells us, the president of Sri Lanka only approved of Anil's visit in an attempt to "placate trading partners in the West" (16).[5] This statement not only provides insight as to why the Sri Lankan government has taken a sudden interest in the human rights of its people, but it also suggests a dubious reason as to why the United Nations has followed suit. As Samuel Makinda explains, human rights violations often become high profile issues when and only when they start to encroach on the economic and/or social well-being of the West:[6]

> [T]he West does not see "rescue" as a matter of affirming that certain things ought not to be done to human beings, and that certain things ought to always be done for them. Instead it, in part, regards intervention as a matter of ensuring that human rights abuses in certain parts of the world are not allowed to disturb global order or threaten the tranquility of life in the West. (357)

The revelation that Sri Lanka is involved in business partnerships with Western industries gives way to other details that would suggest a more complicated "truth" about the human rights violations Anil is sent to investigate. Sarath tells Anil, for example, that the three rivaling factions in the war have been "importing state-of-the-art weapons from the West" (17). Confirmation of this fact comes later on when Ondaatje writes, "It was a Hundred Years' War with modern weaponry, and backers on the sidelines in safe countries, a war sponsored by gun- and drug-runners. It became evident that political enemies were secretly joined in financial arms deals" (43). Of significance in these two passages is the disclosure that Sri Lanka's civil war is big business for Western states and that those states have been capitalizing on the lucrative weapons market that the island's conflict sustains. In that sense, then, Sarath's statement that "we all have blood on our clothes" extends to the West as well (48), for it would appear that Western complicity in the civil rights violations occurring on the island can be summarized—at least in part—in a simple equation: more dollars means more deaths.

This is probably not the story that will make it into Anil's report, however. Charged with the task of investigating *government*-sponsored atrocities, Anil's orders already presuppose a truth that omits mention of US or European involvement. Although not even Gamini can fully appreciate the complexity of the politics underlining his country's war, he knows enough to understand that Western public opinion oftentimes misses the mark: "those armchair rebels living abroad with their ideas of justice—nothing against their principles, but I wish they were here. They should come and visit me in surgery" (132). Gamini's complaint against the facile judgments cast upon Sri Lanka by "armchair rebels living abroad" suggests that the West assumes no responsibility for the situation on the island and yet still plays a role in the conflict from the sidelines, not only as merchants of weapons but as perpetrators of political propaganda: Gamini continues, "these guys who are setting off the bombs are who [sic] the

Western press calls freedom fighters... And you [Anil] want to investigate the *government*?" (133). Again, the idea that "truth" is entangled in politics becomes clear here, and the United Nations, by showing itself to be partial to a particular version of the truth, that is, by supporting a historical narrative that, among other things, exculpates the West from any sort of involvement in the Sri Lankan human rights disaster, appears to deliver a brand of justice that is not fully separate from global politics and its neocolonial impulse.

Abdullahi An-Na'im, like many other scholars, recognizes the potential for global human rights efforts to devolve in this manner:

> [H]uman rights advocates [are presented] with a serious dilemma. On the one hand, it is necessary to safeguard the personal integrity and human dignity of the individual against excessive or harsh punishments... On the other hand, it is extremely important to be sensitive to the dangers of cultural imperialism, whether it is a product of colonialism, a tool of international economic exploitation and political subjugation, or simply a product of extreme ethnocentricity. (37–38)

While An-Na'im allows for the fact that Western-based human rights advocates may maintain political neutrality while conducting their business, Ignatieff asserts that such a point is probably moot. The perception of bias in such operations, he argues, is increasingly apparent: "As the West intervenes ever more frequently but ever more inconsistently in the affairs of other societies,... [h]uman rights is increasingly seen as the language of a moral imperialism just as ruthless and just as self-deceived as the colonial hubris of yesteryear" (19–20). Such a statement is a harsh indictment of Western-sponsored human rights movements; however, it is an indictment that Ondaatje tends to support. Just as Anil's UN mission favors the Western notion of a unitary truth—one that is uncomplicated by internal and external politics, and one that is always ultimately "discoverable"—Anil's mission also favors the Western notion that the "discovery" of truth is necessarily *desirable*. The question of "desirability" amounts to figuring out what the purpose of truth really is, and while Ondaatje refrains from engaging in an explicit philosophical discussion on the subject, he nevertheless suggests that Anil's UN mission to uncover the truth with respect to the Sri Lanka conflict is more about catering to a global (read Western) ideology of justice than about acting in the best interests of the Sri Lankan people.

The struggle over whose philosophy and whose interests will prevail in this matter is once again played out in a competitive drama between the novel's two protagonists, Anil and Sarath. Anil, classic Westerner that she is, seems to be oblivious of the consequences of intruding in the internal affairs of Sri Lanka. Heady with a false sense of her own importance and authority ("I *was* invited here," she says to Sarath with apparent indignation, dismissing his advice to be cautious when it comes to exposing the truth [45]), Anil's perspective is colored by the typical justice agenda of the West, an agenda which, according to Taylor, replicates "the drama of age-old wrongs righted in valor" (20). Her allegiance to "the [Western] imperative to punish historic wrongdoing" (Taylor 20) has her naively pushing for the disclosure of government secrets with little thought to the consequences involved.

Unlike Anil, Sarath is mindful of those consequences. Ondaatje writes:

> Sarath knew that for [Anil] the journey was getting to the truth. But what would the truth bring them into? It was a flame against a sleeping lake of petrol. Sarath had seen truth broken into suitable pieces and used by the foreign press alongside irrelevant photographs. A flippant gesture towards Asia that might lead, as a result of this information, to new vengeance and slaughter. There were dangers in handing truth to an unsafe city around you. As an archeologist Sarath believed in truth as a principle. That is, he would have given his life for the truth if the truth were of any use. (156–57)

In this passage, Sarath outlines reasons as to why the truth under the current circumstances "is of no use." He tries to communicate to Anil that objective truth cannot be translated to social and political realms unproblematically. The foreign journalists who "break the truth up into suitable pieces" and use it to create a distorted rendition of events necessarily compromise objective truth at a great cost. It is this cost that figures as Sarath's second reason for believing the truth to be of "no use." According to his insider's perspective, a forced exposé about the government's role in a campaign of clandestine terror would incite "new vengeance and slaughter." Anil's persistence in revealing "the truth" about the Sri Lankan government (a truth that is partial and politically charged to begin with) thus proves itself to be, in some sense, a careless gesture, a gesture possibly as negligent as the over-sensationalized stories produced by "flippant" journalists on the other side of the world. Her crusade, like theirs, appears to involve little thought as to the costs involved, and therefore runs the risk of being seen as disingenuous in its nod toward justice.

Anil, of course, has little idea of this. The sum of her words and actions reveals a series of ethnocentric assumptions about the cultural and political meaning of truth: (1) that the value of "truth for the sake of truth" is a universally recognized one, even outside of Western religious and philosophical traditions; (2) that the government of Sri Lanka sustains some kind of American-based judicial system that would presumably care whether or not people were being kidnapped and murdered; (3) that the Western privileging of blame and retribution as worthy ends in the search for truth are shared by non-Westerners; (4) that the status of human rights in Sri Lanka is such that human rights claims trump all other moral obligations and commitments, just as they generally do in Western cultures where the primacy of the individual is such an entrenched ideology, supplanting values of social harmony and "the good of the collective"; and (5) that the truth in the form of objective science can be wrought independent of social and political contexts, as it is in Western discourse.

According to the novel, none of the foregoing assumptions is consistent with the situation in Sri Lanka, and yet Anil still takes it as fact that "to do something" in her capacity as a UN forensic scientist is a preferable course of action (53). Not all scholars agree. According to Fred Dallmayr, the enforcement of global human rights discourse is not a given: "rights traditionally have been protective shields of the underprivileged and oppressed, and [yet]...the concrete enactment of rights needs to be assessed in terms of their justice and rightness" (183). Others bolster this claim. Mahmood Monshipouri and Claude Welch, for example, explain that in many cases, prosecuting human rights offenders (especially high-profile government officials) poses such a threat to the stability and order of the state, that such efforts are overridden by a need to preserve domestic security (393–99).

Lindgren Alves offers a related reason for holding back on human rights investigations. According to him, global human rights doctrine has provided an increasing number of would-be separatist groups with a compelling justification for demanding national autonomy, demands that often come at the cost of civil unrest and violence. Lindgren Alves writes, "Arguably, most contemporary identity struggles have as their foundation the general principle of non-discrimination enshrined in the Universal Declaration of Human Rights" (487). In her essay entitled "Self-determination and the Politics of Exclusion," Tamara Dragadze agrees, writing,

> It is ironic...that the UN which was established to unite humankind has, by its very existence, spurred given peoples to define and defend separate pieces of territory with ever greater ferocity. "A seat at the United Nations," as any leader of a separatist movement will tell you, is the ultimate accolade, the final recognition that a people has indeed determined its own self and its own destiny on its very own land. (346)

Of interest in these observations is the claim that the United Nations often sets up situations in which human rights discourse *thwarts*—as opposed to *furthers*—global justice, for rarely does the pursuit of independent statehood occur without intense civil strife. Robert Schaeffer makes this point in his own discussion of the spread of global separatism, observing that the Eritreans' 1991 declaration of independence from Ethiopia—a somewhat typical case—led to 500,000 deaths, not counting the millions of people who perished from conflict-related starvation (298). As Schaeffer remarks, "Although separatist movements in some countries have managed to depart without triggering conflict, for every velvet divorce there has been a 'charred Yugoslavia'" (298).

Monshipouri and Welch offer yet another concrete example of the way the UN potentially undermines the possibility of global justice. They report that at the conclusion of Sierra Leone's eight-year civil war, the soldiers of the Revolutionary United Front (RUF) were exonerated of gruesome war crimes—including the murder, rape, and torture of thousands of civilians—in the interest of national peace and reconciliation (393). Domestic stability could not be obtained, the government determined, without overlooking the very kinds of crimes that human rights organizations like the UN were eager to prosecute. To have pursued those crimes would have led to renewed violence, an end incommensurate with a kind of global justice that means saving lives and ensuring peace. The work of Monshipouri and Welch and the other scholars cited thus prompts us to question both the motives behind Anil's investigative inquiries and the brand of justice that those inquiries are supposed to deliver. *Whose justice?* appears to be the key question at stake.

It is this important question, however, that Anil never reflects on. She is aware of Sarath's opinion on the issue, saying to him, "I know you feel [that]...it's sometimes more dangerous here if you tell the truth" (53), and yet even still, she never comes around to accepting the idea herself. So oblivious is she to the danger her work places her in that she boldly announces her incriminating findings to a gathering of Sri Lankan officials at the end of the novel, prompting Sarath to publicly discredit her by countering, "I believe in a society that has peace, Miss Tissera. What you are proposing could result in chaos" (275). In the end, it turns out that Sarath is at least partly right. Only days—or perhaps just hours—after Anil's report to the assembly, a backlash of civil violence occurs, this time directed at Sarath himself, a man who knew that his own participation in protecting Anil, as well as his own participation in the investigation of Sailor's death, would surely lead to his own demise. His death underscores the irony and possible imprudence of the UN's intervention in the Sri Lankan conflict, for in the novel's final analysis, the search for truth about global human rights violations leads to at least one more killing.

It is perhaps for this reason that Ondaatje's novel is as "apolitical" as its critics claim. If we recall, LeClair wrote that Ondaatje's "apolitical gaze seems irresponsible." From what we have learned, however, it seems possible that it would have been careless for Ondaatje to have done otherwise. After all, if the ending of the novel does nothing else, it demonstrates that what is "responsible" and what is "not responsible" with respect to the politics of another country cannot always be determined through a Western perspective. Identifying an appropriate course of action, like identifying the meaning of "truth" and "justice," is at least partially dependent on context and culture. For this reason, Ondaatje takes a more sophisticated approach to his account of the Sri Lankan civil war. Deliberately skirting issues such as cause and accountability (which appear to cater to a Western need for an unambiguous, univocal reading of truth), he succeeds in avoiding the narration of yet another Western historical account filled with "false empathy and blame." The Western hero of his tale, for example, notably vanishes well before the ending of the novel, never making it onto the symbolic "plane-above-the-clouds" that finishes off so many imperialist narratives of non-Western cultures. Unlike the endings of those stock histories, we never learn of Anil's fate, just as we never learn what comes of the damning report she presumably delivers to Geneva.

Instead, we are left to pay witness to two seemingly random events, both of them significantly located in the heart of Sri Lanka, which is where the novel ends. The first event involves the assassination of the President of Sri Lanka by a man who approaches the leader with a pack of explosives strapped to this chest.[7] The second event, which occurs well away from the violence and noise of Colombo, involves the painstaking reconstruction of an immense statue of Buddha that was destroyed in an unrelated bombing several years prior. Two events. Two bombings. Two tales of destruction. And yet out of the last one comes the promise of peace and reconciliation. The months of labor expended in the careful reconstruction of the Buddhist statue is immanently symbolic of a rebuilding that might eventually reunite the different factions of Sri Lanka into something whole and stable as well.

It is telling that, in the final two lines of the novel, Ondaatje asserts the importance of genuine human-to-human compassion in the resolution of this internal conflict. Ananda, the artist commissioned to perform the ceremonious painting of the statue's eyes, is perched high above the world on a piece of scaffolding, his young assistant holding up the mirror that will be used to give the Buddha its sight. As the artist begins his work, the novel quietly concludes, "He felt the boy's concerned hand on his. The sweet touch from the world" (307). Of significance in this passage is its unique materialist claim in articulating a solution to the Sri Lankan crisis. The solution to that crisis, Ondaatje suggests, is to be found not in the ideals of liberal humanism and not in the politically charged motives of a Western-based human rights discourse, but in the material world itself, in the simple show of compassion that travels from person to person, in the concrete manner in which the apprentice boy shows his care for Ananda, a hand of concern from the physical world, not a hand from the ideological world of global humanitarianism.

It may seem an odd reversal that Ondaatje elects to end his text with an expression of the importance of "the sweet touch [of] the world," and yet *Anil's Ghost* was never about the rejection of human rights principles to begin with. On the contrary, its emphasis on the need for human compassion and the need for global justice ultimately invites us to question not the imperative for a global human rights objective, but the interests, motives, and ideologies of the political monolith called the United Nations, and thus the West's dominant version of civil and political rights as a neutral, universal discourse. As the primary custodian for the Universal Declaration of Human Rights, the UN has made significant progress in promoting social justice worldwide. Its role in that effort, however, has not been an entirely neutral one. Like the Western states from which it derives the force of its authority, the UN necessarily takes sides, promotes agendas, and disseminates ideas that often run counter to the cultural, political, and economic institutions of non-Western states. Because of that fact, Ondaatje makes it clear that the UN might not be the most objective "hand" to extend to the world. More appropriate, according to his novel, would be a global human rights effort devoid of the age-old arch-struggle between East and West that can be seen in the philosophical jockeying between Sarath and Anil. In such classical struggles (whether in real life or in fiction), the former tends to win, creating a narrative of justice that may do more good for Western global power and its economic ambitions than the people for whom it is intended. Of course, there are those who assert that the legislation of global human rights has little to do with this struggle. There are those who argue that global justice is a separate issue from the neocolonial impulse of economic liberalization and the "Western hubris of yesteryear." For such detractors, it might do well to read a page not from Ondaatje's text but from Secretary-General of the United Nations, Kofi Annan:

A fundamental shift has occurred. If the United Nations has a new-found appreciation for the role of the private sector, it is also true that business and industry are deepening their interest in the activities of the United Nations... More and more, through practical experience, joint ventures and various forms of cooperation, the United Nations and business are finding common ground. (73)

Annan's admission that the United Nations has entered a strategic partnership with the world's business community—a business community governed by Western capitalism—signals a key alliance between the high custodian of global human rights and the Western world. Under such circumstances, it is unlikely that the "truths of Colombo" and the "truths of Troy" will ever find a common ground.

## NOTES

1. I use the terms "Western" and "West" in this essay to distinguish those geopolitical areas that have exerted political, economic, and cultural dominance over other parts of the world throughout recent history. This distinction is not meant to imply that the West is fully homogenous in terms of its politics, policies, views, and cultures.
2. For a comprehensive discussion of the rise of NGOs and their involvement in the global human rights movement, see Tuijl.
3. Interestingly, the United States has proved to be more reluctant than its European allies to grant increased authority to global human rights law. Not only has it dragged its feet on the ratification of several international rights conventions, but it remains one of the primary hold-outs on the approval of the International Criminal Tribunal, a tribunal that would bring American military personnel (and the rest of the world's military personnel) under the legal jurisdiction of an international authority.
4. Sri Lanka's civil struggle, which raged from the early 1980s to the mid-1990s, was comprised of three warring factions: a group of political separatists to the north, a group of government subversives in the south, and the Sri Lankan government itself, which eventually took to rooting out both forces in a manner just as ruthless as the practices adopted by the oppositional groups themselves.
5. The Sri Lankan government has since announced the formation of its own domestic Human Rights Commission. The scope and intent of this commission is outlined by Gomez.
6. Admittedly, this relationship can work the other way as well. That is to say, human rights organizations often enlist the help of corporations to enforce the authority of international law by

pressuring such corporations to refuse to invest in states whose human rights records are especially objectionable. For a more detailed explanation of this relationship, see Schrage and Ewing.

7. Suicide bombings now resonate most clearly with the civil strife in the Middle East, another site where the dispute over a narrative of justice is heavily scripted by American journalists and American political interests.

## WORKS CITED

Alves, Jose A. Lindgren "The Declaration of Human Rights in Postmodernity." *Human Rights Quarterly* 22 (2000): 478–500.

*Anil's Ghost*, by Michael Ondaatje. Rev. *The Economist* 17 June 2000: 14.

Annan, Kofi A. "The United Nations and the Private Sector: A New Era." *Natural Resources Forum* 22.2 (1998): 73–74.

An-Na'im, Abdullahi Ahmed. "Toward a Cross-Cultural Approach to Defining International Standards of Human Rights: The Meaning of Cruel, Inhuman, or Degrading Treatment or Punishment." *Human Rights in Cross-Cultural Perspectives: A Quest for Consensus*. Ed. Abdullahi Ahmed An-Na'im. Philadelphia: U of Pennsylvania P, 1992. 19–43.

Dallmayr, Fred. "'Asian Values' and Global Human Rights." *Philosophy East and West* 52.2 (2002): 173–89.

Dragadze, Tamara. "Self-Determination and the Politics of Exclusion." *Ethnic and Racial Studies* 19.2 (1996): 341–51.

Evans, Tony. "Citizenship and Human Rights in the Age of Globalization." *Alternatives: Social Transformation and Humane Governance* 25.4 (2000): 415.

Flere, Sergej. "Human Rights and the Ideology of Capitalist Globalization: A View from Slovenia." *Monthly Review* 52.8 (2001): 52–59.

Gomez, Mario. "Sri Lanka's New Human Rights Commission." *Human Rights Quarterly* 20 (1998): 281–302.

Gray, Paul. "Nailed Palms and the Eyes of Gods: Michael Ondaatje's *Anil's Ghost* Is a Stark Successor to *The English Patient*". Rev. of *Anil's Ghost*, by Michael Ondaatje. *Time* 1 May 2000: 75.

Ignatieff, Michael. *Human Rights as Politics and Idolatry*. Princeton: Princeton UP, 2001.

LeClair, Tom. "The Sri Lankan Patients." Rev. of *Anil's Ghost*, by Michael Ondaatje. *The Nation* 19 June 2000: 31.

Makinda, Samuel M. "Human Rights, Humanitarianism, and Transformation in the Global Community." *Global Governance* 7.3 (2001): 343–62.

Monshipouri, Mahmood, and Claude E. Welch. "The Search for International Human Rights and Justice: Coming to Terms with the New Global Realities." *Human Rights Quarterly* 23 (2001): 370–401.

Ondaatje, Michael. *Anil's Ghost*. New York: Knopf, 2000.

Robinson, Mary. "Human Rights at the Dawn of the 21st Century." *Human Rights Quarterly* 15 (1993): 629–39.

Rosemont, Henry Jr. "Why Take Rights Seriously? A Confucian Critique." *Human Rights and the World's Religions*. Ed. Leroy S. Rouner. Notre Dame: U of Notre Dame P, 1988. 167–82.

Schaeffer, Robert K. *Understanding Globalization: The Social Consequences of Political, Economic, and Environmental Change.* New York: Rowman & Littlefield, 1997.

Schrage, Elliot, and Anthony Ewing. "Engaging the Private Sector." *Forum for Applied Research and Public Policy* 14 (1999): 44–51.

Silbey, Susan S. "'Let Them Eat Cake': Globalization, Postmodern Colonialism, and the Possibilities of Justice." *Law and Society Review* 31.2 (1997): 207–35.

Taylor, Charles. "A World Consensus on Human Rights?" *Dissent* (1996): 15–21.

Tuijl, Peter van. "NGOs and Human Rights: Sources of Justice and Democracy." *Journal of International Affairs* 52.2 (1999): 493–512.

Ariel 37:1 (Jan 2006)
5-26.

# In Defense of *Anil's Ghost*
## Chelva Kanaganayakam

The echoes of Sir Philip Sidney and Percy Bysshe Shelley that my title invokes are, in some senses, deliberate, since there are striking similarities between the situations in which *The Defence of Poesie* (1595) and *A Defence of Poetry* (1821, published 1840) were written and the complex political and literary backdrop that frames Michael Ondaatje's *Anil's Ghost* (2000). Sidney's argument offers a taxonomy of the arts and sciences in order to establish the supremacy of poetry. The abstraction of poetry is turned into a sign of strength as Sidney discusses the limitations of disciplines that merely document and quantify. Shelley's essay, written more than two centuries later, traverses similar ground by exalting the imaginative strength of poetry without jettisoning its social and moral function. Both were written during times of heightened political activity when there were several attempts to reiterate the significance of the arts. Sidney and Shelley assert that poets may well rely on vision and emotion, but they remain, to use Shelley's famous phrasing, "unacknowledged legislators of the world." In a general sense, the opposition between a socially conscious literature and a form of art that is aesthetically complete but distanced from social or political realities has been the subject of recurrent debates, including the well-known exchange between Salvador Lopez and Gabriel Garcia Villa concerning the role and significance of literature in the Philippines.[1]

*Anil's Ghost* compels a reopening of the debate over literature's relation to politics through its overt preoccupation with a complex political backdrop, as well as a carefully articulated ambivalence about its project. Ondaatje's decision to write a so-called political novel is obviously a deliberate one, and the critical responses to it have been unexpectedly diverse. The multiple analyses advanced by critics have specific implications for the evaluation of Sri Lankan fiction in particular and for postcolonial literatures in general. Over the last decade, Sri Lankan

5

writing has been, for the most part, driven by politics, and Ondaatje's intervention needs to be seen as a significant attempt to champion a particular stance. This paper argues that, far from being biased, orientalist or otherwise irresponsible, Ondaatje's novel charts new territory by establishing a careful balance between political engagement and aesthetic distance.

That said, it can be argued that there is no real urgency to defend Ondaatje's *Anil's Ghost*. Despite its political content and its provocative subject matter, it did not invite the kind of censorship and public outcry occasioned by the works of Salman Rushdie. It did not even arouse the kind of controversy that Shyam Selvadurai's *Funny Boy* did.[2] In fact, the opposite is true. For almost a whole year the novel was on bestseller lists in Canada. And the list of awards it gathered is impressive. Within a matter of months it received several prizes, including the Governor-General's award, the Prix Medicis for foreign literature, and the Kiriyama Pacific Rim Book Prize; it was also the co-recipient of the prestigious Giller Prize. In a representative and clearly laudatory review, Silvia Albertazzi concludes that in this novel the author wants "to restate his commitment to pacifism and his denouncement of the brutality of war," a comment that establishes the text as benign and wholly appropriate (74). This defense, then, is of a particular kind in that this article addresses the concerns of "local" or Sri Lankan-born diasporic critics who see the novel as a shameless act of appropriation, essentialism, distortion or blatant prejudice. The fact that the Sri Lankan critics do not have a consensus about why the novel's flawed adds to the complexity of the problem.[3] The dichotomous situation caused by the praise heaped on the novel by the West makes the defense relevant, even urgent to some degree. One does not wish to privilege Sri Lankan critics and imply that their perspective is somehow more significant than that of Western critics, but the fact that the Sri Lankan response is generally negative raises a number of questions about critical practice, readership, and the literary marketplace.

Praise from the West, particularly for books that fall within the general rubric of "South Asian literature," seems fated to invite hostile opposition as well. Arundhati Roy's *The God of Small Things* is an example

6

of a work that elicited very different kinds of response in the West and the East, some very laudatory and others decidedly critical. The manner in which the strengths and weaknesses of such novels get configured points to significant differences in expectations among readers. *Anil's Ghost* appears to have prompted such a duality as well. The dichotomy in critical reception is not simply a matter of stylistics or narrative. Such a response was perhaps true of *The English Patient*, which was, in stylistic and formal terms, more typical of the Ondaatje aesthetic mode that appeals to some and irritates others. With *Anil's Ghost* the situation is arguably more complex, and the objective of this article is to raise several questions about the assumptions and practices that form the backdrop to this lack of consensus.

At the most obvious level, the duality of responses has to do with the relation between the ostensible subject matter and the literary marketplace itself. In this instance it refers to the kinds of circumstances that make it possible for the South Asian novel to find a huge readership in the West. In short, the argument would be that if the novel gave the West what it wanted to read, the success of the novel would be assured. An extension of the argument would be that the West has imagined a Sri Lanka, which the novel then corroborates. In turn exotic and savage in its description of local conditions, the novel, according to this reading, offers the West a biased representation of the Third World. In Edward Said's terms, the novel is part of a discourse that orientalizes Sri Lanka. The conviction that novelists are complicit in promoting a vision of the East for Western consumption also has the effect of forcing a closer scrutiny of the novel in the Third World by critics who are in a position to test the claims of the novel through comparative or "nativist" eyes. They are also aware, quite often, of the complexity of the political and social context that is evoked in the text. The divide between the two critical schools is not necessarily a spatial one, but the fundamental duality in critical reception remains intact. In other words, the comparative or nativist response would provide a corrective to the euphoria of the novel's success in the West. If the West finds in the novel a reassuring affirmation of an imagined nation, the Third World is dismayed by the novel's refusal to engage with the "realities" of the country.

7

As I mentioned early on, *Anil's Ghost* is by no means alone in eliciting both praise and condemnation. The last few decades have been the golden age for postcolonial writers and several of those who achieved tremendous praise in the West have confronted this ambivalence. *Anil's Ghost*, however, has a particular significance. Ondaatje's *Running in the Family* was seen as a semi-autobiographical about a family. It did not remain unscathed as critics faulted it for various reasons, and even his brother Christopher Ondaatje had reason to express some measure of reservation about its portrayal of family history.[4] On the whole, the personal nature of the narrative redeemed it. *The English Patient* was seen as the quintessential diasporic novel, and its internationalism was, given the displacement of the author, predictable. A more recent book of poems entitled *Handwriting* included disturbing political elements, but not enough to cause concern among the critics. *Anil's Ghost* is much more problematic in its subject matter and narrative stance. The novel is about the political events that sharpened animosities in Sri Lanka in the 1980s, and that specific focus, I would argue, makes it far less immune to the kinds of expectations that politically engaged postcolonial literature appears to generate.

Ondaatje's failure to satisfy many local Sri Lankan readers is also based implicitly on the premise that novels such as *Anil's Ghost* have the effect of producing meaning. Such novels become the window to the outside world, but they do more than reveal or reflect local reality. Their power lies in their capacity to generate meaning. It has been said anecdotally that one lawyer in Toronto used the novel as a form of judicial notice in defining the backdrop to his client's case. Presumably, the lawyer's decision to cite the novel as evidence was based at least partially on the premise that the judge would have read the novel and been aware of its relation to the conditions in the country. In such instances the novel is not simply a representation of the real. It is real to the extent that its accuracy cannot reasonably be questioned. In this case, the novel takes on the status of a document whose representation is sufficiently authentic to be considered a form of evidence.

The issue, from a postcolonial perspective, then, becomes one of trying to define an adequate critical stance to read or explicate the

8

novel. If the novel adopts a "public" persona, then its validity is that of allegory, in Fredric Jameson's sense of the term.[5] Unlike *Running in the Family*, this novel almost announces its allegorical stance by saying that what happens in one village may well happen in another. Further, the fact that the novel begins outside Sri Lanka tends to reinforce its allegorical and universal element. Whatever problems one has with Jameson's statement of the postcolonial project, the idea of allegory as a staple feature of postcolonial writing has remained with some measure of stubbornness. *Anil's Ghost* would be seen as an attempt to present in metaphoric form the turmoil of the country. By including an author's note that highlights the political backdrop involving the insurgents, separatists and the government, Ondaatje deliberately forges the connection with "real" conditions before insisting on the fictive aspect of his novel.[6] Even a cursory reading of the "Acknowledgments" at the end would indicate that the author's research was comprehensive and thorough.

Regardless of what the author/narrator claims, at one end of the spectrum is the critic who chooses to downplay the specific political elements of the novel. The novel, from this angle, belongs to a global tradition of writing and what is at stake is the formal aspect of the text. A second category claims the need for accuracy through an interrogation of the prior text that allegory assumes, and by shifting the focus of this critique from metaphor to metonymy. For critics who are committed to this approach, the history of conflict occupies an unambiguous space and what is important for the reader is to discern how close the novel gets to a sense of truth. The benchmark here is accuracy. Often, what tends to dominate this methodology is the position that Terry Eagleton calls a "normative illusion" that refuses to see the object for what it is. Eagleton adds that this approach "'corrects' [the novel] against an independent pre-existent model of which the empirical text is an imperfect copy.... The typical gesture of normative criticism is to inscribe a 'could do better' in the text's margin" (11).

In some ways, these are different approaches that we often encounter in postcolonial criticism. Allegory of a particular kind offers some measure of distance, but it can also be capable of radicalism, depending

9

on how it is structured. A purely formal approach escapes the difficulties of context and tradition, and is particularly useful when dealing with transnational writers who need to be accommodated in national literary histories or when the target readers are not likely to be informed about local conditions. A more context-based approach works with texts that insist on the reader's awareness of local conditions. Topicality is the mainstay of such works.

Depending on who reads *Anil's Ghost* and where, any one of these approaches is likely to be adopted. Typically, the reviews that appeared in the *New York Times on the Web, Queen's Quarterly* or *Maclean's Magazine* appear to underscore the formal aspect, and in the process give the mantle of universalism or internationalism to the novel. Tod Hoffman, in his review, remarks that "Ondaatje's use of language is, it goes without saying, superb. His greatness lies in combining the poet's gift for word selection and rhythm with the novelist's sense of plot" (450). The *Maclean's* review gives priority to Ondaatje as an international writer first and a Canadian writer second. Writes Brian Johnson, "Ondaatje is our most international author. Quintessentially Canadian, his fiction deciphers identity and bleeds through borders" (67). Implicit here are certain assumptions about identity and nationality. Brenda Glover's essay appears to move in the direction of an allegorical reading, where the details of the novel, while important in themselves, also imply a larger process at work. "In each of his novels," says Glover, "Ondaatje creates an extreme situation with a small cast of central characters, through whom he is able to explore the dynamics of displacement, isolation and alienation, as well as strategies for survival" (79). Under this rubric the novel charts a personal quest, and the political context becomes secondary. Glover's assessment is not very different from Heike Härting's conclusion that "*Anil's Ghost* represents and ... regulates diasporic identity through both the construction of Anil as a nomadic subject and its narrative's modernist configuration of history" (50).

It would be simplistic to assume that essays by Western critics have not paid attention to the political events recorded in the text. But there are differences that need to be noted as well. Margaret Scanlan, for example, refers to Bosnia, Ireland, and Guatemala, and adds "one ob-

10

vious difference, however, between Sri Lanka and these other trouble spots, at least for North American readers, is its unfamiliarity" (303). Nonetheless, she claims that Ondaatje's "distinctive achievement in *Anil's Ghost* is to create a narrative structure that replicates the experience of terror" (302). But her main concern is with the function of "abrupt breaks in time" that postmodern novelists use in order to move away from traditional linear narratives (303). Antoinette Burton is equally preoccupied with history and historiography, although her intention is to show how the novel tests the limits of historical narrative.[7] After a comprehensive and valuable explication of the novel, Paul Brians concludes with a reference to Ananda and the boy who reaches out to him: "such small gestures of compassion are all the book offers as counterbalance to the grotesque cruelty all around; but in the long run the concern of one human being for another is the only hope we have" (193).[8] All these commentaries have much to offer, but they do not, for the most part, interrogate the way in which the novel projects the political violence in Sri Lanka.

For the purpose of this article, the second category of criticism is crucial, since the articles that belong to it are ones that are critical of the novel for what they deem an inadequate portrayal of local conditions. And, this is precisely where the critical response becomes complex and problematic. The analysis of three Sri Lankan critics, all living and teaching in the West, demonstrates not only the multiplicity of critical response but also the difficulties inherent in finding a consensus among critics who adopt a similar approach. The three Sri Lankan critics whose work is looked at here are all unhappy with the novel's representation of Sri Lanka, but for very different reasons. Their approaches are remarkably similar, but they arrive at very different conclusions concerning the novel's referential claims. The issue, then, is not so much about methodology as it is about the novel's vulnerability when the depiction of political conflict becomes an overarching concern in literary practice.

The first example is a long review by Ranjini Mendis who offers a comprehensive reading of the novel. Having drawn attention to Ondaatje's failure to counter "the stereotype of the savage, violent South Asian"

· 11

122

(11), she goes on to conclude that "the absence of detail in historical context, however, works against an informed reading, leaving just a general impression of self-destructive violence as the major thread of the novel" (9). Mendis's article stresses the significance of historically informed reading. The position is clearly comparative and mindful of authorial responsibility, of the critic's task and of the urgency of post-colonial issues. She too, working in the West, is aligned with Ondaatje's status as a "native-alien" of sorts, but her critique underscores the "native" element, which in her view the novel fails to capture. In other words, Mendis provides an analysis of the local situation against which the novel needs to be appraised. At the outset of the review, Mendis sets up her interpretation of local conditions. Having made the assertion about what needs emphasis, she goes on to demonstrate that the novel does not measure up. The intention here is not to take issue with the historical and political reading espoused by Mendis. But I would like to raise what appears to be an interesting problematic that arises out of such a stance. Her position is clear. Says Mendis:

> In the last two decades, 'Liberation Tigers of Tamil Eelam,' a guerilla organization ironically called 'Freedom Fighters,' has been attacking Sri Lanka's socialist-democratic Sinhalese government and civilian population. Funded by Tamil immigrants in Western countries ('Terrorism funds'), their goal is to cripple the power base and establish a separate homeland of nearly half the island for the 12% who are Tamil. (8)

Mendis is troubled by the fact that the novel offers a flawed view of the nation by stressing the atrocities of the government while ignoring the crimes of the Tamil terrorists. Again, to quote from the review, "Ceylon Tamils, with a different history from the Indian Tamils brought to Ceylon by the British for tea plucking, have fought for self-government and to move further south in the island ever since the early recorded history of Ceylon" (8). This is an authoritative position, offered not as historiography but as history. There is no ambivalence, no sense of contingency in her statement, and it is from this position that the partial truths and relativism of the novel are judged. In short, Mendis

12

maintains that the novel's perspective is a biased one that implicitly exonerates the Tamil Tigers while blaming the Sinhalese government.

In contrast, Qadri Ismail writes a polemical essay in which he maintains from the very beginning that some form of social commitment is a *sine qua non* for the novelist. Having thus established his critical standpoint, he then goes on to analyze the novel in some depth. He points to several "errors" in the text—a shortcoming that clearly weakens the referential veracity of the novel. His conclusions are totally unequivocal: "When all the significant actants in a story about Sri Lanka are Sinhala, when in addition all the place names noticed by the text when it sees the National Atlas of Sri Lanka are Sinhala ones, and when the novel's only list of the Sri Lankans disappeared contain exclusively Sinhala names, its country begins to seem very like that of Sinhala nationalism" (39, 41, 24). In a position that is the very opposite of Mendis, Ismail claims that in the novel "The JVP ... is portrayed as human; the LTTE [Tigers] in contrast, as inhuman terrorists, killers of children" (26). Ondaatje's bias in the novel, according to Ismail, is clearly in favor of a monolithic Sri Lanka in which the minority groups are irrelevant: "Sri Lankan history, to this text, is Sinhala and Buddhist history. A more humane history than we are used to hearing, yes; but not a multi-ethnic history, either. We now know whose side this novel is on" (27). In short, for Mendis, the novel is clearly anti-Sinhalese, and for Ismail the novel is blatantly against all minority groups and decidedly pro-Sinhalese.

A third position is established by Kanishka Goonewardena, who faults the novel for failing to capture the "truth of history." Clearly unhappy with statements such as "the reason for war was war," Goonewardena argues "beyond that transcendental tautology, anyhow, no character in the novel offers an insight into the condition of the human condition in war-torn Sri Lanka" (43). The universalist dimension of the novel—evident in references to the brutality in Guatemala, for example—and the refusal to engage directly with the origins and history of the violence in Sri Lanka are, for Goonewardena, both inadequate and potentially misleading. Goonewardena writes: "The decision to write an apolitical novel set in the tragic situation of Sri Lanka is profoundly

13

political" (43). In short, Goonewardena does not say that the novel is being partial by locating itself on one side or the other; instead, he maintains, that the author has a responsibility to go beyond effects to focus on causes, and to engage with the origins of the conflict. The approach here is broadly Marxist, and the critic is wary of a text that is inadequately informed about the historical context. Goonewardena is thus less concerned with the political bias of the novel than with the aestheticism that masquerades as universalism while it simultaneously moves away from the tragic realities of the country.

The three critics write forcefully, even authoritatively, about a situation in which their expertise is a given. However, the very fact that they adopt three decidedly different and contrasting positions also points to significant concerns about Sri Lankan literature and its current role. The lack of consensus among the three critics is also a salutary reminder to the reader that "objectivity" might well be an impossible ideal. In the process of insisting on authorial accountability, I would suggest that the critics themselves may have unwittingly foregrounded their own subjective positions. The last twenty years have been crucial ones for Sri Lanka as the country has undergone a number of significant political changes. This has also been a period of intense literary activity in which a number of authors, including Jean Arasanayagam, Yasmine Gooneratne, Romesh Gunesekera, Chandani Lokuge, Ashley Halpe, Carl Muller, Shyam Selvadurai, Rajiva Wijesinha and Rienzi Crusz have produced a body of varied and often controversial work. Their texts are certainly not politically neutral and regardless of whether they are "local" or diasporic, they shape the way the island is seen by the region and the West. Within this framework, no text is inconsequential, and certainly a novel by Ondaatje that explicitly addresses the political situation cannot be taken only as artifice or allegory. Arasanayagam, for example, is predominantly mimetic while Wijesinha is stubbornly allegorical. Importantly, Ondaatje locates himself somewhere in the middle, thereby frustrating the Sri Lankan critics who find the portrayal of Sri Lanka flawed.

It is interesting that Ondaatje himself has offered at least three different perspectives about the novel. In his acceptance speech for the

14

Governor General's Award, he spoke of reconciliation and forgiveness. "'Pacifism,' 'reconciliation,' 'forgiveness,' are easily mocked words," says Ondaatje, "but only these principles will save us" (2). More importantly, in an interview he deflects the attention away from himself and toward individuals, their private demons and their moments of apprehension that matter to him as a writer claiming, "it isn't a statement about the war, as though this is the 'true and only story.' It's my individual take on four or five characters, a personal tunneling into it" (qtd. in Jaggi 6). It is of significance that the novel itself ends on a note of optimism and rejuvenation with the image of Ananda performing the Netra Mangala ceremony, thereby symbolically suggesting a new beginning. Similarly, the novel also begins with a prefatory note in which the author—"M.O."—comments that in the country the war is going on in a different form that the one depicted in the text. The narrator articulates yet another voice that does not always coincide with the author's opinions. I suggest that these are three different positions espoused by Ondaatje and his narrator in a deliberate gesture that maintains a measure of ambivalence. The shift from one register of emotion to another is a purposful one, since the novel reveals a deep-seated anxiety about the process of telling the tale. It is hardly possible to read the novel without an awareness of all three voices, not to mention the indeterminacy of the narrative mode. Any appraisal of the novel must be aware that while all three perspectives at times bleed into one another, they also occupy distinct spaces.[9]

The framing of the text, then, is very ambivalent. While Ondaatje explicates what he wants to do and what he does not want to attempt, the novel at times subversively contradicts him. An example of this can be found in the detailed description of a man being flung out of a moving train in ways that suggest a more personal and self-referential text was not outside Ondaatje's purview. This particular episode eschews all but a minimum of mimetic details, but it does so in a manner that reveals a shadow text that the author chooses not to write. For the critic who wants to see in the text a direct engagement with empirical realities, it is precisely this shadow text, with all its potential for conventional realism, that would have salvaged the novel.[10]

15

Given the multiplicity and complexity of political preoccupations, the novel does what it sets out to do, though there is an inevitable necessity about the way in which it is done. Critical practice might well occupy oppositional stances, but the text itself demonstrates the need for a productive middle ground. *Anil's Ghost* enacts a realization that the personal, the political, and the social are intertwined in ways that problematize clear ethnic, religious, or ideological categories. The novel insists on its artifice, not because life does not matter, but because it is the capacity of art to transform reality that allows for the perception of intersections. Anil's meeting with the old servant at the beginning of the novel is a case in point. Intertextually, the meeting recalls a poem in *Handwriting* that describes the poet's deep sense of guilt at having abandoned a servant. In the novel, the similar episode underscores the deep emotional bond that connects to potential antagonists, Anil, who is Sinhalese, and Lalitha, who is Tamil. For the two of them, ethnicity might not matter, but it certainly does to the granddaughter who works in a refugee camp in the North.

The novel is not autobiographical but it is intensely personal, and its quest is not for realism but rather for truth. The archetypal quest narrative, underlined by its modern counterpart the detective story, provides the structural basis for the novel. However, what drives the text is Ondaatje's own sense of grief, as is evident in the book of poems entitled *Handwriting*, and developed further in the novel. Speaking about what appealed to him in his novel, Ondaatje says: "I was thinking what do I like most about *Anil's Ghost*? It was a scene when Gamini doesn't want to embrace Sarath's wife because she'd discover how thin he is. For me, that was a heartbreaking moment, light years away from the official stories" (7). Memory does not constitute a dominant motif in the novel, but that is what drives the text and determines its form and content. The novel must then "invent" and in the process create a mask that would become a gateway to truth. It is the process by which Ananda, tormented by the death of his wife, deliberately constructs a different identity for "Sailor," thereby subverting the mode of detection, but reaching out to a truth that for him has greater significance. At this point, Anil, whose quest is framed by total faith in scientific rational-

16

ity, recognizes the metamorphosis of which art is capable: "[Ananda] had been standing outside, listening to them speaking in English in the courtyard. But now he faced her, not knowing that the tears were partly for him. Or, that she realized the face was in no way a portrait of Sailor but showed a calm Ananda had known in his wife, a peacefulness he wanted for any victim" (187). By the same token, Palipana begins to "see" when his rational, scientific mode fails him together with his eyes. It could be argued that this is a relativist position, a kind of indeterminacy that sidesteps the turbulence of the present. If that kind of ambivalence smacks of a lack of commitment, it is also likely that Ondaatje's identity may not coincide with that of the narrator.

Among the characters in the novel, Anil, Palipana and Ananda may well be considered artist-figures whose roles offer a metafictional commentary on the text. All three have their own convictions about (re)creating the identity of Sailor. They work together and their varied approaches complement each other, but each espouses different perspectives. Anil occupies one end with her faith in scientific rationality and Palipana occupies the other with his belief in intuition. If, in the end, no position is privileged, it can also be interpreted as Ondaatje's reticence to endorse any single ideological position.

Graham Huggan points out in a discussion of Janette Turner Hospital's *The Ivory Swing* and Yvon Rivard's *Les silences du corbeau* that the quest novel, with some modifications, works admirably well within a general discourse of orientalism.[11] *Anil's Ghost* is clearly a quest novel and its plot line can be read in a manner that reinforces an orientalist perspective. If this novel veers away from such a position and avoids anthropologizing the nation, it is because it chooses to locate itself as a reflective work rather than an authoritative one. There is in the novel a genuine engagement with the dangers of false historiography and with the inability to arrive at a definitive position. The words that Lakma engraves in stone before Palipana dies are a version of the truth that will endure. But they remain 'partial truths,' valid only in so far as a particular mode of communication is privileged. As a novel that self-consciously questions the perspectives it offers, it could not have espoused a position in unequivocal terms. It is hardly an accident that Palipana,

17

the renowned epigraphist, who succeeded in claiming agency from colonial historians, begins to see the limitations of a nationalist historiography. He then "invents" the truth in a move that is described by the narrator as "not a false step but the step to another reality, the last stage of a long, truthful dance" (81). And the narrator adds a comment that is crucial to the novel as a whole: "A forgery by a master always meant much more than mischief, it meant scorn" (82).

When Anil first visits Palipana in the grove, he feels her arm to get a sense of her person. A particular kind of logic is at work here, and Anil is impressed by the scientific rigor of the man who requires a specific kind of objectivity. The reader is at the same time reminded of the allusion to the Biblical story of Abraham and his two sons Esau and Jacob, and the duplicity practiced by his wife Rebekah to ensure that one son is privileged over the other. The two narratives intersect to subvert the ostensible purpose of the scene. If Palipana serves the purpose of questioning nationalist and official versions of history, the allusion insists that Palipana himself is treated with a degree of irony.

It is equally important to remember that the political events in Sri Lanka during the last few years have borne out the risks of easy generalizations. In a country faced with the violence of ethnic strife, it has become increasingly clear that positions of power change, and agency shifts in curious ways, not to mention that categories that were shown to be homogenous have proved to be otherwise. Postcolonial authors, particularly in nations such as Sri Lanka, are confronted with the anxiety of uncertainty and are aware that positions that were once relatively straightforward have become complex.[12]

A comprehensive reading of the novel is not the objective of this article. Rather, the idea is to position Ondaatje's novel as one that is neither aesthetically distanced nor overtly tendentious. That it is a paradoxical position, particularly in a South Asian context, hardly needs emphasis, although it is important to recognize the inevitability of such a standpoint. For writers like Ondaatje there is often no real choice about what they write or how they write. Regardless of the limitations of their perspective, it is also important to acknowledge that the myth of homogeneity can hardly be asserted in most nation states. There can be no

18

unified reading of the nation, any more than a unified reading of a text. Ondaatje is situated as a Sri Lankan-Canadian and therefore an insider whose ancestral memories go back to the time of Dutch rule. However, as a Burgher who left the country in the 1960s he is an outsider to the ethnic conflict between the Sinhalese and the Tamils.

A historically informed position is a necessity for the postcolonial critic. Having moved away from a critical tradition that removes itself from the context altogether, it would now be futile for the postcolonial critic to jettison the need for a nuanced awareness of local conditions. But to insist that the novel must validate a particular position is to reduce the text to an ideological construct. To look for what the text says or does not say from the perspective of the historian or sociologist is also to deny the literariness of a novel. For the critic to wear the mantle of historian or sociologist can be risky, counterproductive, or even unfair, particularly when the effect is to tell both the reader and the author what merits attention. To make this claim is not to revert to a formalist position that subordinates political and social realities to aesthetic ones. Such distancing is likely to be equally hegemonic even when it masquerades as art. A culturally and politically sensitive reading fills the gaps, identifies connections that are made or deliberately suppressed, but in no way ignores the artifice of the novel. It is possible to look for and celebrate books that offer a strong and unequivocal message. And if we look hard enough we are likely to find one whose subjective position coincides with our own. But such texts do not test the limits of language, they do not reveal the struggle of the author to embellish the everyday with invention, they do not challenge the critic to question his or her own biases, and often, they do not endure. Responsible critics play a crucial role in positioning texts, for only they would know where realism ends and artifice begins. The critic's task, then, is to distinguish between realism and artifice in order to elucidate their functions rather than conflate them.

I do believe that it can be difficult to defend the realism of *Anil's Ghost*. The descriptions of landscapes, buildings and even characters do not convince the reader of mimetic accuracy. In fact Ismail documents several errors that have found their way into the novel.[13] The complex-

19

ity of the political situation may well be outside the reach of the novel. However, for critics to say that the novel is wrong-headed, misinformed or naïve is to miss the point that mimetic representation is not the text's primary aim. For the critic who brings to the novel a complex historical consciousness the challenge is to grant the text its autonomy, to appraise the novel within the terms it sets out for itself rather than from a position that reflects the critic's own subjective stance. Surely, the postcolonial critic should not wish to colonize the postcolonial novel.

Among the many approaches to the issue of authenticity is one that looks at vernacular literatures and their response to the events that form the backdrop to the novel. At least in Sri Lankan Tamil literature the response has been one that provides a curious perspective. In this corpus, *it is not often that one encounters the kind of political analysis that one would normally expect in a vernacular text.* The displacement caused by political strife might well be shown from the perspective of an old man who can no longer understand why his daughter-in-law has suddenly become hostile. A text might describe the bewilderment of a farmer who is told that he must move to make way for the security forces and does not quite understand who would attend to his plot of land. It is true that vernacular literatures have also been capable of profound mimetic accuracy and political analysis, but that is not necessarily the norm. In general vernacular writing tends to focus on effects rather than causes, while literature in English often favors abstraction. It can be argued that a novel like *Anil's Ghost* is difficult to write in the vernacular, and that it is also the strength of writing in English to produce such works.

That said, *Anil's Ghost* invites attention to its political engagement. It is, at some level, a rewriting of *Running in the Family*. The time period is approximately the same, and here again is an exiled subject who is returning to the home country after fifteen years. What the earlier work failed to do, this novel attempts, but on its own terms. *Anil's Ghost* offers political engagement without taking sides, and without the realism of mimetic detail. The earlier text pays little attention the insurgency of 1971, since its objective was to foreground the history of a family. *Anil's Ghost* is steeped in politics, but decides to problematize the events it painstakingly describes.

20

The text does, however, embody a deliberately fragmentary style that invites the kind of criticism that has been leveled against it. The novel's configuration of time and space, its gradual filling-in of information, and its micro-narratives that involve several characters, invite a particular kind of criticism. It must be noted, however, that in the micro-narrative that occurs on the train there is the nucleus of a plot, which, even in the hands of a second-rate novelist, could well become the structure of a novel. The story of Lakma, the girl who looks after Palipana, or even the story of Ananda would lend itself very easily to a plot that would lead to a kind of realism. The choice to write a different kind of novel, then, is deliberate.

One of the criticisms is that the novel insists on an allegorical dimension. What happens in one place happens everywhere. Guatemala is the same as Sri Lanka. Goonewardena expresses disappointment with such universalism. Alternatively, it can be asserted that what we have here is not the kind of allegory to which Jameson refers. *Anil's Ghost* is particularly specific about its local concern. The disgrace of a specific person, and the hunt for a specific victim are not peripheral to the narrative. These are not entirely allegorical pursuits. If Anil or Sarath at some stage do not see distinctions between the specific and the general, that does not necessarily deny the specificity of the quest. Individual characters, even minor ones like the old servant who appears at the beginning, do matter in the novel.

In structural terms, the novel is quite straightforward. The objective is to detect and unravel the identity of a murdered person. When that fails, we have a situation in which the form works against content. The identity of Sailor is established at the end, but it leads to no resolution, no *denouement*. It is thus no more than an aside. A whole epistemology is brought into question when the novel's form works against content. Anil, with all her faith in a western way of knowing, is made to understand that not only is rationality sometimes futile, it is also destructive. Sarath dies because of her insistence. He will be her ghost, her shadow. In fact, as the text says at the end, both Ananda and Anil carry within them Sarath's ghost.

And this is where the entire episode involving Palipana becomes

21

significant. Palipana is, in some ways, Senarat Paranavitana's *doppel-ganger*.[14] As readers, we are made to be aware of the intersection of fact and fiction. Palipana is accused of forgery. His is the power of artifice. If his forgery implies scorn, it is the scorn for a particular kind of realism. His power of vision is in direct proportion to his loss of sight. He exemplifies the paradox of existence: you see best when you are not involved any more. His forgery must be seen as imitation and as forging. In the process of distorting he also forges—creates anew—a reality that needs to be recognized as legitimate.

In both Mendis and Ismail, there is a deep concern with official narratives. And that is precisely what Palipana acknowledges and later abandons. Official histories are not dismissed in the process, but they too are seen as textual constructs, often driven by ideology. Palipana is also treated with some measure of irony, but that whole section in the grove reveals that what we know is less important than the artifice, which results from "facts." By the same token, one needs to look carefully at Ananda—a name that recalls the chief disciple of Buddha. He too recognizes the limitations of rationality. As he recreates Sailor in the image of his wife, he privileges metaphor over simile and creates a dichotomy between signifier and signified. At the end Sailor might remain a shadowy presence, but the quest certainly does not fail.

The whole episode involving the *Walawe* to which Anil, Ananda and Sarath retire is in fact deeply problematic. Despite the plausible and rational reasons that are given for this choice, the fact remains that the entire episode can only be a staging of artifice. The entire image is preposterous in realistic terms. One needs to be completely ignorant of tropical jungles in order to accept the realism of that section. But that is also precisely the point. The metaphor is meant to accommodate opposites. The rational is tempted by the instinctual while the intuitive is captivated by the rational. Both succeed, in different ways, at different moments. The sheer artifice of the episode forces the recognition of opposites and contradictions, both of which are important markers in the novel.

It is possible to contend that the diasporic novel is at its best when it works with metaphor rather than metonymy. In practice, however,

22

the two often complement each other in significant ways. To confuse one with the other would be to misjudge the purpose of the text. *Anil's Ghost* is likely to remain flawed in its knowledge of the local scene. But its strength lies in its willingness to capture the contradictions without which a nuanced representation is hardly possible. The moral stance of the novel might well nudge the edges of elitism, but it is also an assertion of its commitment to a humanism that is cathartic. In relation to much that has been written about Sri Lanka in the recent past, by scholars and writers, this novel establishes its unique niche by demonstrating that if artifice takes liberties, it also has the capacity to hone perception and shape realities in ways that are profound. Ideological positions do matter, according to the novel, but more important is the human cost of conflict. By the same token, human misery, the text argues, cannot be decontextualized and aestheticized in universalist terms. Critics may well admire *Anil's Ghost* for its formal sophistication or critique it for its ideological position, but the novel, in the final analysis, defends its stance by establishing a sophisticated rapport between political engagement and aesthetic distance. Edward Said puts these ideas across admirably well:

> Texts have to be read as texts that were produced and live on in all of sorts of what I have called worldly ways. But this by no means excludes power, since on the contrary I have tried to show the insinuations, the imbrications of power into even the most recondite of studies. And lastly, most important, humanism is the only, and I would go so far as to say the final resistance we have against the inhuman practices and injustices that disfigure human history. (6)

*Anil's Ghost* does not jettison its commitment to represent ethnic strife and political violence, but it also insists that any engagement with the referential must recognize the discourse that determines what is said and how it is said.

**Notes**
1   For a comprehensive overview, see Lopez.

23

2  The combination of politics and gay sexuality in the novel did not find easy acceptance in Sri Lanka. During the first few years, the fact that the author did not launch his book in Sri Lanka was an indication of the hostility of the state.

3  I use the terms "Sri Lankan" and "local" in a very specific sense to underline the distinction between Western critics who have viewed the novel favorably and Sri Lankan born critics who are troubled by the politics of the novel. The fact that all three Sri Lankans referred to later live in the West does not alter the substance of the argument.

4  For instance, referring to the death of Lalla, Christopher Ondaatje writes: "In my brother's book, Lalla dies when she is carried off in the great Nuwara Eliya flood. It is a marvelous piece of literature and true to her zany character, but in fact she died of alcohol poisoning. ... That is a sadder and more depressing account than Michael's. Nor was there much charm in seeing that crazy and eccentric old woman sitting on a stool in the busy, chaotic Nuwara Eliya market bragging to bemused strangers about her son, my uncle, then the attorney general of the island" (50).

5  Jameson's well-known essay, which advances the argument that third world literatures tend to be national allegories, appeared in *Social Text* (1986).

6  In the note at the beginning, the author says: "From the mid-1980s to the early 1990s, Sri Lanka was in a crisis that involved three essential groups: the government, the antigovernment insurgents in the south and the separatist guerillas in the north. Both the insurgents and the separatists had declared war on the government. Eventually, in response, legal and illegal government squads were known to have been sent out to hunt down the separatists and the insurgents."

7  According to Burton, "if *Anil's Ghost* does not fully resolve the question of how to recuperate those stories that remain buried or are without a trace in the aftermath of history's violence, past and present—or does not do so to our satisfaction—it nonetheless offers one example of how and why histories are made at a time when the traditional *matériel* of History (whether archives or bones) is proving increasingly unavailable and reliable" (52).

8  It is also of some significance that Brians, in his annotated bibliography, refers to a review by Dinali Fernando, which he glosses as "a nitpicking review in a Colombo newspaper that catches Ondaatje in a few errors of local detail" (193).

9  An interesting comparison with *Anil's Ghost* would be Gunesekera's *Heaven's Edge*. The two texts reveal an "anxiety" about postcolonial realities, but while Gunesekera works at the level of allegory, Ondaatje straddles both allegory and realism.

10  Pages 31 and 32, which are not numbered, stand outside the main narrative, but its effect is to alert the reader to the kind of novel that the author chooses

24

not to write. The episode that is described is all the more horrific because it is not contextualized.

11 According to Huggan, "the formula is a familiar one: a restless Western writer takes temporary refuge in the East, hoping to find physical stimulation and/or spiritual enrichment there but discovering instead the limitations of his/her own culture, a culture to which he/she nonetheless returns, suitably 'enlightened' (46). With minor changes, the definition applies to Ondaatje's novel as well.

12 The intervention of Norway and several countries to bring about a negotiated peace in Sri Lanka amounts to a rethinking of national politics, and the more recent split among the Tigers is a reflection of primordial loyalties that transcend ethnic ones.

13 Unlike Rushdie, who deliberately inserts errors in his novels, Ondaatje in *Anil's Ghost* unwittingly overlooks them.

14 The well-known archaeologist Senarat Paranavitana, who also made claims about interlinear texts, is deliberately invoked through the character of Palipana. Goonatilake refers to "the case of the hallucinatory inscriptions which the well-known archaeologist Paranawithana saw in his dotage" (46).

## Works Cited

Albertazzi, Silvia. Rev. of *Anil's Ghost*. *Wasafiri* 32 (Autumn 2000): 74–75.

Brians, Paul. *Modern South Asian Literature in English*. Westport, CT: Greenwood Press, 2003.

Burton, Antoinette. "*Anil's Ghost* and the Ends of History." *J of Commonwealth Literature* 38.1 (2003): 39–56.

Eagleton, Terry. *Against the Grain: Essays 1975–1985*. London: Verso, 1986.

Glover, Brenda. "'Unanchored to the World': Displacement and Alienation in *Anil's Ghost* and the Prose of Michael Ondaatje." *CRNLE J* (2000): 75–80.

Goonatilake, Susantha. *Anthropologizing Sri Lanka*. Bloomington: Indiana UP, 2001.

Goonewardena, Kanishka. "*Anil's Ghost*: History/Politics/Ideology." Paper given at the Congress of the Humanities and Social Sciences, Université Laval, Quebec City, May 24–26, 2001.

Gunesekera, Romesh. *Heaven's Edge*. London: Bloomsbury, 2002.

Härting, Heike. "Diasporic Cross-Currents in Michael Ondaatje's *Anil's Ghost* and Anita Rau Badami's *The Hero's Walk*." *Studies in Canadian Literature* 28.1 (2003): 43–70.

Hoffman, Tod. "Seeing Ghosts." Rev. of *Anil's Ghost*. *Queen's Quarterly* 107.3 (2000): 446–51.

Huggan, Graham. "Orientalism Reconfirmed: Stereotypes of East-West Encounter in Janette Turner Hospital's *The Ivory Swing* and Yvon Rivard's *Les Silences du corbeau*. *Canadian Literature* 132 (Spring 1992): 44–56.

25

Ismail, Qadri. "A Flippant Gesture Towards Sri Lanka: A Review of Michael Ondaatje's *Anil's Ghost.*" *Pravada* 1.9–10 (2000): 24–29.

Jaggi, Maya. "Conversation with Michael Ondaatje." *Wasafiri* 32 (Autumn 2000): 5–11.

Jameson, Fredric. "Third-World Literature in the Era of Multinational Capitalism." *Social Text* 15 (Fall 1986): 65–88.

Johnson, Brian. "Review." *Maclean's Magazine* 18 Dec. 2000: 67.

Lopez, Salvador P. *Literature and Society: Essays and Letters.* Manila: University Publishing, 1940.

Mendis, Ranjini. Rev. *Anil's Ghost. Chimo* (Fall 2000): 7–12.

Ondaatje, Christopher. *The Man-Eater of Punanai.* Toronto: Harper Collins, 1993.

———. *Running in the Family.* Toronto: McClelland & Stewart, 1982.

———. *Handwriting.* Toronto: McClelland & Stewart, 1998.

———. *The English Patient.* Toronto: McClelland & Stewart, 1992.

———. *Anil's Ghost.* Toronto: McClelland & Stewart, 2000.

———. "Acceptance Speech." *The Globe and Mail* 15 Nov. 2000: C2.

Roy, Arundhati. *The God of Small Things.* Toronto: Random, 1997.

Said, Edward. "A Window on the World." *The Guardian* 2 Aug. 2003: 4–6.

Scanlan, Margaret. "*Anil's Ghost* and Terrorism's Time." *Studies in the Novel* 36.3 (2004): 302–317.

Selvadurai, Shyam. *Funny Boy.* Toronto: McClelland & Stewart, 1994.

26

# THE ✦ INDEPENDENT

# The Cat's Table, By Michael Ondaatje

Reviewed by Roma Tearne

Friday, 26 August 2011

The last time Michael Ondaatje visited Sri Lanka in a novel was in 2000 with Anil's Ghost where, through a series of fragmented narratives, he presented a story of waste in a time of war. Now he returns. Only on this occasion it is not modern Sri Lanka with which he deals, but the lost and mythical island called Ceylon, a country as foreign as the past, and as extinct as the dinosaur. Ondaatje is both poet and novelist and his use of English is elegant and beautiful. He writes, not in the worn-out clichés that are current in Sri Lanka, but with a feel for an international language that post-Ceylonese nationalism tried hard to strip from the education system of a whole generation.

The Cat's Table tells the story of an 11-year-old boy, Michael, on a voyage from the former Crown Colony of Ceylon to England in the 1950s. Like VS Naipaul in The Enigma of Arrival, Ondaatje combines fiction with autobiography. It is an engaging device and hardly needs the author's warning that it provides only "the colouring and location of memoir". We understand perfectly the play between fact and fiction.

As in Anil's Ghost, The Cat's Table employs a deceptively light touch, hiding a carefully constructed and tender hymn to the enigma of journey. Indeed, both the arrival and Michael's subsequent life are coloured forever by the experiences of those 21 days at sea.

The novel opens when Michael, along with two other boys, Cassius and Ramadhin, are let loose on a ship, surrounded by a group of eccentric adults and with no proper parental care. They are destined for England. The description of Michael's pre-departure from Colombo expresses the child's tensions, bound as he is, for the unknown. "On my last day," he writes, "I found an empty school examination booklet... a traced map of the world, and put them in my small suitcase. I went outside and said goodbye to the generator". Here is the young boy's unaccountable ache, the dimly grasped sense of what is slipping forever into history.

Ondaatje knows, as all those children who left their home by boat at that time knew, the sweet sadness of such goodbyes. "What was I in those days?" the adult Michael, changed by that voyage, asks. "I recall no outside imprint, and therefore no perception of myself." Years later a distant cousin describes his behaviour at that time: "You were, I recall, a real yakka, a real demon... I remember you caused a lot of trouble."

During the voyage many things, some real, some imaginary, happen. The boys are like lightning conductors, attracting the kind of trouble that constantly tests their bravery, sometimes foolishly, to its limits. One night during a violent storm two of them, tethered by the third, battle out the night on deck. The ship plunges through a 50-knot gale and only the accidental skill of some reef-knots stops them being washed away. Finally, as the tempest dies down, they are found and rescued, half-drowned, before receiving a lecture from the captain.

The story is constructed in a series of vignettes, stitched together in episodes that move backwards and forwards like the action of a Rubik Cube. One moment we are on board ship and the next on land many years into the future. The narrative both puzzles and unexpectedly pulls us up short.

For Ondaatje the poet, economy has always been a watchword, and his imagery is compressed and sparse. Take, for instance, his description of the ship, the Oronsay, which we are told is "lit like a long brooch". Similarly, through a patchwork of seemingly unconnected fragments, we are introduced to the deaf Asuntha, a girl whom the boys first see, "exercising on a trampoline". Suddenly, "she was in mid-air, with all that silent space around her". Later, this image of mid-air suspension is echoed when a passenger describes cycling to work in Italy in the burning August heat.

The sense of movement is everywhere in this novel, charting the voyage and threading through the story like the pulse of the sea which, "in an unexpected abundant light spilled off the deck". It is present in the sharply focused image of the three boys diving into the swimming pool to retrieve silver teaspoons flung into the water by a steward. We find it in the secret garden that grows deep within the ship's bowels, swaying under artificial light. And it is there, too, in the slow, rumble through the Suez Canal with its onshore runners flinging papers and objects across to the ship.

Woven through all of this are the memories of a vanished past; a mental and physical innocence in a once carefree place that no longer exists in Sri Lanka's complicated and brutal metamorphosis. The Ondaatjes themselves come from an old Burgher family and have always been outsiders to the main struggle between Singhalese and Tamils. As a result, in The Cat's Table, we are shown a place of luminous magic and make-believe. Where else could a single sliver of gold be added to the lime and cardamom betel paste chewed at village weddings? Or a bottle of Kelani River water turn into a talisman?

No serious novel can ignore history, and as the journey to the cold north continues, we notice, here and there, touches of the long arm of the imperial rule, softened by humour, but present nonetheless. Ondaatje does not let us escape such moments but nor does he labour his point: "You are a polecat... a loathsome little Asian polecat. You know what I do when I find a polecat in my house? I set fire to its testicles."

And thus, when the fabulously wealthy Sir Hector de Silva, cursed by a monk, contracts rabies but refuses the local ayurvedic treatment, he is doomed. Why? Because he prefers to embark on a dangerous voyage in search of a Western cure. But "not one English specialist had been willing to come to Colombo to deal with Sir Hector's medical problem. Harley Street would remain in Harley Street, in spite of a recommendation from the British governor, who had dined with Sir Hector in his Colombo mansion." Then, when Sir Hector unexpectedly dies, we are told that his knighthood is instantly forgotten, washed chillingly away, together with his body, into the ocean.

Undeterred, the Oronsay continues onwards while Michael, lying in bed, in his cousin's Emily's cabin, makes a discovery: "Suddenly there was a wide gulf between Emily's existence and mine, and I would never be able to cross it... I felt in that moment that I had been alone for years." Unable fully to express his sadness, he understands the defences "which had marked the outline of me, were no longer there".

Such is the quality of the writing that not until we near the novel's end do we notice a false note in the character of Niemeyer. As the shackled prisoner, so necessary for the plot, he remains two-dimensional, with neither his presence, nor the working-out of his fate, really quite believable. That said, this is a quibble in what is otherwise a beautifully crafted whole.

*Roma Tearne's fourth novel, 'The Swimmer', is published by HarperCollins*